Longman Archaeology Series

Pottery in the Roman World

Longman Archaeology Series

Advisory editor: Barry Cunliffe

R. J. Bradley *Prehistoric Britain: the social basis*
D. R. Brothwell *Early British man: a bioarchaeology from the Palaeolithic to the Middle Ages*
R. W. Chapman *Death, culture and society in prehistoric Europe: theory and applications*
D. P. S. Peacock *Pottery in the Roman world: an ethnoarchaeological approach*
D. P. S. Peacock, J. A. Riley and D. F. Williams *Amphoras and the Roman economy*
R. F. Tylecote *The pre-history of metallurgy in Europe*

D. P. S. Peacock

Pottery in the Roman world:

an ethnoarchaeological approach

LONGMAN
London and New York

Longman Group Limited
Longman House
Burnt Mill, Harlow, Essex, UK

Published in the United States of America
by Longman Inc., New York

© Longman Group Limited 1982

First published 1982

Library of Congress-Cataloging in Publication Data
Peacock, D. P. S.
  Pottery in the Roman world.
  (Longman archaeology series)
  Includes bibliographical references and index.
  1. Pottery, Roman. 2. Rome – Antiquities.
I. Title. II. Series.
TP802.95.P4   666'.3937   81-12356
ISBN 0-582-49127-4   AACR2

British Library Cataloguing in Publication Data
Peacock, D. P. S.
  Pottery in the Roman world.
  1. Pottery, Roman
  I. Title
  338.7'6663'0937   HD9618
  ISBN 0-582-49127-4

Printed in Singapore by Singapore National Printers (Pte) Ltd.

Contents

List of plates

List of figures

Preface

This somewhat unorthodox book was conceived in a fairly conventional manner. Roman pottery ranks among the more common archaeological artifacts of Europe and the Mediterranean region and it is virtually impossible to excavate without finding at least a few sherds. It follows that some acquaintance with Roman pottery should be an essential part of an archaeological education. However, herein lies a difficulty, for much of the relevant information is to be found in specialised ceramic reports published in many different languages, often in obscure journals. Clearly what is required is a broad synthesis and evaluation of both the basic principles and of the more common material. This was attempted in 1905 by H. B. Walters as part of his two-volume work on the *History of Ancient Pottery* and more recently in 1955 by Robert Charleston in his brief but useful sketch entitled *Roman Pottery*. Since then the subject has been treated on a regional basis with the publication of important surveys of material from Spain, Britain and France, in particular (c.g. Beltrán Lloris, 1978; Vegas, 1973; Swan, 1978; M.-H. and J. Santrot, 1979). At the same time certain types of well-travelled pottery such as amphorae or the red-slip wares have been the subject of a broader-based international approach (e.g. Panella, 1973; Beltrán Lloris, 1970; Hayes, 1972).

This book is an attempt to present a more general picture, but it cannot be regarded as the successor to the works of Walters and Charleston, because in the last few decades the aims and nature of archaeology have changed radically. In the 1950s it was customary to assert that archaeologists could be properly concerned with the how, when and where of the past but that the question 'why' generally lay beyond the limits of archaeological inference. However, a subject relegated to a mere descriptive role will rapidly become sterile, practised by those to whom the catalogue or corpus is an end in itself rather than a means of further enlightenment. It is hardly surprising, therefore, that as archaeology has developed into a vital and vibrant discipline, the central issue is increasingly becoming one of explaining *why* certain developments or changes took place. The study of Roman pottery is no exception, for workers are now evaluating topics which a few years ago might have been dismissed as 'speculation', fit for discussion at excavation tea-breaks rather than for serious publication. Of course, unfettered and undisciplined surmises are valueless and publication on the pretext of simply stimulating discussion is indefensible.

Nevertheless, the question 'why' can be brought within respectable academic bounds by adopting an approach involving the generation of hypotheses or models which are then tested against the evidence. This deductive method of reasoning has revolutionised the study of prehistory and is being increasingly employed in Classical archaeology. The present book is a first attempt to apply such an approach to the production and marketing of Roman pottery as a whole. Working from the premise that the present is the key to the past, an attempt is made to understand pottery production in the complex market economies of present-day Europe and the Mediterranean region. If we cannot understand how and why the contemporary system works, what hope have we of unravelling the Roman situation? The ethnographic evidence is then compared with the Roman. In some cases the correspondence is good, in others less so, but both congruences and contrasts are equally valuable in assessing Roman practice. Thus it is not a question of forcing the modern interpretation upon an ancient situation, but of using ethnography as a yardstick to distinguish probable from less plausible explanations.

The quotation at the beginning of this book is particularly apt, for the idea of using ethnographical evidence as a means of understanding classical ceramics arose while processing many tons of pottery from the recent British excavations at Carthage. A visit to the local pottery *souk* at El Kram was a stimulating experience, for it seemed that if the material on sale was to be broken up and placed in boxes, it would differ little from the boxes of material we were studying. Of course the red-slipped wares are now replaced by glazed vessels, but there in the pottery shop were similar proportions of table wares, kitchen wares, hand-made vessels, water jars, lamps and exotica. Some came from Nabeul on the Cap Bon peninsula, some from Sedjenane in the Krouminie mountains, others from Moknine in central Tunisia, while Tunis itself supplied some curious hand-made cooking vessels. It seemed that an understanding of how collections such as these were produced and brought together could furnish ideas of considerable value in understanding ancient assemblages. Thus began a study of modern pottery production, and after several years of concentrated reading, field visits to potteries in Spain, France, Italy, Greece and Tunisia, I feel able to offer a preliminary and tentative synthesis of the main parameters, which I believe are crucial to the Roman period also.

It is not the aim of this book to describe Roman pottery in its multifarious forms, and the reader will search in vain for typological sequences and chronologies. This does not mean that I am unappreciative of the great strides made by ceramic scholarship or that I do not recognise the fundamental importance of classification and dating. It is simply that my objective is different: it is to understand the *processes* operating in the Roman ceramic industry. Of course these changed with time and place and even here it is easy to reassert the prime importance of chronology. In practice however, the evidence is so poor and patchy that at present it is hard to discern more than the barest outlines and diachronic studies must await future improvement of the data-base. If this book does something to stimulate more acute observation in the field, it will have served a useful purpose.

Any new approach inevitably leads to the introduction of unfamiliar terms and concepts. Since this book occupies middle ground between a number of different disciplines I have aimed to communicate widely by avoiding new jargon as far as possible. I am conscious that many of the ideas might have been expressed differently in specialist papers, but modern learning has erected enough barriers to mutual comprehension without multiplying them. Nevertheless it is impossible to be all things to all men and the use of some specialised terms is inevitable.

By selecting Roman pottery as my subject, I have chosen to evaluate a small part of the archaeological ceramic spectrum. However, even within this limited compass it is often hard to do justice to all the evidence in the space of a relatively short book. I have endeavoured to make amends for superficiality and selectivity by adopting a fairly full system of referencing so that the reader can expand the discussion and dispute or concur with the claims I make.

However, although the scope is limited, the principles, lessons and discussions should have wide relevance in the study of ceramic production in early complex societies. In my view the real interest of Roman pottery will only be fully revealed when similar work has been done in other developed cultures so that broad comparisons are feasible. For the present my canvas is more limited. If I have shown that the living but rapidly dying tradition of pottery-making is as vitally relevant to the historical archaeologist as to the prehistorian, I shall be content.

Southampton
December 1980

D. P. S. Peacock

Acknowledgements

One of the pleasanter tasks when writing a book is acknowledging those who have made it possible. The list must be headed by my wife who has constantly encouraged the project and followed its progress, as well as spending many hours reading and checking manuscripts or proofs; it is thus apt that the book should be dedicated to her. However, I owe a particular debt to Dr M. G. Fulford and Dr J. A. Riley, both of whom read the entire manuscript, and their perspicacious comments have enabled me to add certain points or eliminate a number of erroneous ones. In addition, Dr D. F. Williams read and commented on Chapters 5 and 6 with similar benefit.

The task of preparing the drawings was made much easier by Martin Oake, who prepared Figs 2, 7, 16, 43, 71 and 72. Joanna Bailey redrew Figs 77, 78 and 81, while Siriol Mynors and Roberta Tomber drew Figs 3 and 82 respectively.

Many of the plates are my own, but Dr Hugh Chapman and the London Museum kindly allowed me to photograph their particularly rich collection of Roman pottery from the City and most of the illustrated Roman vessels are from that source. I am indebted to Mr G. Marsh and Miss J. Hall for much information about the collections, which is incorporated in the captions.

In addition Mr G. F. Bryant kindly provided Plate 22, and I am grateful to M. A. Vernhet and M. M. Balsan for Plate 30. Plates 1, 13 and 20 were taken by Mr Nick Bradford and Mrs K. Winham of the Department of Archaeology, University of Southampton.

I am grateful to the following for permission to reproduce copyright material: the Doncaster Museum Service for Plate 24; Dr D. F Williams for my figure 22, from Williams, 1977; Professor W. F. Grimes and the Honourable Society of Cymmrodorion for the frontispiece, figures 2 and 19 (my figures 27, 68 and 69) from Grimes, 1930; the Worcester Archaeological Society for figures 1 and 2 (my figures 37 and 38) from Peacock, 1967; the Hampshire Field Club for figure 3 (my figure 54) from Fulford, 1975b; the authors and the Council for British Archaeology for figures 4 and 50 (my figures 57 and 58) from Lyne and Jeffries, 1979; the Council for British Archaeology for figure 44 (my figure 84) from Peacock, 1978. Full details of these publications can be found in the bibliography at the end of this book.

Finally I must thank Mrs A. Hamlin for typing the manuscript so swiftly and accurately.

For Barbara

In that old Potter's Shop I stood alone
With the clay Population round in Rows
And, strange to tell, among that Earthen Lot
Some could articulate, while others not.

Rubáiyát of Omar Khayyám
Trans. Edward FitzGerald
First Edition, verses 59 60

1 Introduction: the study of Roman pottery

'Roman' murmurs Max disgustedly. It is his last word of contempt. Stifling any lingering feeling I may have that the Romans were an interesting people, I echo his tone and say 'Roman', and cast down the fragment of despised pottery.

Agatha Christie Mallowan,
Come tell me how you live: 40[1]

General Pitt-Rivers once said that the most important archaeological finds were the common ones, a precept which has since been accepted and taught by a majority of British archaeologists. If the General is to be taken seriously this must mean that pottery is vitally important, for it is by far the commonest type of portable artifact from the Neolithic period onwards. Certainly pottery has achieved a dominant place in prehistory for it is usually the only medium permitting realistic social and chronological synthesis. At times its role has been so overstressed that, as Cunliffe (1974:10) has remarked, one might think that the pots themselves were animated entities. However, pottery does not seem to have achieved the same status in Classical archaeology and the student can be forgiven for taking a somewhat cynical view: it is not the commonplace but the exotic and the unusual that excite interest and figure most prominently in discussion or writing. Thus while the finer Greek vases have been the subject of detailed and scholarly treatment, almost nothing is known of the common utilitarian wares in contemporary use.

In Classical archaeology, ceramic studies have followed a somewhat biased course predetermined by two factors. Firstly, the subject has developed firmly within the framework of art history which has led to a preoccupation with the more decorative wares, but

secondly and above all it is the overwhelming quantities that have precluded all but the most selective study. The problem can be illustrated with some numerical examples. In 1975, Dr M. G. Fulford published what must rank as one of the most detailed and comprehensive pottery studies ever undertaken. Excavation of over 3700 square metres of the Shore Fort at Portchester in southern England produced some 350 kg of late Roman wares. The prodigious task of processing and publishing this large assemblage has justifiably won praise from reviewers, but credit is also due to the excavator for allocating the considerable funds required for such a venture. However, when we move southwards to the heart of the Roman world, the Mediterranean, the situation is very different. According to my colleague, Dr. J. Riley, 320 kg was the content of one cistern at Bengazi, while at Carthage excavation of a similar area to Portchester produced about 10,000 kg (10 tonnes) of pottery. These figures compare with those from Sabratha, where the late Dame Kathleen Kenyon recovered some seven tons. Quantity and cost-effective processing may disturb British archaeologists but their problems pale to insignificance when compared with those of their Mediterranean colleagues.

Faced with this enormous pottery mountain and the limited size of excavation budgets many archaeologists seem to have acted as though there were but two courses of action open. One was to ignore pottery altogether and the other to be highly selective and concentrate on the 'interesting' wares, in other words those displaying some evidence of artistic or technical achievement. Of these there is no doubt that the first alternative has proved most popular, and alas the somewhat frivolous passage at the head of this chapter still epitomises an attitude prevalent in some circles.

---

[1] I am indebted to Dr J. Riley for this recondite but apt quotation.

However, on the credit side, indifference or downright hostility applies mainly to the coarse utilitarian wares. The fine pottery of both the Greek and Roman periods has attracted *aficionados* so that the typological and artistic development is now well established and understood. The precise detailed knowledge available is the envy of archaeologists specialising in other periods or in other parts of the world.

In view of this serious imbalance, it may seem strange if not foolhardy to write a book on the pottery of the Roman world: it would either mean concentrating on the development of the better documented wares or the text would show a heavy predilection for northwestern Europe where the evidence is more even. To some extent both these limitations will be apparent, but the scope of the work remains very definitely the Roman world, and there are some advantages in reviewing the problem on a wide scale. A broad canvas focuses attention on general rather than particular issues and surprisingly there are many of these that have been inadequately discussed or not considered at all. In addition, the lack of reliable data forces consideration from a theoretical as well as a pragmatic point of view. One of the most exciting growth points in contemporary prehistory has been the development of an approach in which the generation of models is crucial, but these methods have only just begun to influence Classical archaeology even though they offer unrivalled opportunities for new insights. It could of course be argued that the needs of the prehistorian contrast markedly with those of the Classical archaeologist who has access to written records, and it must be conceded that there is much truth in this. However, a major objective of this book is to demonstrate the desirability of looking at well known material from new and often radically different viewpoints. The methods of the prehistorian are not irrelevant, for Roman pottery is, in a sense, **prehistoric**, since there are practically no significant written records bearing directly on it.

This somewhat novel position requires justification and the object of this chapter is to make a case; to discuss the *raison d'être* of the book and to explain the approach adopted in subsequent chapters. Our present needs can be better appreciated by looking briefly at the way in which Roman pottery studies have developed, and hence a short excursus on this theme is pertinent. For obvious reasons it is convenient to consider coarse- and fine-wares as separate entities, although in reality the division can be arbitrary.

The remarkable technical achievement of Roman fine-ware potters has long been noted. For example, the quantities of Arretine ware discovered during the building of medieval Arezzo occasioned astonishment at the subtlety, workmanship and form of the vases (Chase, 1916:5). However, it was not until the turn of the nineteenth and twentieth centuries that wares of the so-called samian tradition received the attention they deserved. Workers such as Dragendorff (1895–96), Déchelette (1904), Knorr (1919, 1952), or Oswald and Pryce (1920) laid a foundation of scholarship upon which later generations have built. Their methods involved careful attention to details of typology and ornament considered in conjunction with the epigraphic evidence of stamps. Their meticulous approach was supported by the excavation of sites that could be historically dated such as those on the German *limes* or Pompeii. This firm foundation has paid dividends for it is often possible to assign small sherds to their maker and to suggest dates within narrow limits.

With the exception of Arretine, fine-ware studies began somewhat later in the Mediterranean. The most influential of the earlier studies were those of Waagé (1933, 1948) in the east and Lamboglia (1941, 1950, 1958, 1963) in the west. Unfortunately, although both were to some extent concerned with the same wares, neither took cognizance of pottery outside their own region, resulting in confusion and a dichotomy now resolved in a masterly survey by Hayes (1972). The study has yet to achieve the precision possible with the earlier Gaulish and Italian wares, but a solid foundation has now been laid analogous to that long ago provided by Oswald and Pryce (1920) for the northern parts of the Empire.

Studies of coarse pottery have followed a rather different pattern, with most of the early developments in Britain and Germany, where a dearth of standing remains may have led to the early consideration of this rather unprepossessing material. Among the first observers was John Conyers, a London apothecary, who in 1677 recorded a Roman kiln discovered during the building of St Paul's Cathedral (Jewitt, 1883:32). However, this is an isolated and exceptional instance and it is not really until the subsequent eighteenth and nineteenth centuries that the subject was considered seriously. The tempo of observation gradually increased with the passage of time, but a particularly significant landmark was reached as early as 1828 when Edmund Artis produced a magnificent publication on the Nene Valley potteries. Inadequate though it is by modern standards, the *Durobrivae* remains an outstanding and precocious work on Roman coarse pottery. However, the systematic examination of coarse pottery had to await the early years of this century when the study was developed by J. P. Bushe-Fox or Thomas May in Britain and by students such as Sigfried Loeschcke or Ernst Ritterling on the Continent. Their method was almost exclusively typological and chronological with relatively little attention paid to origins, for these questions were difficult to discuss intelligently in the current state of knowledge. Thus began a long tradition of pottery study which has persisted to the present day. It would be possible to compose a long list of works that have materially advanced our knowledge of specific points but one worthy of especial mention is John Gillam's (1957) article on coarse pottery in northern England in which he was able to relate many major types to historically dated deposits on Hadrian's Wall. This has proved particularly influential and Gillam is not to blame for the frequency with which his dating has been misapplied.

In the Mediterranean, coarse pottery has generally fared less well, but a clear distinction must be made between amphorae and other utilitarian wares. The former often bear painted inscriptions and hence they attracted attention in the nineteenth century when the great *Corpus Inscriptionum Latinorum* was launched. Schoene (1871), Mau (1898) and Dressel (1891) were responsible for publishing material from the towns of Pompeii and Rome and each included a typological sketch to illustrate the forms to which the *tituli picti* were ascribed. It is a credit to their perspicacity and scholarship that these typologies are still in common use today. However, after this precocious start amphora studies were largely neglected until about the middle of this century when a developing interest in underwater archaeology led Lamboglia (1950) and Benoit (1956) to study the subject anew. Further impetus came in the mid 1960s with Zevi's (1966) evaluation of Dressel's work and in the debate that followed the publication of Callender's (1965) book. From the beginning the emphasis has been upon economics: discussion of origins, contents and commerce have figured more prominently than chronology and this tradition continues, for amphorae are far from ideal for dating.

Study of the remaining utilitarian wares has followed a different path. Most of the early workers seem to have concentrated on Hellenistic pottery and Roman wares did not attract their due share of attention. With a few exceptions the subject does not seem to have been taken seriously until the

mid twentieth century, when the results of excavations at Tarsus and at the Athenian Agora were published (Jones, 1950; Robinson, 1959). In the west, Lamboglia's (1950) account of the Ventimiglia excavations has remained a key work unequalled until very recently when the results of the excavations at Ostia became available (Carandini *et al.*, 1968).

This brief and highly selective historical sketch suggests a marked bias towards chronology, based upon typological analysis. This is hardly surprising, for Roman archaeology has been regarded as an illustrative adjunct of Roman history and chronology is obviously vital if the archaeology is to enhance the established historical framework.

However, within the last decade a number of new aspects have emerged, and the emphasis has moved towards technology and economics. For example, methods of spatial analysis developed by geographers have enabled distributions to be discussed in terms of marketing (e.g. Hodder, 1974a, b, 1977a; Fulford and Hodder, 1975; Loughlin, 1977) while scientific methods of fabric analysis, based on trace elements or petrology have added a new dimension in the discrimination and diagnosis of origins (e.g. Picon, 1973; Picon *et al.*, 1971; Peacock, 1967, 1973a, 1977a). The technology of pottery production is also receiving attention in a number of ways. The study of production sites is forging ahead (e.g. Fulford, 1975b; Young, 1977a), but specific aspects of production and manufacturing are also receiving detailed investigation. Thus Cuomo di Caprio (1972) and Berger (1969) have revitalised the study of kilns, pioneered by Corder (1957) over twenty years ago, while experimental kiln firings begun by Mayes (1961, 1962) have been actively pursued by Bryant (1973, 1978). Little attention has been given to pottery as a tool for interpreting the social status and function of sites and the Colchester pottery shops (Hull, 1958) remain an outstanding if somewhat self-evident example. However, social aspects have not been totally ignored and an experiment involving a meticulous exercise in three-dimensional plotting has been undertaken on the fifth–sixth century site of Cadbury-Congresbury in southwestern Britain (Rahtz and Fowler, forthcoming).

Thus recent years have witnessed a marked expansion and diversification in pottery studies which is encouraging and bodes well for the future. However, it is easy to be complacent and it is important to recognise lacunae as well as achievements. In the past the main thrust of ceramic research has been directed towards the classification and identification of pottery so that we have been much preoccupied with naming, dating and determining the origin of different wares. Obviously this is vitally important and must continue to receive priority, but the study has now developed to a level where broader synthesis and evaluation is not only possible but essential, for much spadework has been done and we have reached a major turning-point offering exciting new possibilities for the future.

Data about Roman pottery can be used in two ways, both of which are equally respectable and desirable from an academic point of view. On the one hand we can adopt an historical viewpoint and consider ceramics in the light of written records, for although these seldom bear direct witness to ceramic activity they do give indications of the economic framework in which it belongs. In effect, pottery can be used to write economic history in a manner which both expands and develops the literary evidence. Alternatively, we can adopt an approach akin to that of the modern geographer and attempt to understand the underlying principles, mechanisms or processes operating in the industry, an aspect we would not expect to be considered by ancient writers because their conceptual basis was insufficiently developed. Of these two approaches the latter can perhaps be regarded as the more fundamental, for unless we understand the parameters involved in the production and distribution of pottery its correct use as an historical document might be jeopardised.

If this argument is accepted it must arouse concern rather than self-congratulation for we are woefully ignorant of these basic issues and the problem has hardly been defined, let alone answered. Of course it could be claimed that the study is young and naturally our activities are concerned with amassing an adequate data base before attempting a deeper understanding. It is axiomatic that archaeological excavation is a form of destruction and it is therefore essential to record and preserve as much of the evidence as possible for future generations. Unfortunately, however, this is not enough, for contrary to popular belief, it is a harsh reality of academic life that facts do not generally accumulate to produce answers. Conscientious preparation of the record must be balanced by a research strategy in which certain questions are posed and emphasised. Any other procedure is liable to accumulate redundant information fit only to answer the questions nobody is asking. Unless our goals are clear at the outset we may never achieve them.

Of course in our ceramic studies we have plenty of specific detailed problems, but what are the general questions we are trying to consider? Rather than marvelling at modern activity and breadth of approach it is perhaps more instructive to pose a few simple questions, to which a non-specialist might reasonably expect an intelligent answer after about eighty years of continuous research. In order to illustrate the type of problem in mind there follows a selection taken from a wide variety of possibilities:

1. To what extent was Roman pottery made in the home?
2. How did the production and distribution systems of the more widely distributed fine-wares differ from that of utilitarian kitchen wares?
3. Under what economic or ecological circumstances can an industry based on primitive open firings co-exist with one based on the kiln, as was the case in Roman Britain?
4. What are the ecological and economic conditions that determine where and how major industries will develop?
5. By what mechanisms was pottery transferred from the producer to the consumer?

Of course it is possible to give a glib answer in each case, but the honest scholar will recognise that we have neither the data nor the framework to seriously consider any of these matters. However, they cannot be dismissed as trivial and I would suggest they are vitally important for two reasons. Firstly, if the ceramic archaeologist could provide answers or at least an informed discussion of such matters, pottery would make a very definite and worthwhile contribution to our understanding of Roman social and economic development. Secondly, themes such as these have very wide relevance regardless of country or culture and this is one way in which Classical archaeology can contribute to an understanding of the general processes and laws operating in complex societies. Without wishing to overstress the importance of pottery it does seem that current ceramic studies are in some ways comparable with chemistry before Lavoisier. By the early eighteenth century new techniques had been developed and exciting data were accumulating. However, the subject was without structure and direction and it was Lavoisier's relatively simple theory of combustion which provided the foundation upon which modern chemistry developed.

It is exactly such a basis, theory or model – call it what you will – that we require in pottery studies today. Its purpose will be to draw the disparate strands into a coherent whole and to add direction to the exercise. It must be of a very simple and general nature so that it forms a framework, not a straightjacket, for future thought and above all it must be practically relevant so that field observation and synthetic thought can proceed side by side. In the first part of this book we shall make some tentative first steps towards developing a simple model which will be firmly in mind in the second part where an attempt is made to review our knowledge of certain characteristic types of Roman pottery.

2 Towards a model for Roman pottery studies

Nowhere do phenomena succeed one another so gradually or so imperceptibly as in the sphere of economics, that domain of necessities and instincts, where every classification and every distinction of kind or time become more or less artificial. Nevertheless differences do exist, and in spite of the vagueness of their outline one can easily distinguish certain groups of facts which belong together and which by the relative position they occupy, give character to the great periods of economic history.

Paul Mantoux (1927:41)

The idea of approaching Roman pottery from a deductive rather than an inductive point of view is new to Classical archaeology, but not to ceramic studies as a whole. Very recently the general need for models has been stressed by van der Leeuw (1976) and it is implicit in earlier works such as that by Balfet (1966) on North African pottery or even in Anna Shepard's (1956) classic text on ceramics for the archaeologist. Van der Leeuw has developed this idea further than anyone else and has propounded a simple model of general application which is in fact very close to the scheme suggested here, although both were derived independently and from different standpoints.

There are a number of ways in which models can be constructed. A common approach is to derive inspiration from the ethnographical record, a method advocated by van der Leeuw who recommends a thorough perusal of the literature as a useful prerequisite. The value of an ethnographical approach cannot be denied, but there are a number of problems in using ethnographical evidence as a guide to the Roman period. Firstly, the data are heavily biased towards the more primitive end of the spectrum, and complex production has attracted less attention from ethnographers. Secondly, much of the evidence relates to ecological zones in no way similar to the area occupied by the Roman empire and different

factors may have been operative. These problems can be reduced by concentrating on modern pottery-making within the restricted area of Europe and the Mediterranean lands. Not only are we considering precisely the ecological zone occupied by the Romans, but it is also an area where ceramic production is extremely complex and perhaps more closely analogous to that of Classical times than almost any other part of the world. In addition there is a wealth of other evidence and the ethnographical record can be supplemented with historical information or with the findings of industrial archaeology. (For the purpose of brevity all forms of evidence bearing on recent production will be classed as 'ethnographical' throughout this book.)

While acknowledging the essential role of ethnography in generating models it is important not to neglect purely theoretical considerations. As Binford (1968:269) has said, 'Archaeologists are not limited to analogies to ethnographic data as the sole basis for offering explanatory postulates; models can be formulated in a theoretical calculus some of which may deal with forms without ethnographic analogy.'

However, once the model has been constructed, ethnography has a vital role to play. It should help define technology and other characteristics of the components and to delineate traits which will be recognisable in the archaeological record. At once the model becomes a practical entity.

Few would dispute that pottery-making is essentially an economic activity, whether practiced at a household or factory level and economic fundamentals make a good starting point. Unfortunately this immediately introduces a complication, for economic anthropology is split into two opposing schools generally known as 'formalists' and 'substantivists.' Formalists stress the 'economising' meaning of the word 'economy' and claim that economic fundamentals are universally applicable, while substantivists interpret the word in the sense of 'livelihood' or 'subsistence'. They assert that in primitive and peasant societies economic transactions cannot be divorced from social obligations and that Western economic theory is inapplicable (eg Polanyi: 1957b). Recently Dowling (1979) has attempted to resolve the conflict by suggesting a middle way. He claims that the substantivists have erred in denying the overall validity of the economist's primary assumptions (eg that people have infinitely expandable wants and that all people behave rationally and are motivated by self-interest), but formalists have wrongly claimed some of their secondary assumptions to be universal (eg that production units proceed on a basis of the profit motive, etc.).

When considering pottery production in a complex society, the great divide between the two factions can seem somewhat academic and fruitless. If, for example, a peasant potter takes part in the commerce of the market-place his objective may be to make a profit and expand his operations, but equally he may merely wish to exchange pots for other goods so that he can live and meet his social obligations. Profit, as we understand it, may be far from his mind. Nevertheless, he is exchanging pots to satisfy his wants and the two situations are distinguished only by the level of 'want' acceptable to the society in which he must work. It is true that many peasant societies possess levelling mechanisms which deter the development of excess desires, but potters are generally among the lower echelons of society and they may wish to progress to some more congenial occupation such as farming (cf. Foster, 1966:58). Profit and price can never be entirely ignored.

Seen from this perspective it appears that formalist fundamentals are appropriate to the study of ceramic production and exchange in complex societies where a market economy was in some measure operative, but substantivist principles could be relevant in assessing anomalies.

Oscar Lange's (1945) basic paper on the scope and principles of economics is still worthy of consideration and makes a useful opening. Economics, he said, is the science of administering scarce resources, and these resources may be used in three ways:

1. consumption, where they are used to satisfy immediate wants;
2. production, which generally involves the

preparation or adaption of the resource to different and more desirable forms; and
3. exchange, in which the resource is used to procure other resources.

Resources are manipulated by 'units of economic decision' of which Lange recognises three:

1. *Households*. These are essentially consumers of goods but they may undertake production for their own benefit, such as the growing of vegetables in the garden. However, we must not let this humble example obscure the other end of the spectrum, for in the seventeenth century the Gobelins furniture works was established to supply the needs of the King of France: from him everything came and to him everything returned. Here then was a whole industry employing a multitude of artisans, but it was one that lay outside the normal economic orbit, ranking as an extreme example of household activity.
2. *Firms or business enterprises*. These are involved in the exchange of goods for profit, and production is an important facet of their activity. In fact, firms are nearly always producers, if only in the sense of modifying a resource by transportation from a less profitable to a more lucrative point of consumption.
3. *Public services*. These are agencies, usually but not always government operated, whose purpose is to contribute towards certain social objectives: the army, navy or medical services are good examples. They may on occasions act like business enterprises, but it is their ultimate objectives that serve to differentiate and define them. One might expect them to produce goods, but only to further their own objectives and not for direct profit.

Clearly it might be possible to use this simple system in Roman pottery studies. It should be relatively easy to distinguish household production, manufacturing firms and public service production of which the Roman legionary potteries provide a textbook example. However, the model is so simple that it would not get us very far and in practice industrial life is much more complex. Thus Tax (1953) cites a common example of household pottery production in Guatemala where the womenfolk make pottery as a sideline but very definitely for the market and with the profit in mind. Are we to class this simple situation as a firm rather than a household? Then again, as everyone knows, firms vary considerably from a single artisan in his cottage workshop to complex factories employing numerous workers under a managerial superstructure. Also estate production, an important facet of Roman life, is difficult to fit into this scheme. Production may be for the sole benefit of the owner and hence it would fall within the household category, but most estates were orientated towards the market, and ceramic production may have been undertaken for commercial reasons or to improve the estate and enable it to produce other commodities more efficiently.

The point that emerges forcefully from this discussion is that the concept of *modes of production* is fundamental providing a basic tool, which if developed could have great potential in analysing Roman pottery production. In the following paragraphs we shall attempt to construct a hierarchy of modes of production from the simplest to the most complex situation, defining the criteria by which each can be distinguished from the others. However, it must be remembered that we are attempting to impose a conceptual framework upon a situation that in practice may be almost infinitely variable, with many examples falling between rather than within the modes here defined, but it is only when the rules have been made that the exceptions can be recognised. The wise words quoted at the beginning of this chapter were written by a distinguished economic historian wrestling with an analogous problem more than half a century ago. They are worth considering for they summarise both the potential and limitations of any attempt to classify ceramic production.

1. HOUSEHOLD PRODUCTION

This is the simplest mode of production, in which each household makes the pottery it requires for its own consumption. Since this activity is of secondary economic importance, it will in most cases be relegated to the women of the household and classed as a chore on a par with cooking or cleaning. The vessel types will be strictly functional and will be made according to time-honoured cultural recipes. Much thought in prehistory has been based upon the assumption that hand-made prehistoric pottery was produced in this way and that therefore the distribution of ceramic styles will directly reflect cultural or ethnic groupings. However, petrological analysis (Peacock, 1968, 1969a/b) has shown this to be over-simplistic. The extent to which this model applies to the Roman period has never been seriously considered because the humble hand-made wares which might be appropriate have been largely ignored.

We must expect production by this mode to be sporadic. Households could fire individual pots as the need arises, but since there are economies of scale in pottery production, we must predict an annual or even longer circle as the norm. However, the limited and sporadic nature of pottery-making will preclude investment in elaborate technology and neither wheel or kiln will be used; moreeover it is unlikely that a turntable will be available.

A clear distinction must be made between sedentary and nomadic households. The latter may obtain clay from a number of places and an analysis will rightly suggest multiple points of production for identical types. A sherd scatter left by nomads might, if taken at face value, suggest a distribution due to a complex system of production and exchange.

2. HOUSEHOLD INDUSTRY

This useful term, coined by van der Leeuw (1976), is used here in a slightly broader sense. In this mode we see the first steps towards craft specialisation. Pottery-making is in the hands of a few skilled artisans, but it does not seem desirable to follow van der Leeuw in restricting consumption to 'group use'. Production is in the hands of professionals who are potting for profit and so if there are facilities for wide marketing, these will be exploited. This will not affect the mode of production because potting is a part-time activity, not an essential means of livelihood and subsistence would be feasible without it. Because of its secondary role, we would once again expect it to be a craft practised mainly by women, particularly those who through some circumstance have to supplement the family income. Since production is of a part-time sporadic nature, perhaps restricted to the months when there are few other essential demands in time, investment in equipment is likely to be slight. The level of activity may warrant a turntable but not a wheel and open firings will be the rule, but some form of oven or rudimentary kiln may be employed since once constructed these tend to be labour saving.

Once again production may be sedentary or nomadic and obviously if the latter is the case a superimposed marketing structure would produce a very complicated archaeological picture.

3. INDIVIDUAL WORKSHOPS

The division between this mode and the previous one is very fine. However, in this case pottery-making is a main source of subsistence. It may be practised for only part of the year, in conjunction with garden cultivation or farming for example, but it remains a vital source of income. Production is orientated towards the most lucrative markets and aids such as the wheel and the kiln are to be anticipated in most cases. The craft will normally be practised by men rather than women since it has now become economically important. Concerns of this nature are usually isolated and hence not subject to great competition so that the most rudimentary marketing system may suffice.

The craftsman may work by himself but since efficiency is important he is liable to employ a small team of assistants, perhaps members of his own family. The labour requirement together with his investment in equipment favour a sedentary existence. However, this is not always the case and there may be good reasons for peripatetic production if for example large and cumbersome vessels are being made or if the markets are very dispersed.

4. NUCLEATED WORKSHOPS

In this mode individual workshops are grouped together to form a more or less tightly clustered industrial complex. Nucleation may be favoured by availability of raw materials, labour, markets or any combination of the three. Pottery-making is a major activity and other means of income may be entirely subsidiary. Sometimes climate may preclude round-the-year production but every effort will be made to extend the season by, for example, constructing special drying sheds. Potting is now almost exclusively a male activity and every available technical aid will be used. The element of competition will help elevate technique to the highest level and the industry will usually be characterised by a fairly standardised range of high-quality products. Co-operation is perhaps the most important advantage, and one thinks in particular of available practical assistance at times of misfortune, or of financing capital outlay through co-operative schemes.

However, above all the scale of production resulting from nucleation will attract the middleman with his wide distribution network, and the community as a whole will benefit from large sales, without the expense or trouble of individual distribution.

5. THE MANUFACTORY

This useful term describes the condition immediately preceding the true factory system of late eighteenth-century Britain. In it a number of artisans are grouped together in a single building or place and they co-operate in producing a single and often highly specialised product. The process can be carefully divided into its component steps with the workers specialising to an extreme degree. Classicists will recognise an analogy with the *ergasterion* system of the Greek and later the Roman world.

The actual processes will be more or less the same as in the workshop and it is the use of the machinery of mass production usually powered by wind, water or steam that differentiates it from the true factory. The dividing line between the manufactory and the potter's workshop with two or three wheels and a handful of assistants is more difficult to discern. It is really a question of scale, and in order to provide an arbitrary dividing line we could suggest a limit of twelve employees for the workshop, since this is about the maximum encountered in the great centres of production at the present day such as Djerba or Nabeul in Tunisia. Archaeologically the manufactory will be distinguished by the size of premises, the degree of specialisation in the products, by the scale of output, and by evidence of worker specialisation.

Marx (1918:369) distinguishes two types of manufacture. In the first, labourers belonging to various independent handicrafts are grouped together and co-operate in producing a single complex artifact.

A carriage, for example, was formerly the product of the labour of a great number of independent artificers, such as wheelrights, harness-makers, tailors, locksmiths, upholsterers, turners, fringe-makers, glaziers, painters, polishers, gilders, etc. In the manufacture of carriages, however, all these different artificers are assembled in one building where they work into one another's hands. It is true a carriage cannot be gilt before it has been made. But if a number of carriages are being made simultaneously, some may be in the hands of gilders while others are going through an earlier process.

The second form of manufacture is exactly the opposite. All the artificers do the same kind of work, and, perhaps with the help of one or two apprentices, make the entire commodity. Marx cites papermaking or needle manufacture as examples. There is a natural tendency, however, for the job to be split into ever more specialised tasks.

Marx (1918:509) also draws attention to a related mode of production, which he terms 'domestic industry' although it is markedly different from the household industry defined above. Marx's domestic industry is really a sort of 'dispersed manufactory'. In this case the proprietor does not group his workers in a single building, but instead the work is done at home and consequently the centres of production may be spread over a considerable region. It differs from our household industry because the work is very much a full-time occupation and it is centrally directed by the proprietor who provides materials, sets standards and buys back the finished produce. Marx cites lace-making and straw-plaiting industries as examples of domestic industry and suggests that nineteenth-century working conditions could be as horrific as anything encountered in the manufactory or the factory.

It is clear that whatever arrangement is developed the injection of capital is necessary and it is this that really differentiates the workshop and the manufactory. In the workshop investment is required but financial outlay may be modest and the largest input will be one of time, for the technology is relatively simple and raw materials comparatively cheap.

6. THE FACTORY

A true factory system did not develop until the Industrial Revolution, but it is necessary to consider the concept here because the term has been too frequently and too loosely used by economic historians and archaeologists concerned with the Roman period. Many seem to fall unwittingly into the common trap of defining a factory as an organisation with a wide product distribution. Certainly, to survive, a factory must have an efficient managerial and marketing structure with a consequent broad distribution of goods, but Mantoux (1927:29) has already drawn attention to the fallacy of assuming that Persian carpets are factory made just because they are sold all over the world.

The definition of the term *factory* has been debated by historians of the Industrial Revolution (e.g. Mantoux, 1927; Marx, 1918:405) and it became of practical concern from 1802 onwards when the first factory legislation was passed. The factory mode of production is thus much less ambiguous than any of the five already discussed. The true factory involves the grouping together of workers and the specialisation of labour as in the manufactory. However it is larger and, above all, a factory must have machinery powered by something other than human or animal muscle.

Factories are thus more or less precluded from our considerations because it is generally accepted that the Roman world failed to exploit mechanical power to any extent. The power of water, wind or even steam were appreciated but their application was, at best, subsidiary to the use of human or animal power. However, the concept is not entirely irrelevant. Thus at Barbégal, in Southern France, a large complex of water-powered flour mills has been discovered, involving no less than thirty-two individual milling tables, and ventures of this nature might just qualify as factories (cf. Benoit, 1940; Sagui, 1948). As far as pottery is concerned, before we can speak of factories we must demonstrate the grouping and specialisation of labour in a special building and that the industry used power-driven wheels or other machines.

7. ESTATE PRODUCTION

This mode of production ranks as a special category because of its importance in the Roman economy. In practice its economic role is variable, sometimes akin to household production but sometimes on a more commercial basis.

Varro (*de r.r.*, i.22.1) and other ancient writers recommend that everything possible should be made on the estate to avoid unnecessary expense and ceramics were certainly included. However, on theoretical grounds one might not expect ordinary household pottery to be produced in this way because, except in a few notable cases, the estate is unlikely to have been big enough to make such an industry viable. However, heavy goods such as bricks and tiles could have been produced very economically on the estate because they do not require as much manufacturing skill as pottery and they would be expensive to import, particularly over land. Once the industry had become established, providing enough competent slaves or artisans were available, exportation and sale elsewhere might have been feasible.

Thus estate ceramic production is likely to begin in order to fulfil internal needs and to enhance the running of the property. However, once established production can assume a commercial role.

8. MILITARY AND OTHER OFFICIAL PRODUCTION

Normally it would make economic sense for military establishments to purchase, or in extreme cases to requisition, supplies from civilian sources, and as we shall see (p. 149) there is good evidence that this was generally the practice in the Roman world. However, under certain circumstances the army or navy made their own supplies, particularly of bricks and tiles required in quantity for building permanent garrisons, a need which the civilian production may not have been geared to meet. In addition the army potters were able to supply pottery to supplement needs where required. After all, it must be remembered that a legionary fortress would have had the consuming capacity of a small town.

From a theoretical point of view we would expect military production to be streamlined so as to produce maximum quantities in minimum time, but using as little manpower as possible since this could be required for more important and directly military tasks. Military production should thus show the hallmarks of efficient planned production and from a technological point of view we would expect it to utilise the best methods available.

Military activities are broadly of three types: the conquest of new lands, the consolidation of victory in a hostile environment, and finally the defence of a largely sympathetic population against aggression by an adversary. In each case it is reasonable to suggest that the ceramic requirements will be different.

During the initial phases of invasion and conquest there would be little scope for military production. It would be necessary to construct forts of wood and any essential pottery requirements would be requisitioned or imported from more peaceful areas. During the consolidation phase ceramics would continue to be imported and perhaps they would be bought from the native population where local production was at the right level and of the right character. However, during this phase the army might also undertake its own ceramic production. A main reason might be the need to maintain a permanent garrison and the desirability of housing this in a durable structure of brick and stone. We would thus predict brick and tile production to be extremely important, but we might also anticipate some involvement in pottery-making, for the skills are related and kiln equipment similar. In the defensive phase the army and civilian population are likely to be working together and so we would expect both brick and pottery supplies to be met by civilian producers. If this reasoning is correct military ceramics should closely reflect military strategy.

Production by municipal and state authorities might be variable, depending on the degree of interest or control exercised. In some cases manufacture and output might be very strictly monitored and destined for official use only. In other cases the works could be leased to an independent artisan who operated in his own way and sold to private as well as official customers. However, as with military production, the emphasis will always be on bricks and tiles rather than pottery.

3 The ethnography of pottery production in Europe and the Mediterranean area

To confine one's studies to mere antiquities is like reading by candle light at noon-day.

Daniel Wilson (1861:vii)

Classical archaeologists have generally eschewed ethnological evidence as a means of illuminating the past. There seem to be two reasons for this. Firstly, ethnographers have been preoccupied with primitive rather than more developed societies and it is with some reason that many would regard the tribal structure of Oceania as irrelevant to the problems of the Roman Empire. Secondly, the existence of a substantial literary heritage provides satisfying insights into the general nature, structure and workings of Greek and Roman society. However, the words of Daniel Wilson remain as true today as when they were first published more than a century ago: ethnography provides an alternative way of considering the past and we ignore it at our loss. Where several viewpoints are available they should be used and compared to counteract the inevitable distortion inherent in a single approach.

However, the use of ethnographic evidence is not entirely straightforward and it is important to be clear at the outset how and why it is used. Orme (1974) has conveniently summarised the changing patterns of thought on ethnographic parallels in prehistory. A major reservation voiced many times is that an observed phenomenon may result from different factors not necessarily operating in the model. Also the archaeologist may unwittingly compare socially contrasting societies. A further problem results from the nature and objectives of ethnographical research, which are seldom oriented towards the archaeologist's needs and the data for effective comparison may be unavailable. However, these reservations apart, there can be no doubt of the impact of ethnology upon current prehistoric studies.

Stiles (1977) has conveniently discussed the problems and objectives of 'ethnoarchaeology' – ethnographical studies specifically oriented towards archaeological problems. He suggests that ethnographic data can be used in three ways: the provision of analogies, as a source of 'inspiration' in the generation of models, or in the testing of hypotheses. To some extent all these approaches are to be found in this book, but our main objective is more specific, namely to illustrate and develop the model derived in Chapter 2. We need an appreciation of the degree of variability and potential subdivision within the broad categories defined above, a discussion of the technology and commercial networks associated with each mode to facilitate its archaeological recognition, and an understanding of what Matson (1966) has aptly termed the 'ceramic ecology' of production. In other words: what physical, biological and cultural factors determine why a particular mode of production occurs when or where it does, and how it has or might respond to ecological change.

Classical archaeology has already benefited from a specifically ethnoarchaeological approach in some areas. Casson (1938, 1951) perceived the relevance of modern Greek pottery trade in understanding its ancient analogue, while Mallowan (1939) has recorded an interesting modern example of exchange involving storage jars. Unfortunately, both writers tended to regard the modern situation as a hangover from the past, and more recently Warren (1978) has described modern Cretan flasks in the same vein. Even if it were possible to prove continuity it would not be particularly relevant because major changes are almost certain to have taken place over a couple of millennia. It is much more interesting to consider general economic questions. Why are the modern industries located where they are and what is their economic basis, or how do rural industries remain viable in the face of competition from industrial giants? An appreciation of these matters should help in explaining and understanding ancient ceramic phenomena.

The most extensive ethnoarchaeological studies relevant to the Classical period are those of Hampe and Winter (1962, 1965) who undertook investigations in Crete, Greece, Southern Italy and Sicily. They record a great deal of invaluable information about ceramic technology but, alas, very little about the social background or the commercial networks upon which the industries must rely. Ideally more studies are now required with rather different priorities and orientation, and Matson's (1972) ethnoarchaeological work in Greece, or Balfet's (1966, 1973) North African observations point the way.

With these reservations in mind we can now begin to look at modes of production through ethnography.

HOUSEHOLD PRODUCTION

It is surprising to discover that this simple mode of production, so favoured by prehistorians, is very rare ethnographically. While much pottery is made in the home, at least some is usually destined for the market.

The best example of household production seems to be the Berber pottery of North Africa already cited by van der Leeuw (1976). Balfet (1966) has admirably summarised the social setting:

the family constitutes a closed economic unit which produces its own essential equipment (with the exception of metal objects). Annually in each home the women replace the vessels which have been chipped or broken in the course of the year. At that time under the traditional local patriarchal family form of organisation, a veritable workshop is organised under the direction of the mistress of the home. The work is shared according to the free time and the ability of individuals. This ensures the carrying out of daily household tasks and the care of the children, and serves as an apprenticeship for the girls who learn the trade by watching and copying the procedure of the more skilful workers.

The pottery produced supplies the family with vessels for the preparation and the serving of meals, for the carrying and storing of water and for preserving yearly provisions. They also provide adornment for the home and give proof of the foresight, care and ability of its mistress, since the vessels are in full view, set out on shelves. The decorative and social role of pottery is far from negligible; it certainly helps explain the great care taken in the finishing process and the richness of the painted decoration. Each woman does that which she can do best, giving to it all the time and attention that her self-respect demands.

From this it will be apparent that the pottery is not intended for sale and in the majority of cases we would expect vessels to have been made very near to the spot where sherds are found. Very occasionally it might find its way onto the market and van Gennep (1911) states that at times of financial stringency a family might sell any household utensils of value such as half-used carpets or new pots. However, he stressed that Berber pottery is only occasionally and sporadically the object of commerce.

The technology of Berber production has been discussed by Franchet (1911), van Gennep (1911), Balfet (1966) and more recently in a thorough survey by Gruner (1973). Pottery-making usually takes place from about March to May with firings in the early summer. Clay is always obtained locally and Gruner (1973) records a maximum of 5 km transportation. Preparation is extremely simple; the clay is dried in the sun, broken down with a stone, sieved, mixed with water and left to cure for at least twenty-four hours. After tempering with sand, sherd or rock fragments it is ready for use. The vessels are ring-built on rectangular or round stone slabs and may be given a wet hand-finish to conceal the coarseness of the paste. The drying time is variable but at least seven days are required in the hottest month, August. When completely dry the vessels may be burnished with a stone and ornamented with painted decoration applied with a simple brush of animal fibre (Pl. 1).

Firing is also a rudimentary process. No kilns are used and small quantities of vessels are stacked

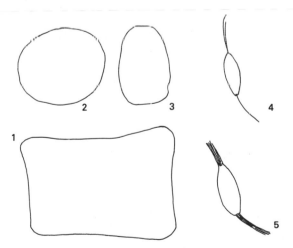

Figure 1 Berber pottery-making tools. No. 1, *estèque* or shaper in wood; Nos 2–3, shapers in stone from Tifra and Aït Lhassen; Nos 4–5, brushes of fibre and unfired clay (after van Gennep, 1911). Scale not given.

Plate 1   Berber painted dish made in 1979 by Saïdani Samir at Sedjenane, northern Tunisia. Diam. 31 cm.

together with dried dung and brushwood on the ground surface or in slight depressions (as at Taher and Tiberguent in Algeria). The object of the depression is to stabilise temperature and at Merkalla a ring of stones is used for the same purpose. The firing time is exceptionally short, 30–60 minutes being considered adequate.

The whole process will leave very few archaeological traces. With the exception of the basal stone and sometimes the shapers, the instruments are of perishable materials (Fig. 1). The firing process generally results in about 10 per cent wastage, but since the sherds will be left lying on the surface of the ground the conditions for preservation are not good. Virtually the only way of demonstrating this mode of

production archaeologically would be to show that there were differences in decorative styles between dwellings and that there was a correspondence between the fabric composition and locally available materials. In order to eliminate the possibility of exchange between settlements it would be necessary to demonstrate a contrast in composition between sites, and unless there were technological differences in, for example, the selection of temper, this could only be done in an area of markedly contrasting geology. Household production is likely to remain extremely elusive archaeologically.

One of the most extraordinary points about this household production is that it still exists at all, for the simple mode has survived conquest by Romans,

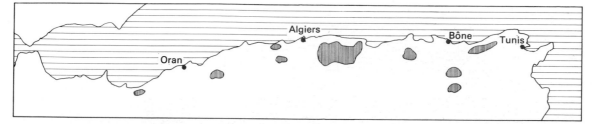

Figure 2 The Maghreb showing the main areas of Berber painted pottery production (after van Gennep, 1911).

Vandals, Arabs, Turks and French. A partial answer may be given by van Gennep's (1911: Fig. 6) distribution map redrawn as Fig. 2. It will be noted that the present-day concentrations lie away from the coast in the recesses of the Atlas mountains and it is presumably here that strong cultural traditions have been fostered by lack of contact with the outside world. No ceramic commerce developed within these areas because there was no market: tradition dictated that every woman should make her own pots and in any case a low level of subsistence may have precluded the luxury of purchase.

However, the situation is changing. The arrival of the French army in the nineteenth century placed a curiosity value on Berber pots and this has been accelerated by the advent of tourism (Gruner,

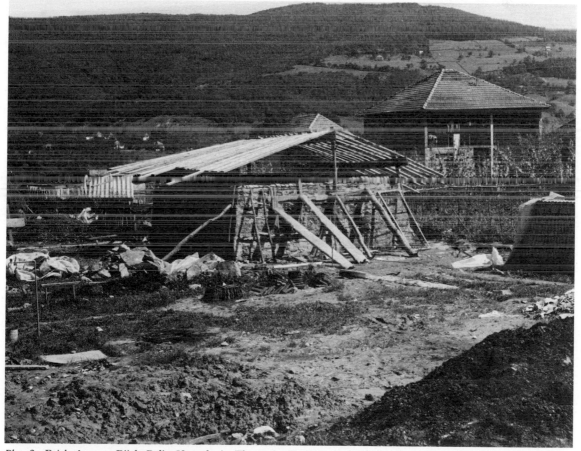

Plate 2 Brick clamp at Bijelo Polje, Yugoslavia. The stack of hand-made bricks has been given a thin skin of clay and equipped with a roof of open wooden laths.

Plate 3   Brick clamp on the island of Thasos, Greece. Although the bricks are machine-made they are fired in simple clamps with walls one brick thick.

1973:160). Some potters now produce for the market and styles are changing in response to consumer demand as well as workmanship becoming more slipshod. Commercialisation is such that at some places such as Merkalla in Algeria, or Sedjenane in Tunisia, the seasonal pattern has been disrupted in an effort to meet demand. Better communication and the development of marketing possibilities is rapidly transforming this ancient mode of production to another commercially more advanced.

BRICK-MAKING

Bricks and tiles require considerably less manufacturing skill than pottery and it is perhaps surprising that their production seldom appears to be a household activity, but unfortunately the brick industry is rather poorly documented. In 1975, during a visit to the autonomous southern Yugoslavian province of Kosovo, I observed peasants firing small quantities of bricks in their gardens. It was impossible to investigate this activity, but it seems plausible that each household was making its own annual requirement.

The manufacture of mud bricks requires even less effort and it is not surprising that there is some evidence of their production on a household basis. Eruin and Tamás (1977) furnish an example of this among the gipsy population of Debrecen in eastern Hungary. In their rehousing programme, the Hungarian authorities allocate land and provide some services such as water supply. The gipsies are left to do much of the rest for themselves including making mud bricks for building their own homes. Activities such as this are but a small step from the household production of ceramic bricks, since clamp firing can be a relatively straightforward process.

Several types of brick clamp are in use at the present day, all of which involve the piling of bricks on the surface of the ground with fuel, sometimes also contained within the clay. Often the raw material is naturally rich in organic matter, but in other cases it is customary to mix additional fuel when the clay is being prepared. The simplest form of clamp is illustrated in Pl. 2, which shows a pile of bricks being fired at Bijelo Polje in central Yugoslavia, perhaps in a domestic rather than a commercial situation. The stack of hand-made bricks has been coated with a thin skin of clay to retain and direct the heat during firing. This example should be contrasted with the commercial brick clamps on the Greek Island of Thasos (Pl. 3) where the enclosing wall is a permanent skin, one brick thick.

HOUSEHOLD INDUSTRY

A situation rather similar to household production existed in the Balkans until recently (Filipović, 1951; Tomić, 1966). Over parts of southern Yugoslavia, Albania, northern Greece, European Turkey, Romania and Bulgaria, it was traditional for a woman to make certain household utensils for herself. However, by the middle of this century many homes were by no means self-sufficient and a considerable degree of specialisation and trading had set in. The women producing these vessels increasingly bartered them for corn or even sold on the open market. Filipović (1951) published a striking photograph showing a peasant selling her wares on the streets of Skopje in 1936.

It must be stressed that a household did not meet its entire ceramic requirements in this way and only certain coarse specialised forms (usually those employed for baking) were made in the home. Water jars and other equally indispensible utensils were purchased from specialist potters who used the wheel.

The making of pans for baking requires extremely simple technology involving neither the wheel nor the turntable. The clay was usually obtained free of charge from the common land on the outskirts of the village and over the years the cumulative effect of many minor diggings often gave rise to a distinctive hummocky topography. Clay digging is hard work and sometimes men assisted in this task. The rest of the process was in the hands of the women who picked out any foreign matter after which the dry material was crushed and sieved. It was then mixed with water and left to cure for five to ten days but sometimes for as long as three weeks. A temper was then mixed in and a wide variety of materials were considered suitable: dung, goatswool, bristle, tow, straw, soot or calcite. This material was thoroughly mixed by kneading with the feet on the floor, after which the vessel was modelled on a piece of board also lying on the floor. The only precaution was a sprinkling of sand or ash to prevent sticking. Drying times were highly variable, ranging from several months to a year if the vessel was not urgently required. In some cases the pans were finished by burnishing with a stone after the surface had been rubbed with soot or dung. Firing was as simple as the clay preparation and forming. Surprisingly in some cases the pots were not fired at all, this operation being combined with the first usage. Where prior firing was considered desirable this was usually done individually by covering a single vessel with ash in an open fire or the domestic hearth.

This rudimentary mode of production is particularly interesting because in contrast to the Berber situation we see the first move towards craft specialisation and commerce, although it should be noted that the ware was never exported outside its general production region. It is interesting to observe that it was often the poorer women who produced for others in order to supplement a meagre existence (Filipović, 1951).

This situation is very reminiscent of the manner in which 'craggans' or coarse household pottery were produced in the Hebrides up to the early years of this century (Holleyman, 1947). They were made by the simplest means and from material requiring minimal preparation. Their production was normally a feminine household chore without market interest, although a minor degree of specialisation and some local trading had set in towards the end.

A slight advance is to be seen in the Canary Islands where a once thriving and widespread industry has now receded to four localities (Gonzalez, 1977; Köpke, 1974; Crawford, 1936; Llorens and Corredor, 1974). Again vessels are made by women without a wheel or turntable, but firing is more advanced and a simple stone-built updraught kiln is sometimes employed as an alternative to open firings. This technological innovation seems to be associated with an increased interest in marketing.

A similar market orientation was displayed by the potters of Corsica recorded by Chiva and Ojalvo (1959). Hand-made pottery was made at three neighbouring villages situated in the hills of the northeastern part of the island, Farinole, Canaja and Monacia. All used the same raw materials, *terra rossa* mixed with asbestos, and hence their wares might appear today as a single petrological group. The industry seems to have been largely in the hands of women who fashioned a limited range of dishes and pans. At both Farinole and Canaja they were fired in bread ovens while at Monacia the firings took place in the open air with the assistance of menfolk. As in our previous examples pottery was a part-time occupation, in this case the six months' season started in April or May.

However, the marketing patterns of the three

Plate 4   Corsican lady peddling pots in the nineteenth century (from Galetti, 1863).

villages were strikingly different. The women from Farinole sold on the coast or journeyed to the Balagne in the west of the island (Pl. 4). The Canaja potters oriented their sales to the north and marketed by peddling around the Nebbio or by selling at the markets of Murato and Bastia as well as Corte and Ajaccio. At Monacia a totally different system operated for the pots were handed over to men who made extensive sales tours of the west and south of the island. It would appear that the potters were trying to seek areas where they could expect a monopoly and competition seems to have been carefully avoided. If so this must be a near-perfect example of the principal expounded by Bradley (1971), who suggested that merchants will tend to select areas that are mutually exclusive.

   At one time this simple mode of production and distribution must have been very widespread. It is particularly striking that an almost identical female industry has been recorded as far away as Jutland by Steensberg (1939, 1940), who has published a number

of articles describing it. Again technological refinement was minimal and neither wheel nor kiln was employed. Firings took place in the open, in a manner resembling charcoal burning, but the unfired vessels were first treated in a specially constructed smoke house (Fig. 3) to seal their pores with fine soot. The industry was definitely oriented towards the market and in its heyday black pots from Jutland found their way by horse and ship all over northern Europe, to Holland, Norway, Latvia, Estonia, Germany as far as Berlin and Dresden, and even in certain instances to Vienna, some 1000 km away. It is particularly striking that times of maximum output during the eighteenth and nineteenth centuries coincided with periods of maximum poverty, when the inhabitants of Jutland found it necessary to supplement their meagre livelihood by turning to peripheral industries such as pottery and wool work. The death-knell of the industry was only sounded when the heaths were ploughed and planted in the second half of the nineteenth century. The resulting

Figure 3 Pots being taken out of a smoke kiln, Jutland (from a photograph published by Steensberg, 1940).

improvement in agriculture had a dramatic effect for it made farming profitable and the old standbys could be abandoned.

An advance on this simple system has been recorded in many parts of Europe. In certain districts of Yugoslavia a hand-wheel or turntable is used to make vessels for the market or exchange (Tomić, 1966; Popović, 1959) and in some places men may be involved as well as women. Pottery is always a subsidiary activity but investment in equipment as well as the involvement of men is a sure indication that these industries are playing a much greater role in rural subsistence. However, systems of this type are admirably documented in Iberia and it is from there that we shall take our more detailed examples.

A primitive mode of production involving female potters still exists in some of the more remote parts of Iberia at the present day. Köpke (1974) has published a major paper reviewing the Spanish evidence, to which should be added Ribeiro's (1962) excellent account of analogous industries in northern Portugal. To illustrate this somewhat higher order of production we shall consider the female potters of the Province of Zamora, where production has been described from Pereruela and Moveros, but a further industry now extinct was based on the village of Muelas del Pan near Zamora.

Cortés Vázquez (1954) has discussed the Pereruela potters in exemplary detail. In his day there were forty-six potting families but twenty years later only eight were left (Vossen, Seseña and Köpke,

1975:244). One of the extraordinary features of this industry is the lack of clay pits. One type of clay is obtained from diggings on common land, but another seems to be collected more or less at random from local estates. In order to avoid paying dues, the extraction is a clandestine affair usually carried out at night or by first light of day, and it is quite astonishing to discover that a once thriving industry should be based upon a form of poaching! However, there is an exception to this rule of local origin, for one of the specialities of the village is the crucible which requires a special refractory body, produced by mixing local clay with material from Tamama about 10 km away.

When the clay has been brought home it is placed in a rectangular hole up to 1 metre long, 60 cm wide and 40 cm deep, where it is mixed with water. After it has cured for several hours some of the *tierra* (or clay obtained from common land) may be added and also a temper usually comprising the decayed granitic 'rab', upon which the village is built. The mixing operation is particularly important and may take three or four hours, more *tierra* being added until the correct consistency has been attained.

No particular area is set aside for pottery-making, which is frequently done in the street outside the house. The basic instrument is the turntable which is shown in Fig. 4. It consists of a heavy disc of wood 6 cm thick and 40 cm in diameter, mounted on a substructure in the form of a cross. A pivot set in a stone socket supports the structure and it is lubricated with olive oil or lard. Before commencing work, a disc of baked clay is mounted on a ring of clay centred on the table. This forms the base upon which

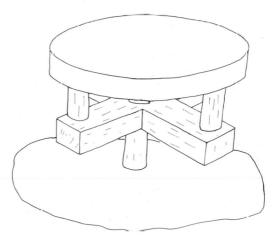

Figure 4 Turntable from Pereruela (Zamora) (after Cortés Vázquez, 1954).

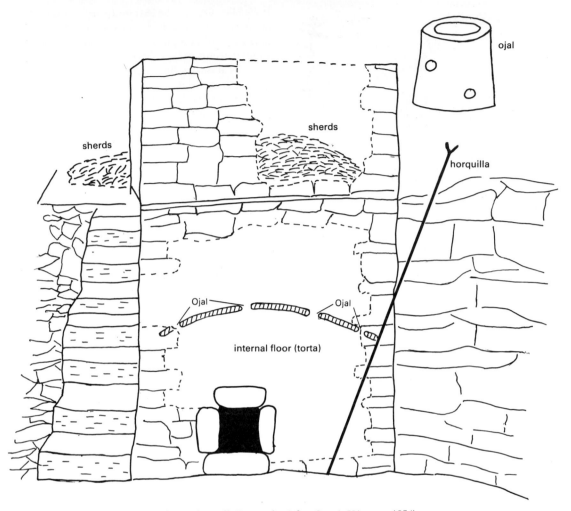

Figure 5　*Horno alto* (high kiln), with iron *horquilla* Pereruela. (after Cortés Vázquez, 1954).

the pot is built. When the bottom of the vessel has been made the sides are built up by adding sausages or rings of clay, the potter kneeling by her wheel throughout. The completed vessels are placed in the sun to dry. They may be finished by glazing with ready-ground galena obtained from Linares in Andalucia. Preparation and dipping may be delegated to other members of the family or to the husband if he is involved in the pottery business.

Men are also involved in the firing process and some men specialise in this, buying unfired vessels from the many women or families who do not possess a kiln. Until recently two types of kiln were in use. The simplest comprises a circular pit about 0.5 m deep and 1.5–2 m in diameter, lined with vertical stones to prevent the pots touching the soil while firing. On one side is a small opening or flue protected by three stones arranged to form jambs and a lintel. One or two large jars, either fired or unfired, are placed in the pit and lined up with the flue. Then the largest vessels are piled up resting upon these and upon the stones lining the wall and the smaller vessels placed on top. The whole pile is then blanketed with sherds. Wood is introduced through the flue and pushed around the jars at the bottom. A kiln of this type has a capacity of about seventy cooking pots and requires about a cartload of wood per firing. Despite its primitive design, it apparently produces excellent results.

The alternative method of firing at Pereruela is to use the high kiln (*horno alto*) shown in Fig. 5. It is an open rectangular stone tower about 1.5 m square built on the ground surface. Near the base is a flue opening and about half way up is a clay floor with perforations over which are placed cylindrical clay *ojales* (Fig. 5). The kiln is filled from the top which is reached by stone steps and once again the load is covered with sherds.

The capacity of these kilns varies between 150–250 vessels. The firing takes eight or nine hours and consumes up to two cartloads of wood. It is no more economic than the pit kiln, and the advantages must be greater capacity and, particularly, less dependence on the variability of the wind. Finally, one instrument ought to be mentioned, the *horquilla* (Fig. 5), an iron rod 2 m long, used in stoking and in lifting sherds from the roof to check the process of firing.

The forms produced at Pereruela are very limited. The main products are cooking vessels, with some jugs, crucibles and bread ovens. The products are not sold through local fairs but are generally distributed by mule to neighbouring villages and to Zamora, and occasionally they are traded as far as León or El Barco de Valdeorras in eastern Galicia, a range of about 150 km. The products are also bought by middlemen who distribute to more distant parts such as Burgos or Andalucia. Despite its broad distribution, the pottery of Pereruela is very much the product of a household system. Potting is never an essential means of livelihood and it always takes second place to the more important demands of agriculture. The pottery season runs from late February or March to June and from September to October, but interruptions are frequent should farming demand it.

Cortés Vázquez (1958) has described an almost identical industry from the village of Moveros some 54 km northwest of Zamora. Here twenty to twenty-five pottery concerns in 1958 had been reduced to ten by 1973. The technology and social organisation is virtually identical with that of Pereruela and thus there is no need to reiterate details. However, it is worth drawing attention to the *mavadero* used to break the dry clay (Fig. 6) for the same instrument recurs on Thasos, Greece (p. 31).

Again a limited range of forms is produced at Moveros, but this time they are principally water jars rather than cooking vessels. However, the marketing system is radically different and forms an interesting contrast with that of the Pereruela potters. Once again the vessels are peddled around the province by the potters themselves but a principal mode of distribution is through numerous local fairs of which Cortés (1958:103) lists examples, all within a range of

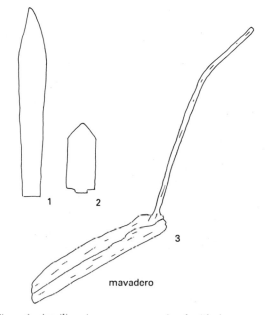

Figure 6 Auxiliary instruments associated with the household industries of north-western Iberia. Nos 1–2, *esquinante* and *fanadoiro* (after Ribeiro, 1962); No. 3, *mavadero* for breaking clay from Moveros (after Cortés Vázquez, 1958).

about 30 km. Particularly important is the *romeria de la Luz* held on the Spanish–Portuguese frontier on the last Sunday in April and through this the Moveros products cross the frontier and find their way into the homes of northern Portugal.

It is hardly surprising that similar industries are to be found across the border in Portugal itself, and Ribeiro (1962) has published a useful comparative analysis of seven pottery-making localities. Space does not permit detailed discussion but it is worthwhile drawing attention to points of difference. Once again production is a domestic affair carried out when agricultural or household duties permit or according to demand. However, in only three of the seven localities listed by Ribeiro is the work in the hands of women and in the remaining four pottery is an exclusively male occupation. This is clearly a natural extension of the situation we have already seen where men help with clay digging or firing, and it implies that pottery may occupy a more essential role in subsistence.

The clay is dug locally and is broken down with a large wooden hammer in stone tubs and is prepared in much the same way as we have already seen though there are local variations. The method of forming the vessel is almost identical and a similar

Plate 5   Turntable used until recently at Rakalj, Istria, Yugoslavia (photographed courtesy Etnografski i Historijski Muzej, Pazin). Table diam 37.5 cm.

Plate 6   Black two-handled cooking pots made on the turntable at Rakalj, Istria (photographed courtesy Etnografski i Historijski Muzej, Pazin). Maximum diam 26 cm.

turntable is employed. Ribeiro's photographs suggest that when men are involved the turntable can be heavier with a broader, thicker table, which tallies with my own observations in Yugoslav museums. The type of turntable greatly affects the appearance of the wares. The products of the light turntable from Rakalj in Istria, shown in Pl. 5, are fairly rough and uneven (Pl. 6), and they contrast, for example, with those from Višnjice housed in Sarajevo museum, which were made by men using a heavy turntable and are almost indistinguishable from true wheel-made products. This also seems to be true of the Portuguese wares, and clearly the distinction between the products of the fast wheel and the heavy turntable is one of degree. Discrimination is important and will be discussed further below (p. 26).

Ancillary instruments are often used with turntables and Fig. 6 shows the Portuguese *esquinante* and *fanadoiro*, both of which are made of wood. The Portuguese products are again dominated by a few household forms and there are differences in typology and ornament, as well as petrology, between the production centres. However, one major contrast with the Spanish centres is that the wares are intentionally black or grey and the firing procedure is adjusted accordingly. Above-ground kilns are available for achieving this but they are rare in comparison with the *soenga* type firing. A pit is dug some 3.5 m in diameter and the pots stacked in the centre with firewood around them, after which the whole mass is enclosed by covering with turf, soil or vegetable matter. The firing takes three of four hours and the potters will watch the progress immediately covering any points where the flame burns through the outer blanket. The whole operation is in many ways reminiscent of charcoal burning, and may be carried out individually or on a communal basis with a number of potters sharing the work.

Ribeiro (1962:413) records little about marketing but it would seem that the wares are usually distributed through local fairs. For example, the potters of Fazamões near Rèsende carry their pots by mule or even on their own backs in the manner of the 'poor cratemen' who distributed wares from the seventeenth-century Staffordshire potteries (Thomas, 1971:4). It is usual for them to attend fairs within a range of about 40 km.

GENERAL COMMENTS

The case histories discussed above have been carefully selected to illustrate variations in household industry

from the simplest facies where incipient craft specialisation can be discerned to technically and commercially advanced systems, so well illustrated in northwestern Iberia. The examples have been chosen because they are particularly well documented or because they illustrate important points, but it is worth stressing that this mode was very widespread in the recent past of Europe and North Africa and we have merely examined certain key localities from a broad geographical spectrum. This mode seems to have existed in Brittany (Franchet, 1911:57), Cyprus (Taylor and Tufnell, 1930; Hampe and Winter, 1962), the Pyrenees (Jagor, 1882), Albania (Nopcsa, 1925; Onuzi, 1974, 1976), Italy (Whitehouse, 1978; Mannoni, 1975), Asia Minor (Dawkins, 1916; Steele, 1971), and in parts of North Africa (e.g. Ginestous, 1947; Herber, 1931), to cite some of the more readily accessible additional examples. Throughout this broad area there are remarkable similarities and it is worth drawing together the salient points.

Firstly, more often than not household industry is operated by women, a point which was anticipated when the mode was defined. Even more striking, however, are the similarities in technology. Although several designs of turntable were known and used (e.g. Popović, 1959; Rieth, 1952), the variety with a cross-bar substructure (Fig. 4) is encountered over wide areas including Albania, Yugoslavia, the Pyrenees, Spain and Portugal. The reason for this homogeneity is far from clear, but it is possible that it is an efficient design evolved independently by different communities.

However, a second point of congruence is even more striking, for it seems that household industry nearly always develops in a closely similar social and economic environment. Almost everywhere it appears to be associated with poverty, and particularly with an inability to maintain a reasonable standard of living from farming alone. In Spain it is found in the western part of the Province of Zamora where the rich farming lands of Old Castile give way to the harsher granite terrain of the Douro Plateau. Again in Portugal this mode survives in the mountainous north rather than in the rich granary of the Alentejo further south, and we have already noted the connection between potting and the impoverished heathlands of Jutland. This relationship can be strikingly demonstrated in Yugoslavia. Figure 7 shows the distribution of turntables superimposed on the basic pattern of land use. It will be seen that there appears to be a concentration along the southwestern edge of the rich arable plain of northern and eastern Yugoslavia, and within the Dinaric area

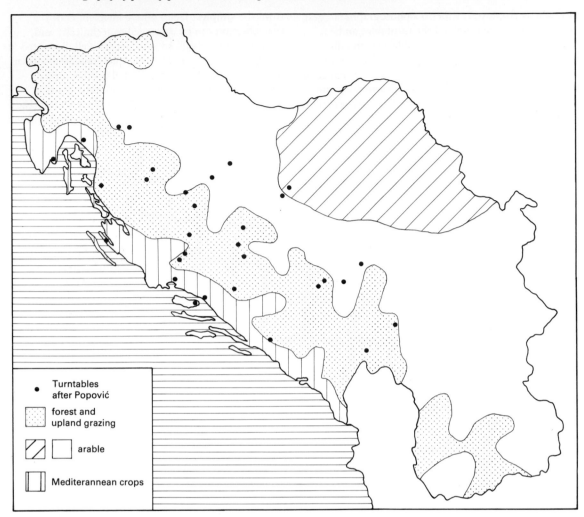

Figure 7   Yugoslavia, showing land use (after Beckinsale and Beckinsale, 1975) and the distribution of turntables (after Popović, 1959).

dominated by forests and upland pasture. The implication seems clear: as farming gets harder, household industries, among them potting, become more attractive. The industry of Mota del Cuervo in central Spain described by Seseña (1967) and Albertos *et al.* (1978) might be an exception. It is situated within the rich and productive plain of New Castile but even here the rule might apply for the nineteenth-century *Diccionario Geográfico de España* refers to the undistinguished nature of the soils around the town.

Finally, it remains to remark that pots produced in this way can be very cheap because potting is always subsidiary to the more important activity of farming and it is merely a pursuit to fill in moments that would otherwise be unproductive. Thus if the potter can obtain but a small price for her wares, it is nevertheless a perquisite that she would be without if she did not ply her trade. This point was noted some years ago by Tax (1953) in Guatemala and it seems to apply equally to Europe. It is presumably the pricing structure that accounts for the extraordinarily broad distribution sometimes achieved by these rough and often blackened wares.

On the other hand it is too easy to impose modern value judgements on pottery which often appears coarse and crude. It must be remembered that in many cases the wares are extremely resilient and the coarse fabric withstands contact with an open flame far better than more refined clays. Thus, often these wares are well adapted to their primary purpose which is usually cooking. In addition the pottery is often held to impart a particularly desirable flavour to food prepared in them and Cortés (1954:147) quotes a local folk song which eulogistically mentions the properties of food cooked in pottery presumed to be from Pereruela (see p. 75).

WORKSHOP INDUSTRIES

INTRODUCTION

The economics of the workshop are vastly different whether they be discrete or nucleated units. By definition the potter must now derive his main livelihood from the clay and as a result he is obliged to work within more rigorous economic constraints. He must produce wares in quantity and sell at a price adequately reflecting his labour. This will normally mean that his output must be of good quality and a substantial investment in technology may be necessary, although the investment may involve time rather than capital. The true potter's wheel and the kiln now have a vital role to play, for without them quantity and quality are harder to achieve.

We might therefore anticipate a considerable technical contrast between the workshop and household industry, and not surprisingly there are also radical differences in the economic settings which tend to foster these developments. I have suggested that household industry is often related to agricultural problems and it is reasonable to expect these to play some part in the establishment of workshops. Llorens and Corredor (1974) cite a number of examples where Spanish potters seem to be operating in an impoverished environment, and it was long ago asserted that the workshops of seventeenth-century Staffordshire relate to the poor farming potential of the Coal Measures (Hollowood, 1940). However, in reality the situation is very much more complex and in many cases the underlying causes are more difficult to unravel.

The economic effectiveness of a workshop will depend on a number of parameters of which the most important seem to be the availability and quality of the clay, the abundance and type of fuel and the distance, density and sophistication of the markets. Obviously the most viable potteries will be those fortunate enough to be near a potential market, but this is not always possible, for both clay and fuel are heavy and expensive to transport and in many cases it will be advantageous to work near to the raw materials. The success of a workshop will depend upon a balance between clay, fuel and markets, but the precise weighting will vary from one workshop to another. For example, if heavy earthenwares are being produced it may be vital to sell in the immediate vicinity for transportation costs will be high and there may be a limit to the price the market will stand. On the other hand table ware may be transported much further because it weighs less and has a much higher value. However, it may require rather better clays which could place a restriction on the number of localities where such products could be made.

Fuel is another variable which will affect the balance, but unfortunately it is very difficult to assess. Some figures serve to illustrate its importance. It is striking to note that the potteries of eighteenth–nineteenth-century Staffordshire consumed 3 tons of coal to every 1 ton of clay (Thomas, 1937). The requirements of wood-burning kilns are more difficult to obtain but they may have been of the same order. The first experimental Romano-British kiln built by Mayes (1961) required 10 units of wood to fire every 1 of clay. Subsequent experiments have significantly improved on these figures, although weights of clay are not generally recorded (cf. Mayes, 1962; Bryant, 1971, 1973).

It is clear that a large pottery or brick industry would demand a great deal of fuel and it is natural therefore that archaeologists should often think in terms of depleting fuel supplies as an explanation of a declining industry. In practice, however, almost all modern industries develop a symbiotic relationship with the natural environment. The coppicing of woodland is one obvious way in which a wooded landscape can be rapidly regenerated in temperate Europe. Frequently, however, pottery-making is finely adjusted to the surplus waste of farming, and this can be seen in the great potteries of Tunisia. At Nabeul and Moknine, pottery-making relies heavily on supplies of *grignons* – the waste from olive pressing – while on Djerba the prunings from date palms and olive trees are sufficient to support a very considerable industry. Elsewhere, ceramic industries obtain fuel from ground that is of little interest to the farmer. At Kairouan for example, the brick industry utilises 'hashish', a coarse heather-like grass imported from the local hills.

From this brief discussion it should be evident that the factors determining the location and development of a ceramic workshop industry are far from simple and contrast with those fostering a household industry. The type of clay available, the nature and distance of the markets, fuel supply and the regional agricultural economy all interact in a complex fashion, and every case is to some extent individual. Unfortunately ethnographers, as well as archaeologists, have failed to consider these parameters in sufficient depth and more fieldwork is urgently required before it is too late. Too often papers on modern pottery-making record all the technical details of the process, but fail to mention the obvious – such as the relationship of the ceramic industry to the local economy.

We must now examine a number of examples of workshop practice and economics and once again an artificial selection has been made to illustrate systems of increasing complexity. It is convenient to treat individual and nucleated potteries together, for although they can display great economic differences they are really the end members of a merging spectrum of ceramic activity. Thus it is easy to conceive a situation where potters work in the same locality attracted by good clay or fuel, but they act as more or less independent units, enjoying few if any of the benefits of nucleation. Firstly, however, we must review certain technical matters.

THE TURNTABLE IN WORKSHOP INDUSTRIES

The individual workshop, if that is an appropriate term, could be seen in a rudimentary form among the Zaër potters of Morocco (Herber, 1931). Here pottery was a full-time male activity interrupted only by rain, cold, or marketing activities. A mixture of two local clays was used and the vessels were fashioned on a simple turntable. After thorough drying in the open air the pottery was fired in a surface bonfire of wood, straw and dung. Marketing was equally basic and the wares were exchanged in the local *souk* or sometimes sold to visiting middlemen. At first sight this interesting industry does not make sense for it would surely be profitable for a full-time potter to employ the wheel and the kiln and this is certainly the case in the great pottery centres of Morocco, such as Fez, Marrakesh or Meknes. However, there are two points that might be pertinent. Firstly, tradition could have been important, the potter preferring to work with a familiar instrument for there is a considerable difference in manipulating a fast wheel and a light turntable (where any momentum comes from the potter's fingers). However, even more important is the social setting, for Herber's illustrations show the potters to be tent dwellers and they would thus lack premises on which to build more permanent

structures leading to greater output or more sophisticated products.

At this point it is appropriate to mention other small potteries in Morocco, well exemplified by those of Karia-ba-Mohammed (Balfet, 1973). During the summer, the slack season in farming, the households in the potters' quarter are transformed into workshops and the menfolk – father and son – become potters with other members of the family taking a subsidiary role. A heavy turntable disc, kept in a corner of the courtyard, is placed on the only fixed part of the installation, a metallic pivot held in a block of wood sunk in the ground and protected by an inverted pot when not in use (Fig. 8). The situation is very close to that of the male potters of Portugal and Yugoslavia and in this area of activity, the dividing line between workshop and household industry can be hard to discern. It is tempting to include Karia under this heading because of the intensity of activity and the fixed installation, but the case for including it in our discussion of household industry is almost equally cogent. Since the boundary between household and workshop industry is, at best, hazy, it is hardly surprising that this applies equally to the principal instruments associated with each, the turntable and the potter's wheel. It is worth considering the matter a little further at this juncture.

Balfet (1973) has stressed the need to consider not only instruments but the techniques involved in achieving a desired result. Thrown pottery involves a certain set of movements which are normally associated with the wheel powered by foot or by a baton. However, it is perfectly possible to use these techniques on a turntable to produce authentic thrown pottery. As an archaeological example she cites a small group of chalcolithic vessels from Beersheba which might normally be classed as 'wheel-turned': Karia-ba-Mohammed provides an ethnographical explanation of this phenomenon, without the need to postulate extravagant technological innovation in the chalcolithic Levant. Balfet argues that the wheel is not used at Karia for good social and technical reasons. Firstly, in the domestic setting there is always a spare pair of hands available to turn the disc while the potter works and in any case the principal form produced is a large jug which involves much handwork so that only a small part of the total process involves the turntable.

The importance of technique is undeniable but attention must also be given to the instrument for surely not all turntables could be used for throwing. Hulthén (1974:69) has suggested that the peripheral speed of the outer surface of the clay is crucial and

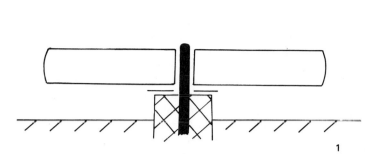

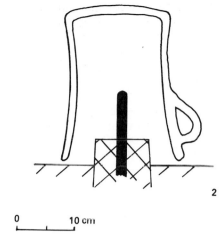

1

2

0   10 cm

Figure 8 Turntable, Karia-ba-Mohammed, Morocco. No. 1, in use, No. 2, pivot covered with a pot during the slack season (after Balfet, 1973).

states that 0.7 m per second or more is required to produce wheel-thrown pottery. Clearly to maintain this speed against the resistance of the clay a heavy disc, able to store momentum, might be desirable. The light turntable illustrated in Pl. 5 would probably be unsuited for throwing pottery even in the hands of the most skilled potter working with an assistant. At present it seems difficult to draw firm lines but perhaps a programme of experiments using different designs of turntable or wheel in various ways might be instructive.

Hodges (1964:28) has suggested a morphological difference between the two instruments: a wheel is composed of two parts, the head on which the clay is formed and the flywheel which stores and transmits the momentum, whereas the turntable comprises but a single disc serving both purposes. This definition is certainly useful when considering and classifying instruments, but the nature of the product must also be taken in account. If we adopt this terminology rigidly it would lead to the statement that Greek painted pottery (which most people would regard as wheel-thrown) was often produced on a turntable.

Although the turntable is rarely a principal instrument in present-day workshops it can play a major subsidiary role because it is particularly well suited to the production of large vessels. It is not surprising, therefore, that Dudley-Buxton and Hort (1921) should have recorded the co-existence of both the turntable and foot wheel in a pottery at Birchircara in Malta.

The potters of Thrapsanos on Crete also use both. The wheel is employed in the potteries of the village for producing normal everyday wares but the turntable is used for making the giant *pithoi* required for storing oil, wine and cereals (Voyatzoglou, 1973; Hampe and Winter, 1962). Since these vessels are large they are both expensive and cumbersome to transport. The problem has been solved in an interesting and unusual manner, for from 21 May to 14 September the potters depart in groups for different parts of the island where they rent a piece of land with all the necessities of potting – good clay, water and fuel. Here they build a kiln or repair an old one and they make simple huts of material ready to hand. These serve as sleeping and eating quarters as well as for the preparation of clay. Outside, a trench is dug and a line of turntables built in it, so that the potter is able to work at ground level while the assistant turning the table squats in the trench. Each vessel is built up, one coil at a time with about an hour's drying between steps. By working along the line of turntables it is possible to maintain a constant flow of work and at the end of the day eight complete vessels can be removed to dry in the sun. When a sufficient number is ready they are fired in the updraught kiln which has a capacity of about twenty-four vessels. Remarkably the firing lasts but four or five hours and the kiln is emptied the next day. About 400 or 500 vessels can be produced in a season, the majority of which are sold locally.

The organisation behind these undertakings is particularly interesting for traditionally the potters arranged themselves into guilds of six, each member of the team having a clearly defined role: the master potter, the second potter, the wheeler, the clay man, the wood cutter and the carrier. At the end of the season they return to Thrapsanos where they engage in farming or other potting activities. This well-known example illustrates an ingenious way of overcoming the difficulties and costs of transporting exceptionally heavy vessels. The turntable is particularly well suited for it is readily portable and ideal for the construction of large jars.

WORKSHOP EQUIPMENT

So far we have been considering the exceptions rather than the rule and at this juncture it seems pertinent to consider the technology normally associated with workshop industries. We will commence with the most important innovation, the potter's wheel. It should be evident, in the light of the above discussion, that the distinction between a heavy turntable and the true potter's wheel is bound to be somewhat arbitrary.

Some of the different types of wheel associated with workshops today and in the recent past are illustrated in Fig. 9. Perhaps the commonest variety and the one which immediately springs to mind is the double or kick wheel which comprises two wooden discs of unequal size mounted on a vertical spindle (Fig. 9.2). The lower flywheel is driven by the potter's feet. It is normal to employ either foot, resting the other on a crossbar, and a seat is often, though not always, an integral part of the design.

Another common design is the large spoked variety resembling a horizontally mounted cartwheel (Fig. 9.1). The potter sits astride the wheel, which he propels by placing a pole in the spokes. It is somewhat more cumbersome than the first variety as the hands must be periodically removed from the clay, but at one time it had a very wide distribution and is recorded from parts of France such as Provence, the Auvergne, Brittany and Haut-Berry (Serre, 1961; Franchet, 1911; Fabre, 1935; Chaton and Talbot, 1977). The basic design is still employed over much of India and Pakistan (Rye and Evans, 1976; Saraswati and Behura, 1966).

A more unusual design is the rope wheel shown in Fig. 9.3. Here the horizontal head is driven by a larger vertical wheel turned by an assistant or apprentice. It has the disadvantage that two men are required, but it does permit rather precise control over the speed of the head. This type of wheel was used both before and during the industrial revolution in Britain and remained in use until very recently in the Truro pottery (Brears, 1972).

These are the principal types but there are other varieties which may have been employed in certain parts of Europe. For example, in Agricola's *De Re Metallica* there is an illustration of a spoked kick wheel of a type that was presumably popular in sixteenth-century Germany and a rather similar version is found in the lower Rhineland two centuries later (Myer-Heisig, 1955).

Various attempts have been made to establish a sequence of turntables and wheels from the simplest to the most complex devices. Franchet (1911:55) was among the first to propose a simple evolutionary scheme, and saw the double or kick wheel as a descendant of the pivoted turntable which in turn derived from the unpivoted turntable. Foster (1959) has suggested a more elaborate sequence: unpivoted turntable → pivoted turntable → simple wheel (i.e. the cartwheel variety described above) → double or kick wheel. His scheme has been marginally modified by Scheans (1965). At this juncture it is worth recalling Balfet's (1973) point, that an instrument cannot be dissociated from its mode of use.

While it is helpful to think in terms of technical evolution, any scheme of progressive development is bound to be an artificial oversimplification, for artifacts can only really be considered in relation to the social and economic circumstances in which they were employed. To regard one instrument as more advanced than another is to venture a technical value judgement which may be of little worth. The slab of stone on which the Berber lady builds her pot is simple but well adapted to circumstances where small quantities of pottery are made on an annual or even longer cycle. The turntable is ideally suited to the woman engaged in household industry but it would be as economically ludicrous for her to invest in the full paraphernalia of the workshop as it would be for the full-time potter to work without it. It cannot be stressed enough that artifacts and techniques must be considered in their social and economic contexts.

The use of the wheel demands a number of specialised instruments to assist in forming the pot. Unfortunately these are not always rigorously described, but studies such as those of Ribeiro (1969) or Petrucci and Poteur (1976) are of greatest value in assessing the purposes to which archaeologically discovered tools could have been put. Figure 10 shows a small selection of potters' 'spoons' and these should be compared with the tools previously illustrated in Fig. 1 and Fig. 6.

However, the use of the wheel has even greater archaeological implications for it is generally a fixed installation housed in a workshop which might be expected to leave rather clear archaeological traces. This contrasts markedly with household industry, where to search for specialised buildings would in general amount to chasing a will-o'-the-wisp.

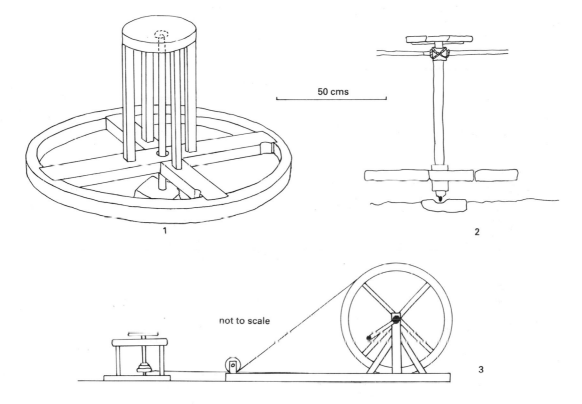

50 cms

not to scale

Figure 9 (above) Potters' wheels. No. 1, simple wheel from Saint-Quentin-la-Poterie, Provence (after Serre, 1961); No. 2, kick wheel from Thrapsanos, Crete (after Voyatzoglou, 1973); No. 3, rope wheel (after Brears, 1971).

Figure 10 (below) Auxiliary instruments from Vallauris, near Cannes, France (after Petrucci and Poteur, 1976). No. 1, *estèque* of pottery used to compress the clay around the bottom of the vessel interior; Nos 2–4, *estelles*, now of metal but originally of wood, used to shape the exterior profile.

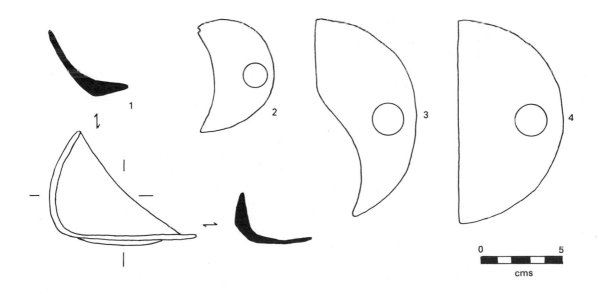

0   5
cms

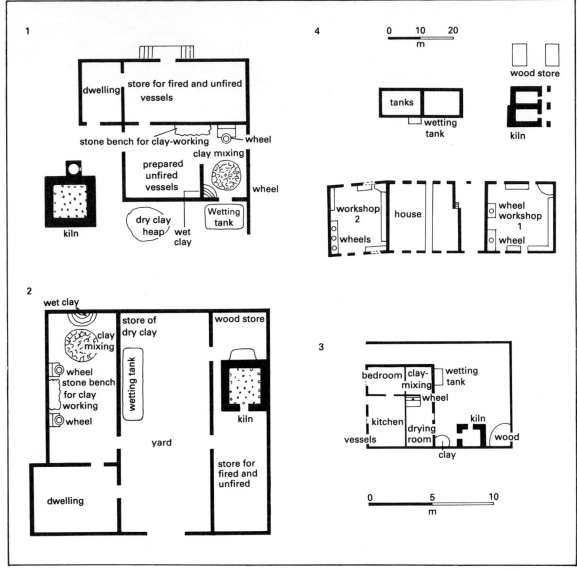

Figure 11 Workshop plans. No. 1, Orei, Euboea, Greece; No. 2, Istiea, Euboea (after Hampe and Winter, 1965). No. 3, Viana do Alentejo, Portugal; No. 4, São Pedro do Corval, Portugal (after Parvaux, 1968). Nos 1–3 are drawn to a common scale.

The design of workshops is naturally variable, particularly as some previously served other purposes, but an indication of the variation in size and layout is provided by the selection of plans shown in Fig. 11. It will be observed that wheels are nearly always situated near windows or by doors but in some cases they lie against the back wall illuminated by a shaft of light from the door. Kilns may be internally or externally sited. The former have the disadvantage of polluting the workshop atmosphere, but the marked advantage of providing a warm room suitable for storing timber and drying pottery; this arrangement might thus promote an extension of the potting season.

The structure of present-day kilns is variable and some examples are shown in Fig. 12. They are almost invariably of the updraught variety, with a grate separating the firing chamber from the source of heat below. Most are constructed of brick or stone laid upon or partly sunk into the ground surface, while in plan they are square, rectangular or round. The reason for this variety is hard to discern, and is worthy of further thought and investigation. One might expect round kilns to be designed for pottery while the quadrangular ones might be better suited for bricks. However, in practice this bipartite division is not sustained and the two types are used more or less indiscriminately. In some cases it is possible to explain anomalies rationally. For example, a brick works on the western outskirts of Nabeul in Tunisia employs round kilns because the site was originally used for pottery-making a quarter of a century ago. The Kairouan brickyard shows a remarkable mixture of round and square structures. The round kilns are traditionally lime kilns but nowadays they are also used for brick-making. However, in the majority of cases it is hard to explain why a particular design has been chosen. Thus in southern Italy (Fig. 13) kiln types display little rational patterning except for a homogeneous group in southern Sicily.

THE INDIVIDUAL WORKSHOP

The workshop can be seen in its simplest form in the isolated pottery which is normally found in a rural rather than an urban setting. Although very common, these humble concerns have seldom been the subject of detailed ethnographic report. Hampe and Winter (1965) briefly describe a number of examples from southern Italy, Sicily and Greece, while Llorens and Corredor (1974) give further examples from Spain, but in most instances significant and useful data is missing. Nevertheless, the majority of these small producers make coarse earthenwares for a very local market, often comprising little more than the community in which the pottery is situated. This would appear to be the norm and fine-wares are seldom produced in these simple concerns. There is evidence that this was precisely the situation in North America during the eighteenth century, for Olton (1975:25) records that an attempt to set up a pottery factory in Philadelphia was beset with difficulties. It lacked the technical ability to produce china of the quality demanded by a sophisticated market accustomed to English imports, but could not sell cheap red-ware and earthenware in the hinterland because the countryside abounded with small potteries supplying local needs. The implication seems to be that the small workshop is a rather efficient means of producing everyday coarse-wares, doubtless because the type of clay is not crucial and long-distance transport is avoided.

A good example of an individual workshop is to be seen on the island of Thasos in northern Greece. There are two potteries on the island, both situated just outside the main town; one now produces much for the tourist market, but the other remains traditional in both methods and products. The pottery is located in a long building with a kiln at one end and it serves for throwing, drying and storing the finished vessels (Pl. 7). Two types of clay are used deriving from different sources on the island and most of the preparation takes place outside. The material is dried, broken and sieved (Pl. 8) after which it is mixed with water in pits (Pl. 9) conveniently situated near the well. When it has settled and dried out to the correct consistency, it is dug, wedged and thrown on a typical kick wheel (Pl. 10). When sufficient vessels have been made and dried they are fired in the rectangular kiln, which is fueled with olive wood and prunings. The product comprises internally glazed casseroles and unglazed water jars. Potting only takes place in the summer months and during the rest of the year the two potters find employment in forestry. Most of their wares are sold locally either to visitors or to stores throughout the island.

A rather similar situation has been recorded at Amolocho on the Aegean island of Andros (Birmingham, 1967). The potter supplied his own village with everyday wares, seldom venturing further afield, for the competition on the coast was too great due to good sea connections with the mechanised potteries of Euboea. In this case pottery making was even more of a part time activity for the winter was considered too cold, and although pottery-making was previously an important activity in the summer, it has now been largely replaced by vegetable-growing. Details of technique need not be reiterated for they differ but little from those observed on Thasos.

Brick-making

Before the coming of the railways the brick industry was almost invariably organised into small units scattered irregularly across the countryside as clay and fuel permitted. The economic factors which affect the production of pottery are even more acute since the end product is very heavy and expensive to transport, but weight for weight bricks have a much lower market value than pots. Ideally a brickworker must try to minimise transportation costs and the most successful industries will be those near to the market. However, this may not be possible because the location is restricted by outcrops of suitable clay,

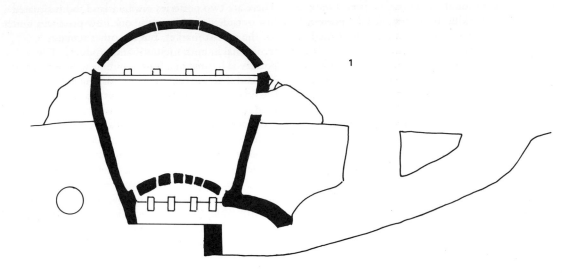

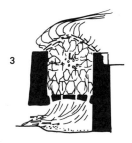

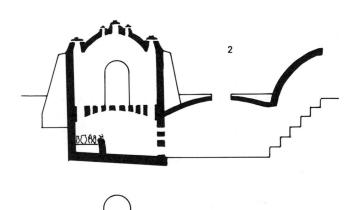

Figure 12 Some modern pottery kilns. No. 1, Djerba (after Combès and Louis, 1967); No. 2, Nabeul (after Lisse and Louis, 1956). No. 3, S. Lucia, Calabria; No. 4, Cariati, Calabria; No. 5, Phili, Cyprus; No. 6, Kliru, Cyprus; No. 7, Squillace, Calabria; No. 8, Pisticci, Basilicata (all after Hampe and Winter, 1965, except Nos 5–6, *idem*, 1962). The symbol by each section indicates the general form of the ground plan. For nos 1 and 2 scale not given: the remainder are at the scale indicated.

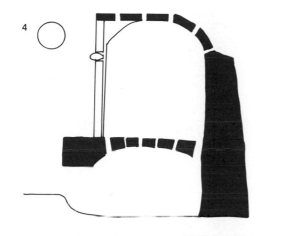

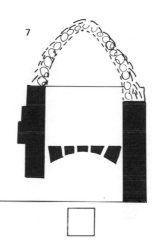

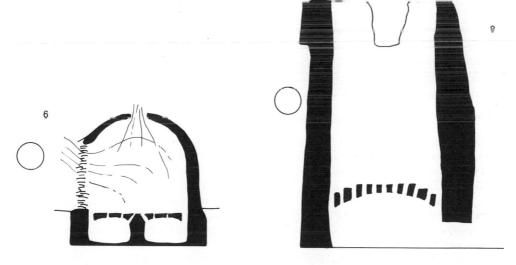

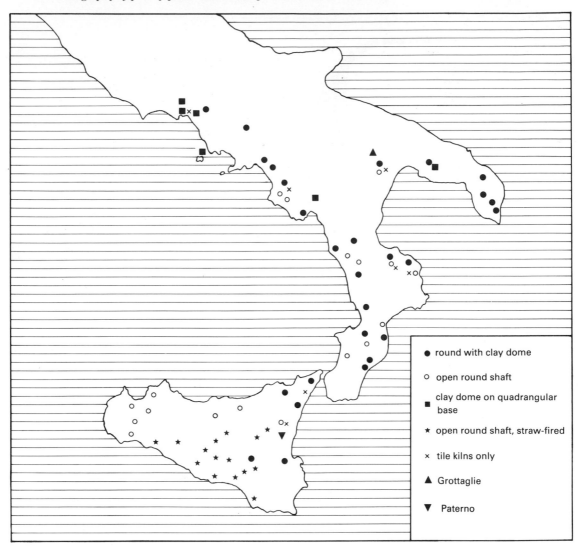

Figure 13   Kiln types in southern Italy and Sicily (after Hampe and Winter, 1965).

and since this is required in quantity even limited transportation of raw materials would be prohibitive to the normal brickyard producing undistinguished and unspecialised products.

The pattern of Victorian and more recent brickworks is now fairly complete for the English county of Hampshire thanks to the work of White (1971) and his co-workers. It displays precisely the characteristics one might anticipate: a broad scatter of yards across the Tertiary and Cretaceous clay beds of the Hampshire basin with a marked concentration in the country around Southampton. The same dispersed pattern can be seen in southern Dorset

(Young, 1968) and in the Walloon brickworks of Belgium (Vandereuse and Pinon, 1961).

A good example of a country brickyard is provided by that at Broadmayne, situated some 6 km (4 miles) southeast of its principal consumer, the county town of Dorchester in Dorset (Young, 1968). Markets of lesser importance were scattered over a 15 km (10-mile) radius and occasional exotic orders led to transportation as far as London or Cosham in Hampshire. Discussion of the techniques of production is best reserved until the somewhat similar estate kiln at Ashburnham is considered (p. 46).

Plate 7 Small pottery worked by two men on the island of Thasos, Greece. Note the kiln appended to the workshop, the woodstore in front and the moistening pit in the bottom left of the picture.

Also worthy of mention is the tilery at Civry-la-Forêt in the Ile de France, which supplied the town of Mantes some 18 km away (Gault, 1952). This small works was operated in conjunction with a farm and achieved an annual output of 1,000,000 or 1,500,000 tiles. Clay was dug in the winter and production began in April. Most of the seasonal labour seems to have been recruited locally but the more skilled workers such as the tile moulders came from Normandy. To judge from Gault's brief account it would seem that once again techniques of manufacture were very similar to the Ashburnham example to be discussed below (p. 46).

Brickworking equipment is fairly simple and it is not surprising that workers are much more mobile than potters, a point well illustrated by the Walloon industry (Vandereuse and Pinon, 1961). Like so many concerns in northern latitudes, activity was of necessity confined to the spring and summer, with factories or mines providing alternative employment during the winter months, although at one time the domestic production of hand-made nails was an important pursuit. In the spring the workers grouped themselves into teams of five under the leadership of a moulder who could be either a man or a woman. The *table* as it was called comprised a mixer, a barrower, a loader and two porters who were usually children of either sex upwards of seven or eight years old. The teams either worked locally or spent the season abroad in France, Germany, Switzerland, Turkey, Spain and even Russia. Of course, long-distance travel was greatly facilitated by the advent of the railway, but teams are known to have travelled on foot some ten hours' journeying beyond Paris, a distance of well over 200 km.

In Kenya today bricks are frequently made on the building site by teams of itinerant workers firing in surface clamps (information Dr S. Wandibba). This mode of production seems to have been a major factor in the building of Victorian housing estates in

Plate 8   Sieving the dried clay outside the workshop shown in Pl. 7, Thasos, Greece.

Plate 9   Removing moistened clay from the pit. Thasos, Greece.

Plate 10 Potter at the kick wheel, Thasos. Note the seat and the shaping instruments in the bowl of water.

Britain and has been recorded for Portsmouth, Southampton and London (White, 1971; Woodforde, 1976).

A migrational tendency seems to be a recurrent feature of rural brick industries and this is relevant to the Roman situation, for where the same brick stamp is found in widely separated places there is at least a strong possibility of movement in personnel rather than products.

NUCLEATED INDUSTRIES

We must now turn from the individual unit so well exemplified by rural brickmaking and begin to consider the phenomenon of nucleation. A transitional stage is to be seen in the activities of a William Smith who worked in the Farnham area during the early nineteenth century and whose activities have been vividly recorded in a delightful book by George Bourne (1919). Of course there were many potteries in the area and thus technically Smith was part of a large nucleated industry, but he seems to have worked independently and enjoyed few of the potential benefits of nucleation apart from the services of the specialist kiln builders and the turf cutters who supplied fuel. The reason for an agglomeration of potters in the area seems to relate to the excellent fuel and above all to the proximity of the insatiable London market, but 65 km (40 miles) distant: clay on the other hand was brought from quarries about 13 km (8 miles) away.

Smith learnt the trade as an apprentice and eventually managed to amass sufficient capital to purchase his own pottery in which he employed his brothers as assistants. Bourne records Smith's methods which seem to have been fairly conventional: after digging, the clay was mixed with water and sand and matured in pits for about twenty-four hours after which it was thoroughly wedged by treading on the floor with bare feet. The pots were thrown on a wheel (presumably the usual double or kick wheel) after which they were glazed and dried in open sheds warmed with fires. Firing took about three days to complete.

Marketing is a particularly interesting aspect of Smith's activity for as in small isolated workshops he seems to have taken charge of this himself, selling almost exclusively in London. In view of the high cost of road transport it is hardly surprising that he fully utilised the Basingstoke Canal. However, in later life he bought a farm which he ran in conjunction with his pottery business and it is astonishing to learn that he then preferred to send his goods by road. Presumably he had carts on the farm and their use would have obviated the need to load and unload barges. Most writers on the Roman period seem to regard water transport as a more efficient way of transporting pottery because of rough road surfaces and high costs, but clearly the number of times goods have to be loaded and unloaded may offset these benefits (cf. Duncan-Jones, 1974; Peacock, 1978; Hartley, 1973; see p. 159).

It is very common to find potteries clustering together as at Farnham, but in the majority of cases the benefits of nucleation are much more evident. At this juncture it is pertinent to distinguish two types of nucleation, each with slightly different characteristics. The first category, *urban* nucleation, is very common for potteries are frequently grouped in or around towns. Numerous examples can be cited such as Moknine or Nabeul in Tunisia; Fez, Marrakesh or Meknes in Morocco; Grottaglie in southern Italy; Vallauris on the French Riviera and many places in Iberia. It is hardly surprising that potteries should multiply where good clays and adequate fuel are to be found near to a concentration of potential customers. The second category, *rural* nucleation, is decidedly less common and the reasons for development often less self-evident. The potteries on the remote island of Djerba in southern Tunisia comprise a classic example, but the same phenomenon can be seen elsewhere, as in the potteries around La Borne in Berry, central France. Obviously rural agglomerations contain settlements and the categories can be difficult to distinguish in some cases, although the general distinction seems clear enough.

Urban nucleation can be further subdivided. In some cases, such as Fez, Moknine or Vallauris, pottery-making is accommodated within the confines of the town itself and obviously such an intimate location may be determined by social, commercial or defensive parameters, in some cases a combination of the three. However, pottery firing presents a fire hazard and generates a great deal of smoke which can be distasteful to other citizens and so it is not surprising that potteries are often to be found outside town boundaries, usually concentrated near the clay pits or a major arterial highway out of town: Nabeul provides an admirable illustration of this.

From a technical point of view the needs of the urban workshop differ little from the small concerns described above. However, because of increased demand there is a tendency for establishments to be larger with more equipment and more personnel. At Nabeul the industry is very large and is a major craft

Plate 11 A pottery on the Tunis road, Nabeul. This establishment specialises in heavy ceramics, particularly sanitary ware and glazed roofing tiles. Note the moulds against the wall. The picture shows flower pots drying in the winter sun, but in summer they would be accommodated in the large cool workshop

in the town. Lisse and Louis (1956) record that in 1955 there were 160 workshops and about 1252 craftsmen, so that each unit would employ six to eight men. At Moknine the average workshop has a staff of six or seven people (Sethom, 1964) which is again larger than one would expect in isolated rural potteries.

One of the features of nucleated potteries is that the season is longer and work often continues the year round. This normally means that some special provision must be made for pot drying during excessively damp or hot seasons. At both Moknine and Nabeul, where work continues throughout the year, the problem finds a natural solution, for the kilns are located externally, releasing large areas of the workshop for cool even drying during the intense heat of summer (Pl. 11). On the other hand, in other urban centres such as Grottaglie or Vallauris the kilns are situated internally (Hampe and Winter, 1965:73; here Pl. 12). This could be dictated by tradition but it might also reflect the need for a warm drying place during damper winters

It must be stressed that while there is a tendency for nucleated potteries to become full-time and work throughout the year, this is not always the case. William Smith successfully combined pottery-making and farming and presumably this was true of other potters in the Farnham complex. At Moknine, pottery production was traditionally linked to farming, providing employment in the summer slack season, and other instances could be cited (Sethom, 1964:55).

One of the features of urban industries is that they characteristically produce a wide variety of pottery types. Of course some workshops specialise in certain forms, but by and large there will be an attempt to

Plate 12   Firing casseroles at Vallauris, near Cannes, southern France. The kiln is wood fired and sited within the workshop complex.

meet the multifarious requirements of the town and its hinterland. This is well illustrated in Nabeul which produces a wide range of kitchen wares, table wares, storage jars and various industrial ceramics, all of which may be glazed or unglazed. To this must be added the exotica such as candlesticks and the arab drum, the *derbouka*, used by bands in both Tunisia and Algeria. Some of the wares are traditionally decorated and the ornament is dominated by motifs of vegetable derivation. Of course the advent of tourism has done much to stimulate the 'artistic' end of the spectrum and new forms or new ornament have been introduced to meet the questionable tastes of the holiday-maker.

The kitchen wares are worthy of especial comment for casseroles are a characteristic Nabeul form (Pl. 13). However, they owe much to recent Italian inspiration and it is extraordinary to note that the

clay used in their making is imported from Hammam Sousse, some 50 km to the south. Such long-distance movement of raw material is only feasible for specialised wares comprising a small part of the output of an established industry which relies for the most part on local clay deposits.

Lisse and Louis (1956:221) describe the marketing of Nabeul pottery. It appears that there originally was very little interest in direct sales for the traditional pottery has no shop attached. Sales are made through the Friday market frequented by dealers as well as the local population, but this far from absorbs all the output. Particularly important are the pottery dealers, who visit the workshops buying up lots to transport and sell in other parts of Tunisia or even Algeria and Libya.

Turning to rural nucleated industries, we cannot do better than consider the complex on the island of

Plate 13   Casserole from Nabeul, Tunisia. This type of vessel is made of clay imported from Hammam Sousse 50 km to the south, and is a form recently introduced from Italy. Diam. 12 cm.

Djerba described by Combès and Louis (1967). Djerba, often identified as the land of the lotus-eaters by commentators on the *Odyssey*, possesses one of the most interesting and important pottery centres in the entire Mediterranean. At first sight it is remarkable that an industry is able to survive here for it is a relatively barren place which seems to scrape its living from the cultivation of olives and dates. Yet surprisingly the annual prunings from this activity provide all the essential fuel upon which the industry depends; an instructive warning to those who suggest that major Roman pottery industries must have been surrounded by large remnants of forest which they might in the course of time deplete.

However, even more striking is the size of the industry and its relationship to markets. The 157 workshops recorded in 1967 are spread over about 12 square km at Guellala on the southern side of the island. The clay is particularly good here and may have been worked since Roman times. There is thus every reason to expect some form of pottery industry here, but why should it develop to such a size where

there is no major market in the vicinity? The local market town of Houmt Souk is of minor importance, and most Djerban produce is distributed through the major towns of Tunisia such as Sfax, Sousse, or Tunis, while its wares can also be purchased in Tripoli or in Algeria. Of course the potteries are on the coast and the sea provides a main means of dispersal, but even so there is no major port. The bay of Bou Grara, which the potteries encircle, is so shallow that even small boats have to anchor offshore and await charges of pottery brought from the land on the backs of camels and donkeys. The industry is thus something of a paradox and it is difficult to appreciate why it should not only survive but thrive in the face of competition from potters more favourably located elsewhere. Part of the answer must rest in the reputation of Djerba for certain specialised products, such as the large amphora-like oil jars (Pl. 14). Although the potteries produce a wide range of wares it is these that attract the attention of the middleman who distributes them very widely. Indeed, the markets are so dispersed

Plate 14   Djerba, Tunisia. A consignment of jars awaiting purchase at a pottery.

that the industry could not survive without the attentions of the specialist dealer and he is certainly the key to understanding the success of Djerba. On the other hand the vitality of the industry cannot be ascribed to the possession of a trade secret for similar jars can be, and are, made elsewhere, at for example Moknine (Sethom, 1964). Furthermore there are clear contacts between Djerba and many other pottery centres in Tunisia and the seasonal or permanent migration of Djerbans is well attested (e.g. Lisse and Louis, 1956:15; Combès and Louis, 1967:25). However, perhaps the costs of working in the countryside are less, in some ways compensating for the extra expense of transportation.

The workshops of Djerba are in many ways similar to those of Nabeul, and once again they incorporate large drying rooms to afford protection from the summer sun (Combès and Louis, 1967:43; here Fig. 14). However, there are certain points of difference between the two potteries. For example, the clay is quarried underground on Djerba, a practice which is dangerous and has claimed many lives. After extraction the clay is taken to the workshop usually by a specialist transporter owning a camel and it is then broken down and dried after which it is moistened in small stone tanks 2–4 m long and 1–1.5 m wide. Naturally the kilns can be very large to accommodate the large oil jars: about 160 can be fired at once, the whole operation taking about 10–15 days (Fig. 12.1). The kilns are constructed of refractory bricks and are usually made by the potter perhaps with the assistance of a specialist kiln builder. Smaller kilns are of course available for firing lesser quantities of table or kitchen wares.

could be seen in the potteries scattered across the wooded landscape around La Borne in central France (Chaton and Talbot, 1977). It doubtless owed its existence to accessible fuel supplies, but above all to the remarkable clay which forms an attractive stoneware, and which has been a main factor in the recent resettlement of the area by art potters (Hanssen, 1969). Although differing in technical details, the sales pattern is very similar to that of Djerba. Most of the table ware was consumed locally, but the more specialised forms for which the potteries were renowned were sold much further afield. Thus the large salting pots found their way to

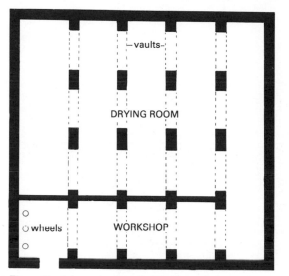

Figure 11 Schematic plan of a Djerba workshop (after Combès and Louis, 1967).

regions of animal rearing such as the Auvergne, Bourbonnais or Limousin, while containers for confectionary or *rillettes* were sold in Paris, Clermont Ferrand or the Touraine (Chaton and Talbot, 1977:53).

These selected examples serve to illustrate the main features of nucleated potteries. To expand the argument would be repetitious, but corroborative information is available from Iberia (e.g. Llorens and Corredor, 1974; Curtis, 1962; Griffith, 1965; Parvaux, 1968), Yugoslavia (Rusić, 1957) or in the Buckley potteries of Flintshire (Messham, 1956), and of course the list is far from complete. The main features can be summarised as follows: urban and rural centres differ but little except that the latter often produce more specialised wares and rely heavily on the professional dealer for distribution. Both differ from isolated workshops in the size of premises and in attempts to extend the season as far as possible, which has technological implications. The size of the complex is important for large-scale production attracts the middleman which leads to wide distribution. Nucleated industries benefit from the natural development of ancillary services, in fuel supply, transport, material supply or kiln building. In addition, co-operation rather than competition seems to be the rule and mutual aid is commonplace.

The brick industry
Although small isolated brickworks make good economic sense, they are sometimes found in nucleated agglomerations. However, clustering will only be viable if at least one of three conditions is met, namely:

1. that adequate clays are only available in one area; or
2. that there are exceptionally efficient communications enabling produce to be widely distributed without making costs prohibitive; or
3. that the yards are located in an area of high population and hence demand.

Nucleated brick industries have seldom been studied ethnographically but a few examples can be cited. Nucleation is often found around towns which are naturally areas of high demand. In Tunisia, for example, they are found around Nabeul where, in 1955, they constituted about 10 per cent of the concerns operating; they can be seen at Moknine where they occupy a distinct area on the opposite side of the town to the potteries, and at Kairouan a splendid traditional industry connected with lime burning is to be found (Pl. 15). Nowadays good road connections enable bricks to be moved considerable distances by lorry at low cost, but originally the works would have supplied their own areas.

An extreme example of nucleation in the Puebla-Tlaxcala basin of Mexico has been described by Seele (1968). Here numerous brickworks are very closely concentrated presumably because excellent clay is available. The area is densely populated and hence much of the produce is consumed locally but considerable quantities are transported to Mexico City, 140 km distant over the Rio Frio Pass which is 3150 m high.

In conclusion a word on the technology of brickmaking is apposite. Traditional methods of moulding differ but little in different types of yard (Pl. 15), but kilns can display some contrast. Isolated concerns may be equipped with kilns of the type described on p. 48 or they may rely on clamp firing (p. 16), but in nucleated works a kiln is invariably employed and it is in this environment that technical developments take root most readily. At Moknine and Nabeul large-capacity tunnel kilns are employed, in contrast to Kairouan where firing remains traditional.

THE MANUFACTORY

Since this term generally refers to conditions preceding the industrial revolution, it is worth attempting to illustrate the concept with reference to pottery-making in eighteenth-century England.

Plate 15   Hand-moulding bricks at Kairouan, Tunisia.

Although the term 'factory' was defined as early as 1802 in the first Factory Health and Morals Act, a grey area persisted for some time as concerns which we would now call factories were persistently referred to as manufactories, largely in an attempt to avoid inclusion under the provisions of the Act. In 1816 Josiah Wedgwood II argued before a commission of enquiry that the Staffordshire potteries were 'manufactories' in contrast to the textile 'factories' (Thomas, 1971:10). His case rested on three grounds: the size and structure of the premises with its scattered workshops of no more than two storeys, the size of the workforce and its distribution among several workshops and, thirdly, the limited extent to which power driven machinery was used. Wedgwood's appeal was successful and the potteries were not declared factories until 1864. It is

clear that they were vastly different from the textile factories, a principal subject of the first factory act, but an alternative judgement might have been possible as the problem is essentially one of where to draw a fine dividing line. It should be noted that as early as 1790, Wedgwood's 'Useful' branch alone employed 160 workers with a further 110 in the 'Ornamental' division and there is evidence of intense worker specialisation (Bladen, 1926). Furthermore, Wedgwood frankly admitted that he used 'a steam engine for grinding the materials and some of the lathes are turned by the steam engine' (Thomas 1971:11).

The question of the use of power is particularly difficult since long before the industrial revolution it was customary for potters to grind their materials in a wind or water mill, often a converted corn mill,

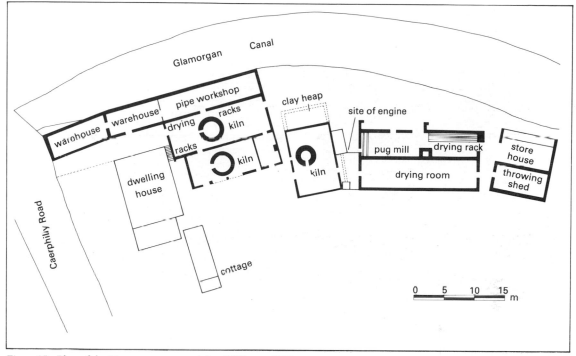

Figure 15 Plan of the Nantgarw pottery (after Williams, 1932).

and the potter with easy access to such a facility would be in a very fortunate position. It has been suggested, for example, that Thomas Wheildon's rise to fame in the early eighteenth-century can be attributed to an advantageous position in this respect (Thomas, 1937:405). It could be argued that as soon as a pottery has its own specialised flint mill it becomes a factory rather than a manufactory, but this is an extreme position and additional consideration must be given to the workforce which should involve hundreds rather than tens of people with worker specialisation under a managerial superstructure.

It would thus appear that the term manufactory has been somewhat loosely applied and it is in the period before 1760 that we should look for the types of industrial organisation defined above (p. 9). In her book, *The Pottery Trade and North Staffordshire 1660–1760*, Lorna Weatherill (1971) has transformed our views of the developing Staffordshire potteries. We can no longer think in terms of industrial revolution superimposed upon a primitive peasant production, but rather that it was preceded by a long period of gradual expansion and innovation. Statistical evidence shows that there was a steady almost linear increase in the number of potteries working, the raw material consumed and in output;

the trend is particularly clear in the period 1734–60, where the data are most numerous.

From the end of the seventeenth century there were also marked technological developments. Methods of preparing raw materials were improved and a new type of wheel was introduced – presumably it was during this period that the rope wheel began to replace the traditional kick wheel. Also lathes and moulds seem to pre-date 1760, and firing techniques were substantially developed before the industrial revolution.

However, changes in the size of workforce employed in individual potteries is particularly striking, for around 1710–20 the recorded establishments could boast about ten employees, which is near the maximum encountered in workshop industries at the present day. However, in the decade 1750–60 twenty or more workers was the norm, and clearly these establishments might qualify for the term 'manufactory'.

Unfortunately it is difficult to relate these interesting historical conclusions to existing or archaeologically investigated structures and it is particularly hard to find a groundplan showing the layout of one of these larger concerns. Hopefully this is one of the lacunae that will be filled by industrial

Figure 16   A view of the Nantgarw pottery (from Jewitt, 1883).

archaeologists, but for the present we must turn to a rather later period for an illustration that *might* be relevant. The small pottery works at Nantgarw in South Wales had a very short life and was used intermittently from 1813. It was surveyed in some detail by Williams (1932) and his plan is reproduced as Fig. 15, while Jewitt's (1883) engraving (Fig. 16) gives a good impression of the general appearance. The groundplan shows a complex of throwing rooms, drying facilities and kilns on a far more impressive scale than those encountered in the average workshop, and although power was employed to drive the pug mill, the works has the general size and shape that might be appropriate to a manufactory.

ESTATE PRODUCTION

It is difficult to find good examples of estate production of ceramics, even though, until recently, this mode must have been of considerable importance in certain parts of the world such as Britain, where estate development has been fostered by particularly favourable economic and social conditions in the eighteenth century.

Unfortunately, however, ethnography seldom begins at home and it is only in recent years that an attempt has been made to record and preserve fast disappearing facets of urban and rural life. Ceramics have been particularly badly served and it is now almost too late. Documentary references indicate that estate production of commodities such as bricks, tiles or drainpipes was at one time commonplace. However, of these numerous rural industries only one has been adequately described: that on the Ashburnham estate, Sussex, where simple techniques survived until the last firing in November 1968. Nevertheless, this example is particularly apt from our point of view and worth discussing in some detail. Not only does it provide an insight into the workings of an estate industry, but rudimentary methods were employed. The kilns were similar in groundplan to Roman ones, and were unique in being the last wood-fired kilns operating in Britain, thus providing potential technological as well as economic analogies. The following account is based upon a popular article by Gordon (1969) but more particularly upon the excellent paper by Leslie (1971).

The production of ceramics at Ashburnham probably has a long history, but the phase that concerns us here began in 1840 when new kilns were built on their last and present site at Lower Spring Field. The main products were bricks but a tilery was attached and later in the nineteenth century there are records of a wide range of products including drainage pipes and flower pots.

The new kilns were built to furnish domestic needs. In 1830 a certain Edward Driver had surveyed the estate and observed that too many of its buildings were of timber, recommending that future buildings should be in brick that would 'last for ever'. Further impetus came in the 1830s when plans were made to reconstruct Ashburnham Place with a facing of brick as the Regency-Gothic casing of cement was cracking and flaking. The works were thus established with the needs of the estate firmly in mind but their subsequent history is complex and interesting. Leslie (1971) has conveniently summarised the main phases:

1840–5   Mainly estate production, with small commercial sales
1846–55   Ashburnham Place restoration and enlargement
1856–96   Expansion of commercial sales
1897–1927   Estate repairs and building
1928–68   Expansion of commercial sales

It would appear that although the estate was the main *raison d'être*, commercial sales were important as they kept the industry alive when internal demand was at a low ebb. The commercial expansion in Victorian times is particularly significant for it corresponds with a great period of building in Britain of which East Sussex enjoyed its share. The estate yard rose to the demand and exported its products as far as Eastbourne 20 km (12 miles) away. In 1877 a load went to Faversham in Kent, about 80 km (50 miles) distant, but this was quite exceptional. The importance of Ashburnham from our point of view cannot be overstressed. It provides an admirable ethnographical example of estate production and illustrates very clearly its unique economic situation intermediate between the domestic and commercial world.

The technology is well documented and supplementary information for the non-estate yard at Broadmayne (Young, 1968) provides corroborative data. At both Broadmayne and Ashburnham clay was dug from within the yard itself presumably to avoid carting large quantities of very heavy material (Fig. 17 shows a plan of Ashburnham). This was usually done in the autumn or winter so that the action of rain or frosts would improve quality and enhance ease of working of the clay. However, in the

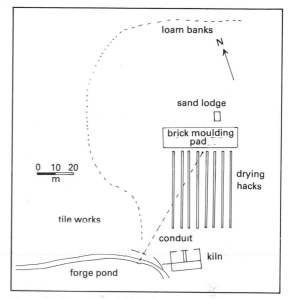

Figure 17 Plan of the Ashburnham estate brickyard (after Leslie, 1971).

last few years of operation at Ashburnham the clay was often dug just one week before use, a practice which, according to the brick-makers, merely made the work of preparation and moulding a little harder but did not affect quality. On the day before use the clay would be mixed with water to achieve the desired degree of plasticity and hard lumps would be eliminated by working with shovels and mattocks. At Broadmayne a small quantity of sand might be added but apparently no extra temper was required at Ashburnham.

The moulding took place in open portable sheds with the base of the moulds fixed to a moulding bench. They were of beech wood shoed with iron and before use would be dusted with dry sand to prevent the wet clay sticking. The art of moulding was to dash the pug or prepared clay into the mould with such force and at such an angle that it would spread evenly throughout the mould avoiding air bubbles. Afterwards the excess clay would be removed by scraping the mould with an instrument rather like a rolling-pin.

At Ashburnham the rate of production was 500–600 bricks a day which compares favourably with Broadmayne where a moulder could make 700–800. These rates assume a staff of two, but with extra assistance the output would have been greatly increased. A moulder assisted by a mixer or by a pug-mill could increase his output to 1000 bricks a day (Young, 1968:320).

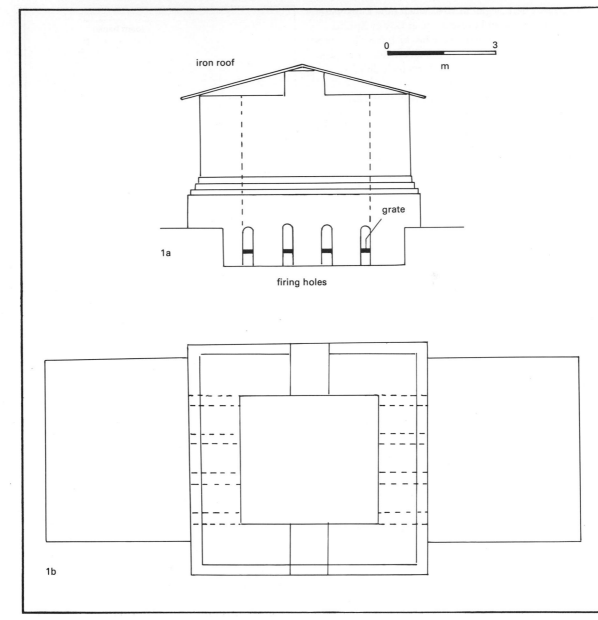

Figure 18   Brick kilns. No. 1, Broadmayne (after Young, 1968); No. 2, Ashburnham (after Leslie, 1971).

The green bricks were taken to the hacks for drying. These consisted of long narrow concrete strips which could be covered with a portable wooden roof if the weather was wet, although in earlier days loose straw was apparently used for this purpose. The drying process would take between three and six weeks depending on weather conditions.

When dry the bricks would be loaded into the kilns for firing, the plan and elevation of which is shown in Fig. 18. These structures, highly reminiscent of the typical Roman brick kilns, were square or rectangular in shape with thick walls presumably to provide insulation and reduce temperature variation throughout the kiln. At the bottom was a flue system above which was a brick-built grate upon which the unfired green bricks were stacked. At Ashburnham each of the two kilns had a capacity of 20,000, a

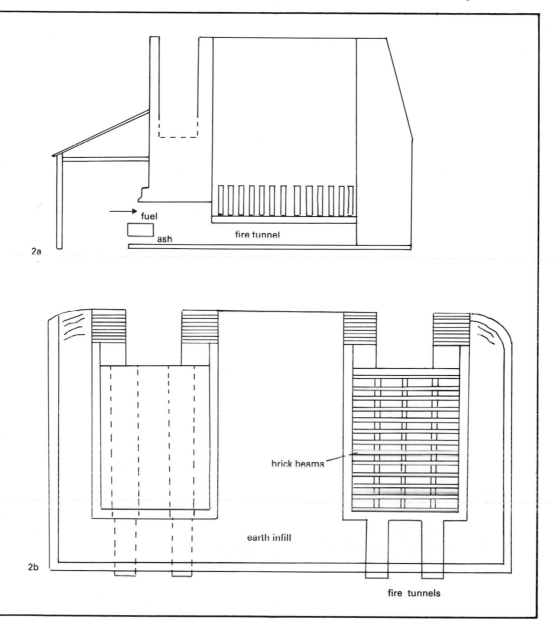

figure which is of the same order as the 25,000 at Broadmayne.

The kilns at Ashburnham relied on wood as fuel, particularly favouring silver birch or hornbeam, but unfortunately quantities required for each firing are not recorded by Leslie (1971). However, some 10 tons of coal were used in each firing at Broadmayne and so the quantity of wood used must have been considerable. In both cases firings took around 50 hours and temperatures in excess of 1000 °C were attained. During this period careful observation of the colour of the fire-tunnel enabled temperatures to be gauged and constant fuelling was necessary. The subsequent cooling stage required a further five days at Ashburnham but only three at Broadmayne. It should perhaps be added that both kilns were essentially open at the top apart from a layer of rough bricks acting as a heat barrier. A portable corrugated iron roof protected the load before firing if the weather was bad during the burn. At Broadmayne, however, it was customary to leave this on for the first day. There were of course variations in quality of bricks depending on their position in the kilns, but the number of wasters that had to be rejected is of particular interest. At Broadmayne these amounted to 4 per cent of the load and the figure may have been similar at Ashburnham where Leslie records that 75 per cent of the products were of first-class grade.

PRODUCTION BY OFFICIAL ORGANISATIONS

It is difficult to use recent examples to illustrate the types of production grouped under this heading for military and municipal ceramic supply has proved of little interest to the ethnographer or historian alike. This is one of the few fields in which it is reasonable to claim that the Roman situation is better documented than the more recent. Nevertheless it is useful to discuss a few examples which provide instructive insights into some of the facets mentioned above (p. 11).

Ceramic supply to a military garrison under stress is well illustrated by the American frontier fort of Michilimackinac, occupied by both the French and the British during the eighteenth century (Miller, 1970). Not surprisingly the structure was entirely of wood and architectural ceramics are absent from the assemblage. However, the pottery has been the subject of rigorous analysis and comparison leading to the conclusion that the ceramic suite is very similar to that in use in urban settlements behind the lines. At first sight this is a remarkable claim, for common sense would suggest delicate and expensive table ware to be out of place on a harsh and dangerous frontier. However, this is exactly paralleled in the Roman world and perhaps both phenomena can be explained in terms of common supply mechanisms or by soldiers carrying the requisites of civilised life with them.

The supply of bricks to an army playing a defensive role is well illustrated in the building accounts of Sandgate Castle in Kent, a Henrician fort built between A.D. 1539–40 (Rutton, 1893). Several different sources of bricks are mentioned, of which the most important seem to be in the Elham district about 5 km (3 miles) away. However, some came from brickyards 25 km (15 miles) away and a load of 7000 was brought by water from Rye, 35 km (22 miles) distant. Thus, whereas a fortress built from local military kilns might show extreme uniformity in fabric, the deployment of civilian resources is

likely to produce a range of distinct fabrics. This is very relevant to the study of Roman fortification and it is notable that many of the Shore Forts built on the southern coast of England during the late Roman period display a considerable variety of materials (p. 146).

Equally it is hardly surprising that municipal authorities should show little interest in such a trivial matter as pottery production, but the production of building materials is a different matter. Both could be seen among the Moravian communities of North Carolina (Bivins, 1972) but neither are worthy of detailed study in the search for general observations, for the Moravians, who comprised a closed religious community, were exceptional by any standards. It is worth noting, however, that their enterprises were run on a commercial basis by brethren who were supervised by the *Aufseher Collegium* or ruling body of the community. A further example of a town brickworks has been briefly described from Mölln in northern Germany and this could have been typical of other Medieval towns on the Continent (Hermann, 1961). The works continued in operation until 1906 and provided for official buildings, churches and fortifications. They were owned by the council and leased to a brickworker who operated on their behalf. The total output was always low and never exceeded 40,000 building bricks and 10,000 roofing tiles per annum, the majority of which may have been destined for official projects, although the possibility of private sales cannot be discounted.

CONCLUDING COMMENTS

In this chapter the production of pottery has been described in a hierarchical scheme progressing from simple to more complex organisation. It must be stressed that the modes of production and their variants cannot be seen as the 'stages' of an evolutionary system, for industrial arrangements merely reflect social and economic organisation. It is erroneous to talk of 'primitive' or 'advanced'. On the other hand industries do change with the passage of time and, in general, ethnography has the drawback of presenting a static picture drawn at one particular chronological point. Dynamic transformations can account for certain anomalies in the ethnographic record. Thus, the potter of Andros does not now make a major part of his livelihood from the clay but he possesses the full technical paraphernalia of the workshop because it is a legacy from an era when pottery-making played a much greater role in his life.

The small demand for pots at the present day would hardly justify such an investment now.

On the other hand Steele (1971) has described an industry at Sorkun, near Ankara, where it seems that pottery-making is a major activity. However, surprisingly, it is still primarily a female occupation and the men are employed more or less full-time in distributing the products by lorry all over Turkey. At first sight this does not fit the rules for we might expect such heavy demand to be met by the establishment of workshop industries with more sophisticated equipment. However, this paradox can be explained if we assume that the industry began as a part-time female occupation of the Pereruela-Moveros type, but became more and more important economically because of increasing demand. Presumably this enhancement was facilitated by clays of exceptional quality which enabled outstanding pottery to be made – in other words wares well able to withstand thermal shock.

Pottery industries are not static but dynamic entities changing in response to external stimuli, but unfortunately we have only a sketchy perception of the way in which change can take place. This is particularly unfortunate because such matters are of greatest importance to the archaeologist. It would seem that we now need new studies which place surviving industries in a chronological perspective. Perhaps this could be achieved through co-operative studies involving ethnographers, historians and archaeologists. We may then be able to model change more perceptively.

4 Ceramic technology in the Roman world

Relics of by-gone instruments of labour possess the same importance for the investigation of extinct economical forms of society as do fossil bones for the determination of extinct species of animals. It is not the articles made, but how they are made, and by what instruments, that enables us to distinguish different economical epochs. Instruments of labour not only supply a standard of the degree of development to which human labour has attained, but they are also indicators of the social conditions under which labour was carried on.

Karl Marx (1918:200)

In the previous chapter an attempt was made to indicate some of the main features of traditional pottery and brick industries functioning at the present day or in the recent past. The discussion will be expanded in subsequent chapters, but we must now begin to consider Roman pottery, evaluating the extent to which our model applies. It should be evident that the modes of production described above are each fostered by rather different social and economic facies, thus providing a tool which could be of value in more general debate about social and economic conditions in the ancient world. The mere recognition of modes of production is an important step which can have useful implications in itself, but ideally we should try to assess the importance and interaction of different modes, a goal which still lies a long way off in Roman studies.

Each of the systems described above can be distinguished by the location of the industry, the types of ware produced, the techniques employed in their making, and the distribution of the products. It is interesting to note that all these parameters are capable of archaeological investigation; and it is not the concept but the paucity of recorded information that is a main stumbling-block in realising our goal. Of these parameters there is little doubt that a study of production technology is vitally important, but archaeologically this field has remained unfashionable for far too long and all too often technology is considered an interesting sideline rather than a central issue in economic analysis. One chapter will not redress the balance, but it seems desirable to draw together the disparate scraps of evidence about Roman practice.

The production of pottery involves five basic steps. The clay must first be *dug* after which it must undergo some form of *preparation*, for no clay is immediately ready for working. It must then be *formed* into the required shape and decorated if necessary, after which thorough *drying* is required before the final stage of *firing*. It is convenient to consider ceramic technology under these five headings reviewing the apparatus required and the way it might have been used.

RAW MATERIALS

Although a large number of Roman production sites is known, very few have produced evidence for the extraction of clay or of the coarse materials required for tempering heat-resistant cooking wares. This is hardly surprising, for very little material is required to make a pot and the extraction of raw materials can have a relatively slight impact on the landscape.

Some sites however, have revealed traces of pits situated, as one might expect, in the immediate vicinity of the kilns. Brockley Hill and Stanground are good examples in Britain, but Young (1977a:16) gives a more extended list. In many cases the size and positioning of the pits implies small-scale and perhaps intermittent operation. Larger-scale systematic extraction must be anticipated in the more sophisticated potteries and the quarry at Heiligenberg

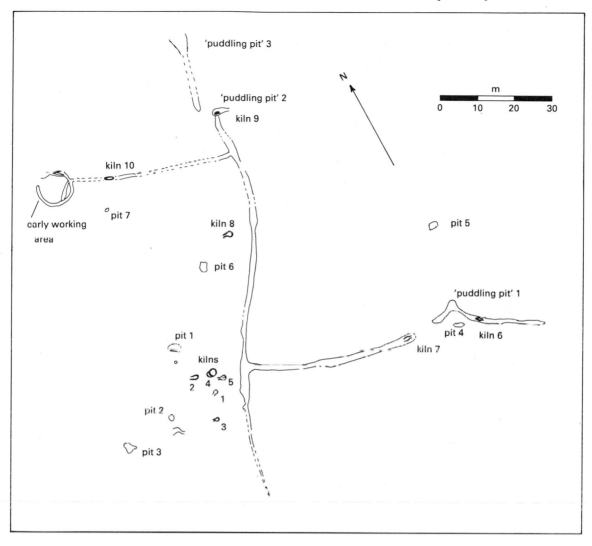

Figure 19 Plan of excavated pits, ditches and kilns at Highgate Wood (after Brown and Sheldon, 1975).

serves as an example (Forrer, 1911:13). Young suggests that in the Oxford potteries, it was usual to transport clay and other materials over a short distance to the kiln site as most kilns are not sited on clay beds.

Our knowledge of extraction methods is far from satisfactory but it would appear that quarries were opencast rather than underground as on contemporary Djerba. Very few digging instruments have survived in the context of a pottery but Chenet and Gaudron (1955, Fig. 8a) illustrate an iron shoe which would have fitted on a wooden spade, and presumably this was a major tool.

PREPARATION OF RAW MATERIALS

The evidence for preparation techniques is marginally better, for in many cases special facilities were needed. Some of the less sophisticated wares might require little more than hand-picking of extraneous matter from a clay naturally tempered with numerous rock and mineral inclusions, but in a majority of cases much more preparation is required.

Today it is common practice to dry the clay and break it down with a wooden mallet, but obviously this process is unlikely to be visible archaeologically. The comminuted material is then mixed with water and it is hardly surprising that wells are a common feature of Roman production sites. They are known, for example, from Oxford, Halder in the Netherlands or from Rheinzabern in Germany, to select but three localities from a wealth of published data (Young, 1977a; 16; Willems, 1977; Ludowici, 1905, Fig. 44). However, wells have not been found on all sites despite fairly extensive exploration in some cases, and this raises the question of alternative means of water supply. The answer is not always evident, but sometimes their place may have been taken by a network of drainage gullies and ditches, well documented from sites such as Highgate Wood or the New Forest (Brown and Sheldon 1975, here Fig. 19; Fulford 1975b, Fig. 4). On the other hand these do not always seem to drain towards reservoirs as one might expect if their purpose was catchment rather than drainage, but perhaps they could have been directed towards clay heaps (since demolished) with the object of keeping the material damp and facilitating the breakdown of hard lumps.

Mixing procedures would vary according to the type of production; large jars and cooking wares would require the addition of temper to give the clay 'tooth' or to increase resistance to thermal shock, although naturally tempered clays might be selected for this purpose where possible. However, Roman pottery is often devoid of large inclusions and there is little doubt that it was common practice to purify the raw material by the process of levigation, which involves mixing with water and allowing the coarser fraction to settle out. A number of clay or stone-lined tanks about a metre or so long and rather less across have been reported from sites in Britain such as Oxford, the Nene valley or Brockley Hill (Young, 1977a:16, here Fig. 20). These have been interpreted as clay storage tanks, but they are very close in size and shape to the mixing tanks used on Djerba for example, and it seems better to regard them as such. In some cases they may have served to moisten rather than to levigate clay. Similar structures have seldom been reported from the Continent, but excavations at Halder have produced a large post-lined pit about 5 m by 6 m which was filled with clay, and pits of roughly the same size are known from Rheinzabern (Willems, 1977; Ludowici, 1905, Fig. 44, here Fig. 20). However, the most spectacular levigation tanks were recovered during the nineteenth century in Arezzo, for one belonging to the *Perennius* establishment had a capacity of no less than 10,000 gallons (Pasqui, 1896, here Fig. 20).

Clay is usually worked with the feet to mix in any additives and to remove air bubbles which might

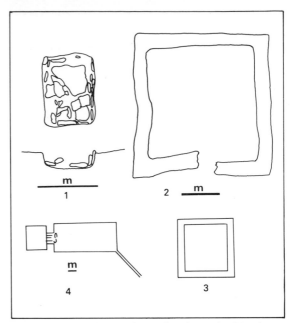

Figure 20 Levigation or clay moistening tanks. No. 1, Churchill, Oxford (after Young, 1977a); Nos 2–3, Rheinzabern (after Ludowici, 1905); No. 4, Arezzo (after Pasqui, 1896). In each case the scale is one metre long.

cause spaling during firing and this usually demands a dry flat area which may be paved to prevent contamination. The puddling pits, so beloved of the nineteenth- and early twentieth-century antiquarians find few parallels in the recent past of Europe and the Mediterranean area and it is possible that the 'puddling holes' reported from sites such as Oxford or Brockley Hill were used for the damp storage of clay with the objective of breaking down hard lumps in clay derived from older geological formations. Puddling pits are still employed in the Kairouan brickworks where they are used to make a fairly sloppy mixture which would be difficult to contain on the floor.

Paved areas have been reported from a number of sites such as Cowley, Dorchester or the New Forest, and Young (1977a:18) rightly infers that these may have been for clay mixing, although they are only about 1 m long and 0.5 m wide, which is rather small by modern standards.

It is possible that some form of pug-mill or mechanical mixing device was used on occasions, but the evidence is tenuous and it seems unlikely that the practice was very common. Ribeiro (1972) has argued that the horse-driven pug-mills used today in central Portugal (Fig. 21) might be of Roman origin, and she draws attention to a very similar device used

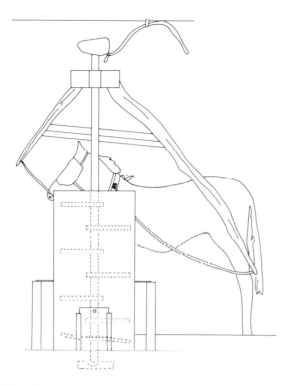

Figure 21 Horse-driven pug-mill, Asseiceira, Tomar, Portugal (after Ribeiro, 1972).

for mixing the ingredients of bread, represented on the tomb of *M. Vergilius Eurysaces* (Beltrán Martínez, 1949). However, it is difficult to accept arguments for continuity between the present and the Roman period since Rasmussen (1967) has recorded a remarkably similar device from Dokkedal in Denmark, where Roman influence is decidedly improbable.

Nevertheless as analogous devices were used in the Roman period the existence of the pug-mill is far from impossible. Negev (1974) reported a cylindrical stone structure from the Nabatean potters' workshop at Oboda in Israel, which he interpreted as the foundation of a wheel. This is difficult to accept, as it is hard to see what type of wheel it would have accommodated and furthermore, unlike wheels at the present day, it is neither situated by the door nor by a wall that might have contained a window or have been illuminated from a door. It resembles the mount for a Pompeian style mill and hence it could be the podium for a conventional mill for grinding materials, if not a pug-mill of the general type described by Ribeiro, although as Fig. 21 illustrates the modern examples are not raised above the floor.

FORMING AND FINISHING METHODS

There is no doubt that pottery was formed by a variety of methods in the Roman world, but unfortunately we know little of them. Many of the wares classed as 'hand-made' are smooth enough to have been fashioned on a turntable and in some cases the finish of the rim clearly bears witness to some form of turning device. This is illustrated in the well-known Romano-British black-burnished cooking pot (Fig. 22, 1, 5, Plate 16), which has a body displaying the hallmarks of hand forming, while the rim appears to be wheel turned. This curious mixture of techniques could be readily explained if the vessel was made on a turntable with varying degrees of rotation. Unfortunately, however, no Roman turntable has survived, and we can only assume that they were in some measure comparable with the example illustrated above in Fig. 4 (p. 19).

There is no doubt that the bulk of Roman pottery was produced on a fast wheel and here we know a little more, for occasionally parts of wheels have been discovered. By far the commonest finds are the socket stones in which the wheel axle turned and a number have been reported from sites such as Oxford, Rheinzabern, or the Argonne (Young, 1977a: Fig. 4; Ludowici, 1905:150; Chenet and Gaudron, 1955: Fig. 9; here Fig. 23, 3–4). They are all remarkably similar and consist of carefully rounded stones or natural pebbles about 7–9 cm across with a worn central depression. They seem to have been deliberately selected to withstand wear, for the rock is always hard fine-grained material such as quartzite or basalt. It has been assumed by some writers, such as Rieth (1960), that these are the basal pivot stones of double or kick wheels. This is possible but perhaps unlikely, for they are very small and unless set in the ground with mortar (for which there is no evidence), they would not withstand the constant impact of footwork. It is worth observing that present-day kick wheels such as those on Djerba or Crete have much more substantial basal stones (Combès and Louis, 1967:49; Voyatzoglou, 1973:14). On the other hand the simple wheel can be designed to rotate either on a fixed spindle or on an axis that is fixed to the wheel and pivots on the ground. Both pivoted and socketed wheels have been described from India by Saraswati and Behura (1966), and the former seem to be rotated in a manner to which the Roman socket stones are better suited (Fig. 24). Socketed wheels also require a bearing which can be of stone but if these are to be secured to the table they would require shaping, a point well illustrated in the

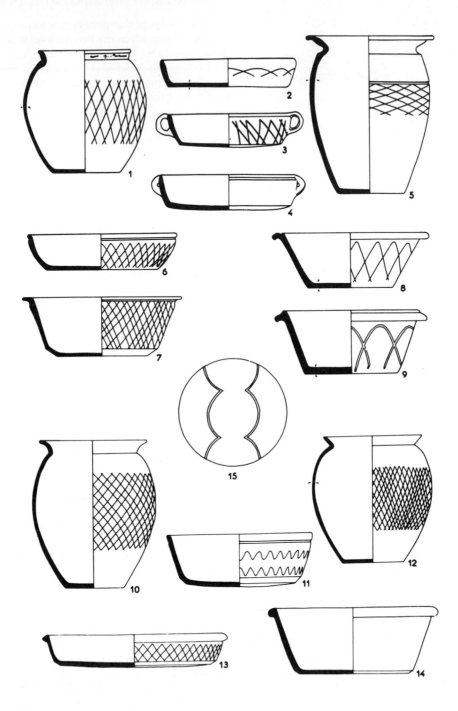

Figure 22   Black-burnished ware (after Williams, 1977). Nos 1–9 and 15 (base with 'Redcliff' motif), category 1 from Dorset; Nos 10–14, category 2 from southeast England. Scale ¼.

Plate 16 Category 1 black-burnished cooking pot, fourth century A.D. Made in the Wareham–Poole Harbour area and found at Minories, London. London Museum ac. no. 2993, height 17 cm.

stones used at La Borne in France (Chaton and Talbot, 1977:78).

Other parts are much rarer but an iron spindle from Engelhof in Upper Austria has been interpreted as the axis of a potter's wheel (Jandaurek, 1956; here Fig. 23). If this is correct it is far too short to be from a kick wheel for it is about 48 cm long.

Most Roman flywheels must have been of wood for very few have survived. A remarkable exception is a wheel from Speicher, now in Trier Museum, which is fashioned from Mayen lava (Eiden, 1951; here Fig. 23). It looks rather like the upper stone of a flour mill but it lacks the characteristic wear pattern and has holes on the upper periphery which could have accommodated the tip of a pole used in turning. A similar stone, 74 cm across, with two holes, was found at Rheinzabern and it is almost certainly another wheel rather than a mill for colorants as Ludowici (1905:172) suggested. Fragments of querns or mills have been found on other production sites (e.g. Wild, 1973; Swan, 1973), but as Fulford (1975b) has warned they could well be from querns used to grind materials and unless a substantial portion is recovered it is difficult to be certain of the original use.

The evidence of the socket stones, the iron spindle from Engelhof and the two flywheels combine to suggest that most Roman wheels were relatively small and of the simple variety, perhaps somewhat akin to the Indian pivoted block wheel shown in Fig. 24. If so Roman wheels would have been only marginally different from those of the Greek period, a number of which are shown on painted vases. A well known black-figure vessel now in Munich shows a low flywheel turned by an apprentice or slave while the master potter forms a large storage jar (Noble, 1966: Fig. 73).

However, the existence of double wheels cannot be entirely dismissed, for one is illustrated in a Hellenistic relief from Egypt, although it is very different from the kick wheels we have been considering (Rieth, 1960). On the other hand, two unequally sized terracotta discs from Cincelli near Arezzo are less convincing for fired clay would hardly be strong enough to form a flywheel subject to foot action (Fabroni, 1841). They apparently had lead weights around the edge and could perhaps have been wheel heads like earlier examples from Crete (e.g. Hampe, 1968).

A much larger stone, which might relate to a kick wheel, has been reported from the production site of Tocra in Libya and it has been compared with a similar pivot from Boutovo in Bulgaria (Riley, 1975b:29). It is of course possible that several types of wheel were employed in the Roman world, but unfortunately we cannot yet be certain that these large pivots were not for doors or pug-mills.

One of the features of Roman pottery is the frequent use of a mould, particularly for the finer wares (Pl. 17). These were produced on the wheel and then decorated internally while the clay was still wet. The principal ornament comprised animal and human figures impressed from fired clay (Fig. 25). Many of the motifs are paralleled on metalwork and in the case of Arretine ware it has been suggested that the *poinçons* were made by casting from silver originals (Strong, 1966:139). Once made and fired moulds could be centred on the wheel and elaborately decorated vessels thrown in them with great rapidity. Moulding is thus an efficient way of producing highly ornate pottery, but it was not the sole method and other more laborious decorative techniques were employed from time to time. Slip trailing (*en barbotine*) was particularly common and involved the application of a liquid clay slurry in the manner of icing a cake (Pl. 18). In other cases the ornament resembles *cut glass*, with star or leaf shaped patterns cut with a U- or V-shaped tool, and of course there is

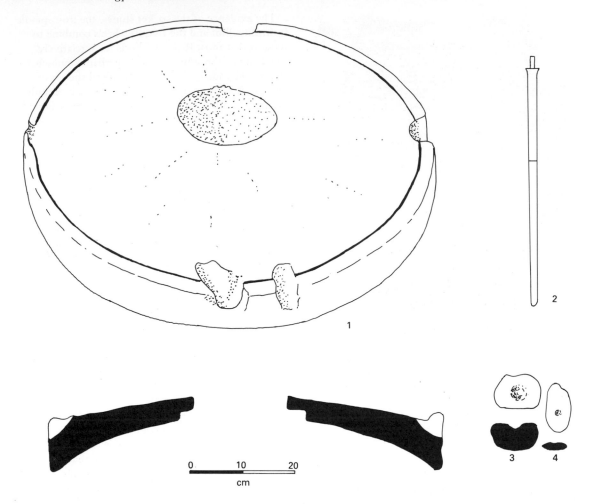

Figure 23   Parts of Roman potters' wheels. No. 1, flywheel from Speicher (after Rieth, 1960); No. 2, iron spindle from Engelhof, Upper Austria (after Jandaurek, 1956); Nos 3–4, pivot stones from Lavoye, Argonne (after Chenet and Gaudron, 1955).

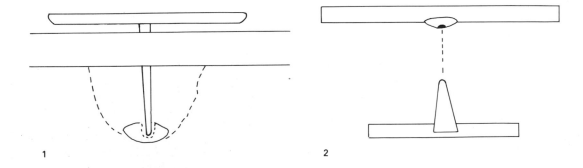

Figure 24   Indian pivoted and socketed wheels (after Saraswati and Behura, 1966).

Plate 17 Imitation samian mould, London Museum. Many similar pieces were produced in the nineteenth century by Kaufmann of Speyer and sold to leading museums throughout Europe. These imitations are very difficult to distinguish from ancient moulds. See Simpson (1976, 247) Diam. 25 cm.

little doubt that these motifs were inspired by glass prototypes (Pl. 19). Applied decoration, in which the motifs are cast separately and then stuck on with liquid clay was never very popular, doubtless because it was excessively laborious, but it was commonly used for the lion heads ornamenting mortaria of the form Dragendorff 45.

We know all too little of the potter's ancillary equipment required to assist throwing and it must be assumed that most of these tools were of wood, as at the present day. A remarkable shaper (*estèque*) of schist was found at Lavoye in the Argonne and it is closely similar to those in use at the present day (Chenet and Gaudron, 1955: Fig. 8c; here Fig. 26 which should be compared with similar instruments shown in Fig. 10). However, this find is exceptional and pieces of polished stone or bone which could

have served a similar purpose are much more common (Fig. 26; Young, 1977a:17). Iron instruments are comparatively rare, but the Musée National at St Germain near Paris possesses a remarkable collection of tools from pottery sites dominated by iron spatulas which could have had a number of uses in shaping and trimming (Champion, 1916; here Fig. 26). Other iron tools have recently been reported from the kiln site of Aspiran in the south of France and they seem to be essentially scrapers for trimming excess clay from the rotating vessel (Genty, 1980; here Fig. 26).

A variety of methods was used to give vessels an attractive surface finish. For many of the coarser wares a simple wet hand finish sufficed, since this is a very simple way of concealing coarse temper and sealing the surface to some extent. An alternative,

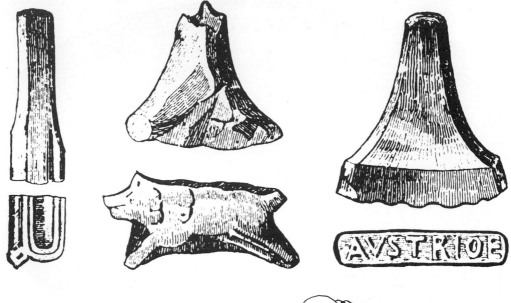

Figure 25 Pottery *poincons* (from Walters, 1905).

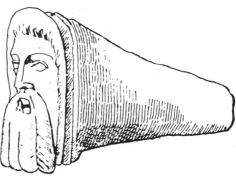

although rather more laborious, method is *burnishing* or polishing with a smooth piece of bone or stone. This process mechanically orientates the plate-like clay minerals so that they lie parallel to the surface and act like tiny mirrors reflecting light. This has the advantage of producing an attractive shiny finish, while the pores are filled and the vessel is better able to hold fluids. It is interesting to note that burnishing is often used to finish vessels made by hand or on the turntable, but it is less commonly found on wheel-turned products, presumably because burnishing by hand would generally offset the advantages of the wheel. Nevertheless there are exceptions, such as the Severn Valley wares produced

Plate 18 Small black-gloss beaker decorated *en barbotine* with white clay. Found in London, but possibly from Central France, second century. London Museum ac. no. 3308, height, 11.5 cm.

Plate 19 Samian ware decorated in the 'cut-glass' technique from Lloyds Bank, Lime Street, London. East Gaulish, late second century. London Museum ac. no. A 27867, height 12 cm.

in Roman western England (p. 98). A useful comparison can be made with the *botijas* produced today at Salvatierra de los Barros in the Spanish Extremadura, from whence they are transported and sold all over Spain. It is interesting to note that the flasks are made by men using the wheel but the burnished decoration is applied by womenfolk using nothing more than a naturally smooth river pebble (Llorens and Corredor, 1974:95; here Pl. 20). It would appear that the economics of the workshop and household industry are combined to great effect.

Many of the finer Roman wares were coated with a *slip*, a fine slurry of clay which can be used to cover blemishes and to give the surface an attractive colour. An artificial distinction is usually made between the red-gloss finish of samian ware and the generally duller, less accomplished, surfaces known as colour-coat. Both are produced in a similar manner, by dipping the leather-hard vessel in a liquid slurry of fine iron-rich clay, and not surprisingly there are innumerable gradations between the two. This method of producing an attractive finish has a very

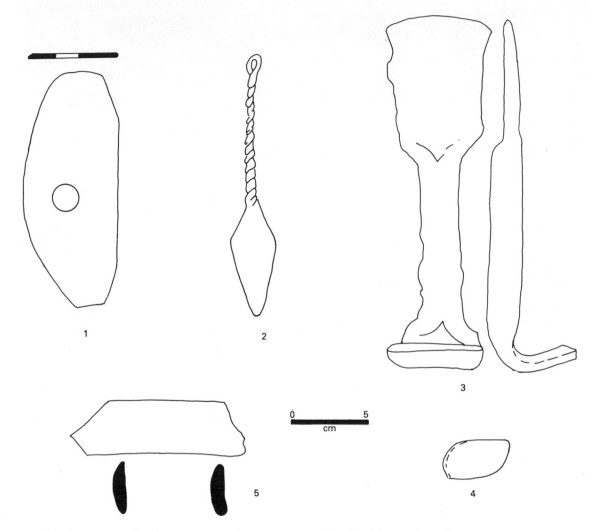

Figure 26   Roman potters' tools. No. 1, *estèque* from Lavoye, in schist (after Chenet and Gaudron, 1955); No. 2, iron spatula from Compiègne (after Champion, 1916); No. 3, iron *tournassin* or shaver from Aspiran (after Genty, 1980); No. 4, polished stone from Rheinzabern (after Ludowici, 1905); No. 5, polished bone from Churchill, Oxford (after Young, 1977a).

long history, particularly in its black or reduced version, for samian red-gloss seems to be a direct translation of the Hellenistic and Greek black-gloss which can in turn be traced back in more or less unbroken sequence to Minoan Crete.

In recent times the better Greek and Roman pieces have attracted considerable attention from both the art historian and the commercial potter anxious to emulate the success of Antiquity. It is hardly surprising, therefore, that the secret of slipping to produce a high gloss finish has been the subject of much speculation, experiment and scientific analysis,

but it is salutary to note that the problem was not solved until 1942 when a German chemist, Theodore Schumann, published a definitive discussion. His findings have since been confirmed and amplified by other workers such as Bimson (1956), Farnsworth and Simmons (1963), Winter (1959, 1978) and Noble (1966).

A number of factors seem to be involved, the principal of which is the creation of a suspension of very fine clay, achieved by mixing clay with water containing a peptising or deflocculating agent. Calgon has been used in present-day experiments but

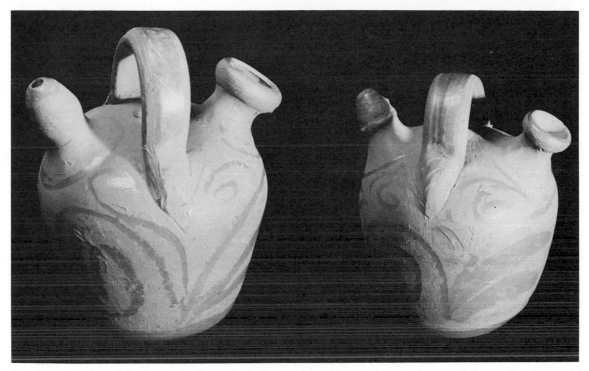

Plate 20 Botijas from Salvatierra de los Barros in the Extremadura of Spain. These vessels are made by men but decorated by women using a smooth river pebble.

in antiquity a solution of potassium carbonate, produced by soaking plant ash in water, might have served the same purpose. The presence of a peptising agent helps to keep the very fine material in suspension so that it can be decanted and concentrated separately, by evaporation if necessary. When applied to the surface of a vessel this material tends to melt or sinter at a lower temperature than the clay body producing a red or black gloss slip depending on the firing atmosphere. Picon (1973:99) has shown that Arretine and samian ware is characterised by the almost invariable use of a calcareous clay. It is possible that the lime acted as a flux effectively lowering the sintering point of the slip.

While the fineness of the particles is crucial, their shape is also important. Most clay minerals have a plate-like habit which promotes alignment with the surface and an optimum gloss is produced from small aligned particles (Oberlies and Köppen, 1953).

It follows that the type of clay is crucial and not all materials are equally suitable for making gloss slip. It is often claimed that only those clays rich in the mineral illite are suitable and certainly this was a dominant in the raw material used by the Classical Greek potters (Farnsworth, 1970). However, illite is a common constituent of clay and as yet it is unclear how much must be present to produce an acceptable gloss. There is unlikely to be a simple answer, for this property must be set against other desiderata such as fineness of particle size and perhaps the presence of iron hydroxides which apparently promote deflocculation in water without an added peptising agent (Picon, 1973:43). In addition firing temperature must also be crucial for Tite (1969:140) has shown that samian ware was fired at a considerably higher temperature than that used for ordinary colour-coat.

An alternative way of producing an attractive surface is the technique of glazing which was very popular in the Medieval world but markedly less so in the Roman. Gloss finish is sometimes referred to as glaze but it is better to restrict this term to pots bearing a coating of glass on the surface. Glass is a super-cooled liquid, generally produced by fusing silica with a modifier to lower the melting-point. In the case of a glaze, the silica is often derived from the clay and quartz in the body and it is merely necessary to coat the surface with a modifier before firing.

Lead salts were favoured throughout much of the Roman empire, and the sulphide ore, galena, was commonly used for it dominates most lead deposits. It can be readily ground to a powder and then dusted on the surface of the leather-hard vessel or it can be mixed with water to form a suspension suitable for painting; both are equally effective in producing a pleasing glaze after firing. Nearly all clays contain traces of iron oxide and these would produce a self-coloured yellowish or brown glaze (green when reduced), which could be intensified by the deliberate mixing of iron oxide with the lead ore. However, many Roman glazes are characteristically green resulting from the deliberate addition of copper salts or copper filings.

The production of glazed pottery is technically very simple and requires a minimum of ancillary equipment apart from a quern to grind the constituents. However, there is evidence from Holt and from Tarsus that vessels were sometimes fired upside down inside round saggars which would protect them from the adverse effects of fire (Grimes, 1930:182; Goldman, 1950; here Fig. 27). On the other hand these were by no means universal and most production sites have failed to yield any indication of saggars.

The technique of lead glazing has a very long history in the ancient world. The idea may have originated in the Near East or Egypt from whence come the earliest examples, dated to the early first millennium B.C. However, the Roman tradition could stem from Asia Minor where a foundation was laid in the strong Hellenistic tradition (Hochuli-Gysel, 1977; Schäfer, 1968). There is no doubt that the technique was increasingly used in the east from the second to the first centuries B.C., while in the latter part of the first century production began in Italy from whence it subsequently spread to central Gaul and perhaps Rhaetia (Pl. 21). Later it was introduced into Britain where Arthur (1978) has recognised nine local groups. Most of these wares were probably produced within the region where they were used but only two

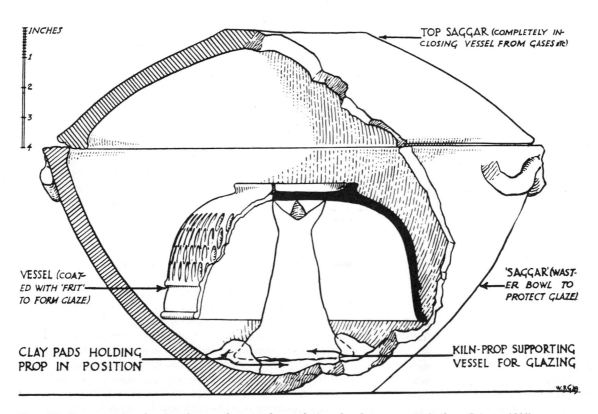

Figure 27 Reconstruction showing the use of saggars for producing glazed pottery at Holt (from Grimes, 1930).

Plate 21 Beaker with green glaze from London. Probably Central Gaulish, pre-Flavian. London Museum ac. no. A 28316. Height 12.5 cm.

kiln sites are known, namely the legionary works at Holt, where details of the technique could indicate connections with the east, and the civilian site at Little Chester (Greene, 1977; Brassington, 1971). The general pattern seems clear; lead glazed pottery was always subsidiary to some more important product and even then the main centres seem to lie in the eastern empire. The situation is vastly different from that of the Medieval world where practically every village potter from Britain to Persia was making glazed ceramics in considerable quantity. It is difficult to discern the reason for this marked disparity between Roman and Medieval practice, save to note that a shortage of galena in the Roman world hardly seems an adequate explanation, for even those potteries fortunate enough to be located near lead outcrops failed to exploit their resource to any extent.

Before concluding this brief discussion it is worth mentioning that, as an alternative to lead, the oxides of sodium or potassium can be used as a modifier producing what are collectively termed *alkali* glazes. This simplest way of producing an alkali glaze is to throw salt into the kiln fire, so that it volatilises, reacting with silica and steam to produce a 'salt glaze'. Although this technique was very popular in post-Medieval Europe it was not employed in Roman times, probably because the reaction requires very high kiln temperature, which lay beyond most Roman potters.

Alternatively sodium can be obtained from soda-rich felspars or from carbonate salt, both of which occur naturally, while potassium salts are also a constituent of plant ash. Some of these materials could be applied in much the same manner as galena, plant ash furnishing a good example since it contains all the ingredients of glaze. However, many sodium and potassium salts used in Antiquity are very soluble in water and if painted on the surface of a pot tend to be absorbed. One way of overcoming this is to fuse or 'frit' the constituents in a crucible and then make a suspension from the comminuted insoluble product.

Again metal salts can be used to colour the glaze and copper was a particular favourite, for in an alkali glaze it yields an attractive turquoise blue.

Alkali glazed wares are interesting from a technical point of view but they were never very common except in the extreme eastern fringes of the Roman empire, where traces of manufacture have been recorded from sites such as Dura Eurapos, Seleucia, Warka and Nippur (Charleston, 1955). A kiln at Bavay in northern France has been claimed as a strange isolated outlier of the industry, but the structure is most unusual and is almost certainly a glass oven (cf. Hénault, 1928).

Charleston (1955:27) draws attention to an interesting variant of the alkali glaze tradition, produced in Roman Egypt, which is usually referred to as *faience* or glazed quartz frit. The body is composed essentially of pulverised quartz which differentiates it from normal pottery and it is better suited to beads and figurine-making rather than containers. Faience has a long history for it was employed in pre-Dynastic Egypt and is still made in parts of Persia today. It can be produced in a number of different ways, all of which seem to yield more or less the same end-product. For example a core of fine quartz cemented with alkali can be packed into a glazing mixture of plant ash, copper oxide and lime, or alternatively a frit can be prepared and painted onto the fashioned core before firing. On the other hand Noble (1969) has suggested that Egyptian faience was produced by a self-glazing process, whereby, as the quartz core dries, the alkalis are drawn to the surface so that on firing they fuse with the colorant to produce the characteristic brilliant blue glaze. It is far from clear which of these methods was used in producing Roman faience and it is particularly unfortunate that the one kiln site known (at Memphis) was excavated before modern techniques of observation and recording had been properly developed (Petrie, 1909).

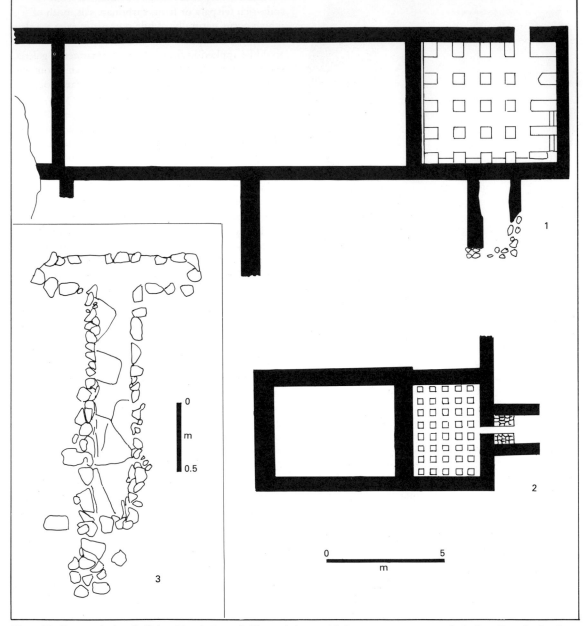

Figure 28   Pottery drying facilities. Nos 1–2, probable workshops with hypocaust system attached, from Engelhof and Holt (after Jandaurek, 1956; Grimes, 1930). No. 3, 'T'-shaped drying oven from Churchill, Oxford (after Young 1977a).

Roman faience is found in a range of forms including substantial vases, which were made by moulding as it is difficult to turn a quartz frit on the wheel. However, it must be stressed that faience is an interesting technical curiosity of little account in the Roman world as a whole.

DRYING

Before firing it is essential that pottery be thoroughly dried to remove excess water which might otherwise cause warping or spaling in the kiln. In seasonal potteries with low output there might be no special provision for drying as the wares could stand outside or be accommodated in part of the workshop. However, high output industries functioning for as much of the year as possible might require specialised drying facilities. This has been appreciated by many excavators, but the search for drying sheds has not been very fruitful.

At Mancetter, Hartley (1965) found a rectangular building 5.8 m long and 3.65 m wide, enclosing rough stone kerbs retaining a system of flues. The structure, which is dated to the mid second century, was of two phases and in the later usage the drier could have functioned as two separate halves. At Holt a building interpreted as a workshop had a hypocaust room annexed and it is thought that this was for drying pottery. A striking parallel is to be seen in the supposed workshop at Engelhof in Upper Austria (Grimes 1930:22; Jandaurek, 1956; here Fig. 28). Again in a military context, a wooden structure from Dormagen has been interpreted as a shed for drying bricks (p. 140).

In Britain drying ovens have been found in the Churchill potteries at Oxford, at Norton in Yorkshire and Hampstead Marshall in Berkshire (Young, 1977a:20). They are generally small 'T'-shaped structures about 1.5 m long and indistinguishable from the characteristic Romano-British 'corn drier' (Fig. 28). Indeed it could be argued that they *are* corn driers, which might imply a close integration of potting and farming activities. However, this view has little to recommend it and the dearth of charred grain, typical of so many corn driers, argues strongly for their adoption by the pottery industry.

FIRING

Roman pottery was fired in a number of ways. The simple hand- or turntable-made wares are seldom found associated with kiln structures and it is reasonable to infer that they were fired in surface bonfires or clamps. It is almost certain that much brick and tile was also clamp fired (p. 16). Unfortunately surface firings are very difficult to detect because the waste will be left lying on the ground and readily destroyed or dispersed, while most of the wares fired in this way were heavily tempered resulting in a rather low failure rate. Furthermore rejects tend to be discoloured or cracked rather than warped and it may not be easy to recognise them as wasters.

Brick clamps have been postulated for a number of Romano-British sites but few claims can be

regarded as reasonably substantiated (cf. McWhirr and Viner, 1978). However, one site deserves especial mention, for careful excavations at Itchingfield in Sussex failed to produce evidence of kiln structure and even extensive exploration of the unexcavated area with a magnetometer failed to reveal the strong anomalies to be expected from a kiln (Green, 1970). It seems almost certain that clamp firing was practised here.

Pottery clamps or bonfires are equally elusive and the only area to yield sites identified with tolerable certainty is the Wareham–Poole Harbour region of Dorset where they seem to relate to the production of black-burnished ware (p. 85; Farrar, 1973:91). Unfortunately none of the sites has been excavated on a large scale and it is difficult to be certain that kilns do not exist, but since only one has come to light in many years of *sondage* the possibility of an extensive complex is not great. The majority of sites produced little more than layers of ash and sherds of black-burnished ware, many of which were uncharacteristically oxidised. The full exploration of one of these sites could enhance our knowledge of Roman firing technology.

There can be no doubt that it was normal practice to fire in a kiln because innumerable examples have been discovered throughout the Roman world, and in fact we have more information available than on any other aspect of Roman ceramic technology. However, there are great problems in using this data, for in many cases the published records are inadequate. Before we can synthesise our knowledge of kilns it is necessary to know something of their morphology, to assess their products and to be able to date them within broad limits. As Duhamel (1973a/b) has pointed out, less than 30 per cent of all recorded kilns from Gaul fulfil these requirements and this could be typical of the Roman world as a whole. Another factor seriously affecting any attempt at broad synthesis is the uneven spread of data since certain key areas such as Anatolia are almost totally unexplored. However, this is to some extent offset by the wealth of information available for other countries. At present we know much about the kilns of Italy, Gaul and Romania (Cuomo di Caprio, 1972; Duhamel, 1973 a/b; Floca *et al*, 1971), while in Britain Corder's (1957) pioneering study is being updated by Vivien Swan. Iberian kilns have been reviewed by Fletcher Valls (1965), Gamer (1971) and Fernando de Almeida *et al*. (1971), but the quality of the original reports on which these surveys are based places severe limits on the inferences that can be made.

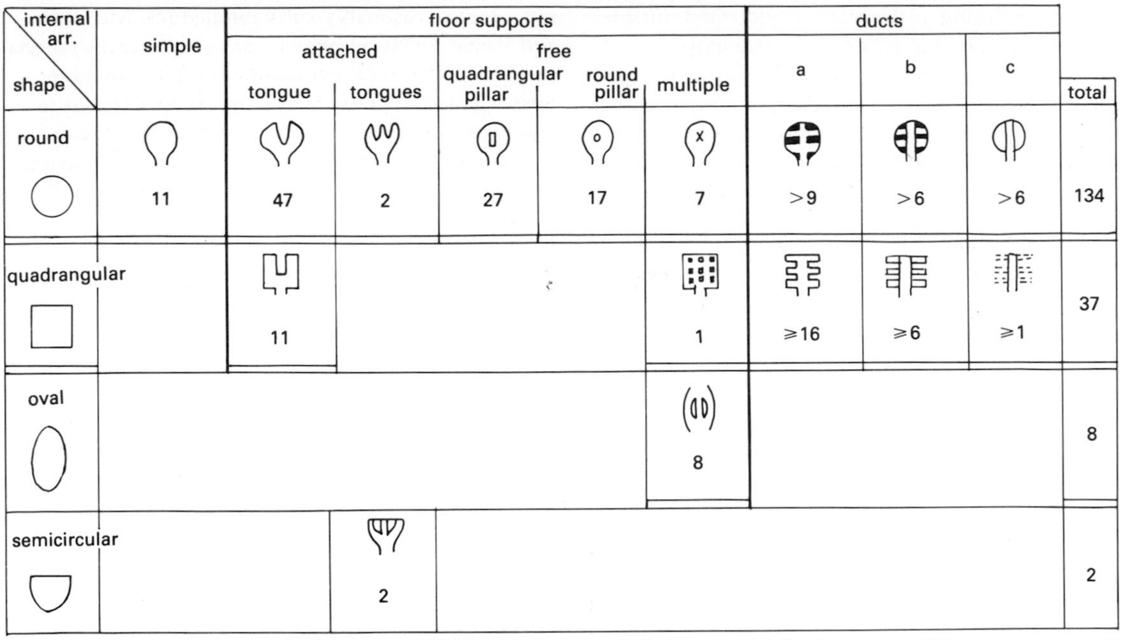

internal arr. / shape	simple	floor supports					ducts			total
		attached		free			a	b	c	
		tongue	tongues	quadrangular pillar	round pillar	multiple				
round ○	11	47	2	27	17	7	>9	>6	>6	134
quadrangular □		11				1	≥16	≥6	≥1	37
oval ○						8				8
semicircular ⌄			2							2

Figure 29   Diagram showing the frequency of different kiln types in Roman Gaul (after Duhamel, 1973a). In type *a* the floor of the open lateral ducts is horizontal, in type *b* it slopes up from the central flue to the sides and in type *c* the ducts are enclosed within the floor and emanate at the sides.

It will be clear that an adequate statement on Roman kilns must await the development of a better data-base, but nevertheless sufficient has been done to consider, however tentatively, two fundamental questions:

1. what is the reason for observed variation in kiln structure; and
2. is it possible to establish technological correspondences between different parts of the Empire?

Most Roman kilns were of the updraught variety, in which pots were stacked on a perforated floor serving to separate the oven compartment from the fire chamber below. Horizontal, or more accurately downdraught, kilns have been claimed from time to time. In this type hot gases are drawn from the stoke pit, deflected from the roof of the firing chamber and exhausted from a chimney at the other end of the structure. Twin-flue kilns are known from a number of places including the Farnham region of Surrey, but Clark's (1949) excavation of fourth-century examples at Overwey demonstrated that they were unlikely to have functioned in this way. There was no evidence for a vertical exhaust-vent superimposed above one of the flues, and it seems more likely that there was a central vent in the superstructure. If this is correct, the flues were presumably alternatives to be chosen according to variations in wind direction. On the other hand Farrar (1977) has described a twin-flued kiln from Ower in Dorset which had an intact dome devoid of a vent. The possibility of downdraught kilns cannot be dismissed out of hand, although clearly they are very rare.

The classification of kilns is, of necessity, based upon the groundplan of the firing chamber and flue for it is unusual to find more than this preserved. In particular great importance must be attached to the general shape of the structure and the method of supporting the floor. A range of designs was used, some of the more important of which are shown in Fig. 29.

The variety of Roman kilns is both complex and bewildering and there is no doubt that a fuller evaluation must await the future discovery of more scientifically excavated examples. For the present it seems best to concentrate the few common types which comprise the bulk of all discoveries, leaving the exotica for consideration when more examples are available.

Most kilns are either round or quadrangular in plan: there are very few examples which are oval, semi-circular or pear-shaped. Some common designs are shown in Fig. 30. Within the circular group it is

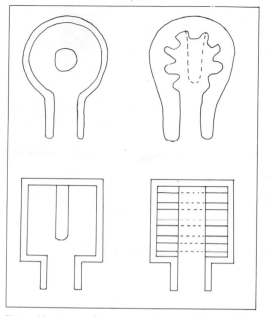

Figure 30   Some of the principal types of Roman kiln, as classified by Cuomo di Caprio (1972).

possible to distinguish four important types which recur with some frequency.

1. Kilns with no recorded support for the floor (this must inevitably include some poorly preserved or inadequately excavated examples).
2. Kilns with a round central pillar supporting the floor.
3. Kilns with a central tongue projecting from the rear wall. Examples with a detached rectangular pillar are probably a variant of the same theme.
4. Kilns with a central flue spanned by a series of arches.

Among the quadrangular types there are but two common varieties.

1. Kilns with a projecting tongue as in type 3 above.
2. Kilns with a central flue spanned by arches as in type 4 above.

The variation in shape presents an initial problem to which a fairly obvious answer is that round kilns were for pots while the quadrangular varieties were for bricks. On the fringes of the empire in both Britain and Romania this seems to be an almost unviolate rule (McWhirr and Viner, 1978; Floca *et al*, 1971). However, elsewhere the division is less clearcut: in Gaul, Italy and Greece (Cook, 1961) quadrangular kilns seem to have been used for

pottery as well as for bricks, while most of the kilns recorded from Iberia are rectangular, which seems to imply that some, at least, were used for pottery although the type of product is infrequently recorded. On the other hand, round kilns were seldom used for bricks, but exceptions are known from Velia in Italy or Avenches in Switzerland (Berger, 1969). The general picture is far from simple but is paralleled in the recent past of southern Italy where round and square kilns seem to have been employed more or less indiscriminately (Fig. 13). The reason for this mixture is not understood but in some cases the model of changing usage might apply (p. 31). However it is worth noting that brick- and pottery-making are not altogether discrete activities and today some brickyards are equipped with wheels for producing certain coarse forms of which the flowerpot is a good modern example. There is evidence that 'brickyard pottery' was also a feature of Roman production and amphorae or dolia were commonly made alongside bricks (p. 130). In some cases the pottery fired in quadrangular kilns was of exactly this type and it is not by chance that the separate roles of the two kiln shapes are least clear in amphora-producing lands. However, at best this is a partial explanation, for square kilns were sometimes used in firing Gaulish samian, furnishing a striking, although by no means unique, anomaly.

The variation in internal structure is even more difficult to explain adequately, but there is no doubt that size is an important consideration. It is hardly surprising that kilns without any internal support are seldom more than about 1 m across, while those with the flue spanned by a complex of arches are large, generally upwards of 3–4 m or more. However, the choice between a tongue or central pedestal attached to the rear wall seems to be much more arbitrary. The tongue is of course an excellent support for the arches of a very large kiln and it is sometimes found in this context, but both tongues and pedestals were used in quite small kilns and it is hard to discern logical reasons for the choice. If one had advantages over the other these remain elusive, and it is difficult to escape the conclusion that the matter was determined at least partially by the tradition and training of the potter. If this is accepted, it follows that an analysis of these traits chronologically and geographically might tell us much about the movement of ideas and perhaps personnel in the Roman pottery industry. It cannot be denied that some relationship to other technical matters, such as choice of fuel, may one day be discerned, but at the moment this seems less than likely.

Plate 22 Experimental kiln built by G. F. Bryant (photo by H. Atkinson, courtesy G. F. Bryant).

While the analysis of the total empire-wide distribution of kiln types must await further collection and publication of data, the study has progressed sufficiently to reveal some emerging patterns. It would appear that tongues are commoner than pedestals in Britain, Germany, France, Austria and Switzerland, but not in Italy where tongues are very rare and virtually restricted to certain earlier Greek and Punic colonies in the south. This dichotomy is curious and demands an explanation, but since the kiln was not a Roman invention the relationship of these two types is unlikely to make much sense without considering pre-Roman developments.

It is true that kilns were infrequently used in pre-Roman barbarian Europe, but a number of examples are known on Continental late La Tène sites and full distribution lists have been given by Meduna (1970) and Németi (1974). La Tène kilns are found over a wide area stretching from western Romania to Germany and eastern France, with a principal focus

in present-day Czechoslovakia, Hungary and southern Poland. While some of these kilns are of the simple variety lacking any form of floor support and others have a central pedestal, the majority are of the projecting tongues variety which can therefore claim to be a characteristic pre-Roman Celtic type. Many of the discoveries are difficult to date accurately but they seem to have been particularly popular in the latest La Tène phase, and in some of the more westerly finds it is difficult to decide whether they were in use before or after the Roman conquest.

Before the late La Tène, the tongued kiln had a long history in the eastern Mediterranean. The earliest seem to be of Mycenaean date with splendid examples from Pylos and Tiryns (Blegen and Lang, 1960; Dragendorff, 1913), but not all contemporary kilns were of this type, for one with no internal structure was discovered at Sitea, closely similar to an early Bronze Age example from Ay Mamas in Macedonia (Platon, 1952; Heurtley, 1939). A tongued example dating to the tenth century B.C. is known

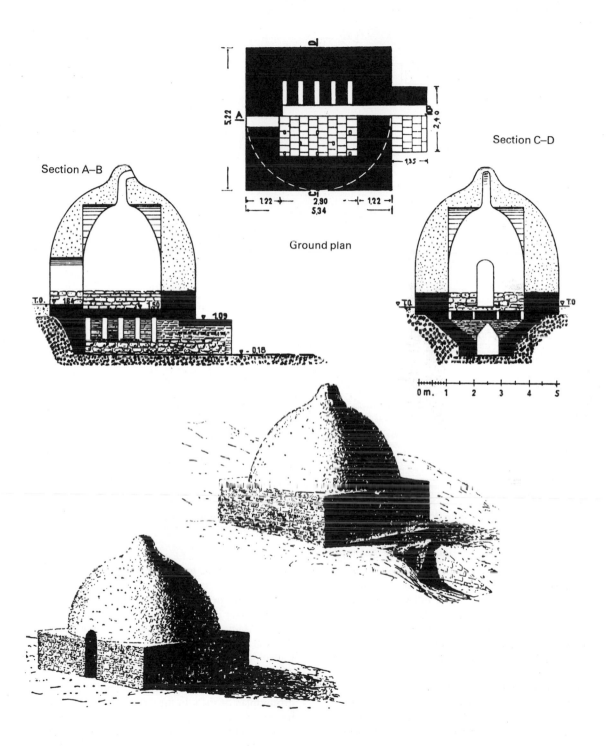

Section A–B

Ground plan

Section C–D

Figure 31 Suggested reconstruction of the Roman brick kiln excavated at Speicher, Germany (from Locschcke, 1931).

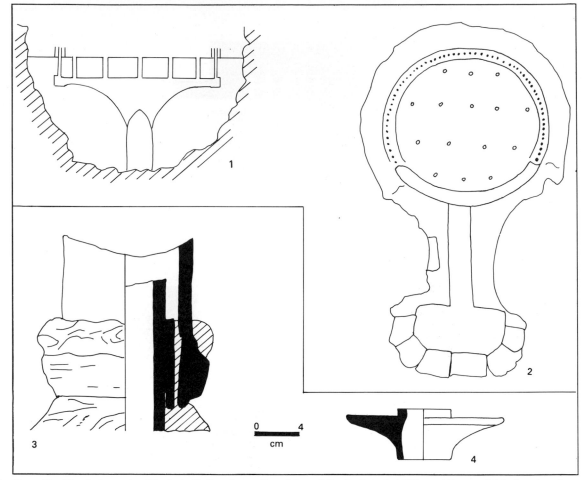

Figure 32   Nos 1–2, samian kiln from Heiligenberg, diam 2.5 m, (after Duhamel, 1973b, and Forrer, 1911) showing the peripheral arrangement of pipes. No. 3, method of mounting pipes on the kiln floor at Lavoye, Argonne; No. 4, so-called 'tournette' or pot support from Pont-des-Rémes, Argonne (after Chenet and Gaudron, 1955).

from Argos but another probably of the same date had a central pedestal (Daux, 1957, 1959). The tongued theme recurs on certain iron age sites in Palestine such as Tell Nasbeh and Megiddo but few can be accurately dated (Delcroix and Huot, 1972). Presumably from thence the idea was transmitted via the Phoenicians to Carthage and other colonies such as Mozia in Sicily (Cuomo di Caprio, 1977).

Classical and Hellenistic Greece reveals a great range of kiln shapes, square, round and pear-shaped, with a variety of internal structures (Cook, 1961; Ducrey and Picard, 1969). The reasons for this diversity are far from clear but tongue supports are present and they could have served as models for the barbarian world beyond.

The evidence is decidedly sketchy and there are many hiatuses in the record, but it seems reasonable to suggest that the tongued kiln, so common in northern and western parts of the empire, was derived from pre-Roman models which in turn were influenced by certain higher civilizations in the eastern Mediterranean. This contrasts with the pedestal variety which may have been typical of the Italian peninsula from whence it was spread by the advance of Rome.

This discussion has inevitably concentrated on the groundplan of the kiln furnace and minor variations have been neglected in an attempt to see the more general picture. Before concluding, it is perhaps worth discussing the question of superstructures in so far as the evidence permits. There is little doubt that certain Greek kilns were capped with a clay dome for at Latô, Ducrey and Picard (1969) found a piece of burned clay forming part of an orifice which they plausibly interpreted as a fragment of the chimney on the top of a dome. It is generally thought that Roman kilns might have been capped in a similar manner, but unfortunately there is little indisputable evidence in support of this. Corder (1957:14) was of the opinion that the typical Romano-British pottery kiln was 'normally a temporary domed structure formed of turves, straw and clay, built upon a framework of branches around the pots as they were stacked and removed when firing was completed'. The only evidence he was able to cite were the plates or slabs of clay found on some kiln sites which, he suggested, were used to reinforce the oven wall. It is true that kilns with clay domes completely or partly preserved have been found on a number of continental sites, such as Bavay, Bussy or L'Hay les Roses (Duhamel, 1973b), but since soil pressure will ultimately cause vertical walls to curve inwards, the evidence is not as conclusive as it might appear at first sight.

It would be very laborious to rebuild after each firing and Bryant's (1971, 1973) experimental work has shown that other alternatives are equally plausible. In fact, a temporary cover of turf, clay plates, or bricks is an adequate way of conserving heat and fuel and it is easy to envisage a permanent cylindrical structure with a temporary capping of such materials (Pl. 22).

Similar arguments might also apply to the quadrangular kilns usually employed for bricks. Loeschcke (1931) was among the first to consider the superstructure and he postulated a clay dome by analogy with modern Turkish practice (Fig. 31). However, kiln excavations have generally failed to produce the clay masses that might indicate a collapsed dome, and the modern kilns at Broadmayne or Ashburnham (p. 48) furnish a more convincing model for reconstruction. On the other hand a superstructure is by no means essential and the flues we see today could have been grates upon which it was customary to build free-standing clamps (cf. Cunliffe, 1973:118).

One final technical point concerns the special kilns in which samian ware was fired. These are usually associated with a curious assemblage of clay pipes, rings and plugs (Fig. 32). Hull (1963) suggested that they were employed to lead gases from the furnace to the oven chamber in order to prevent contact with the pots. However, this is not very practical as it would be immensely difficult to load and unload a chamber riddled with pipes. It is more reasonable to accept the clear evidence from Lezoux and the

Argonne where the pipes were arranged in the walls to form a more or less continuous insulation jacket (Chenet and Gaudron, 1955: Fig. 40; here Fig. 32). Presumably this would greatly facilitate the high temperature firing that seems to be a characteristic of samian. On the other hand, it is curious that this technique was not invariably used in samian production nor was it employed, as far as known, in the black-gloss tradition of the Greek and Hellenistic world.

Finally it remains to mention supports used to separate and stack vessels in the kiln. Figure 32 shows one variety particularly common on samian production sites, but supports took a variety of forms and cotton-reel-like objects of clay were commonly used for this purpose.

THE LAYOUT OF PRODUCTION SITES

There is little point in pursuing this topic at length for the information available is sparse and unsatisfactory, largely because few sites have been

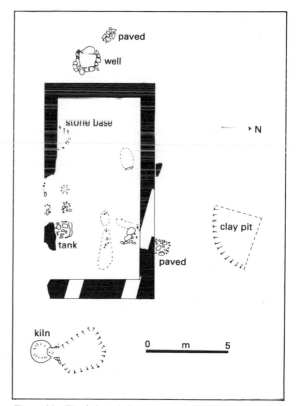

Figure 33 Workshop, kiln and clay pit, Stibbington, Nene Valley (after Wacher, 1978).

explored on a sufficient scale. Some have revealed fragments of rectangular buildings but interpretation is difficult. In Britain round houses are occasionally associated with pottery-making sites as at Oxford or Highgate (Young, 1977a; Fig. 11–12; Brown and Sheldon, 1975; here Fig. 19), while an excellent plan of a rectangular workshop and ancillary structures has been published from Stibbington in the Nene Valley (Wacher, 1978: Fig. 40, here Fig. 33). However, the only general rule to emerge is that kilns seem to have been placed outside rather than inside buildings providing a point of contrast with common practice at the present day.

Some exceptional sites have produced more information. Holt and Holdeurn, to be discussed below (p. 138), provide excellent illustrations of military establishments and show the relationship of the different elements with some clarity. A number of civilian sites have been excavated on a comparable scale, but often, as at Oxford, our understanding is limited by the poor preservation of many of the buildings. There is no doubt that Soultov's (1976) work in Bulgaria will fill an important gap and full publication is awaited with much interest, for a wealth of rectangular buildings has been discovered. One building at Hotnitsa is of particular interest for it is interpreted as a workshop and associated dwelling. Of course ethnography leads us to anticipate potters living on site, but this has seldom been demonstrated in the Roman period and most buildings on production sites have been interpreted as workshops rather than houses.

5 The role of the household in Roman pottery production

En la plaza de Zamora
he de comprar a mi amor,
pucheritos y cazuelas
que al guiso dan buen sabor.

Folk song from Zamora, quoted by Cortés Vázquez
(1954:147)

Emphasis on the art-historical aspects of pottery in the Roman world has had some unfortunate repercussions. While we now know a great deal about samian or Arretine ware, our knowledge of the humbler hand- or turntable-made products is minimal. This is doubly regrettable, for the art-historian has a totally biased impression of Roman ceramic 'achievement' while the archaeologist lacks evidence of the simpler modes of production, which can be particularly informative of the social and economic conditions in pottery-making communities.

Study of the published literature gives the impression that wares made without the wheel or on the turntable are absent from large areas of the Mediterranean world, but the dearth of information almost certainly reflects selective publication policy and a predilection for the better quality wares. A recent study of about ten tonnes of pottery from British excavations on the site of Carthage has shown that 'hand-made' wares are a persistent element of nearly all the later deposits examined, and while never *very* common, they comprise about 5–10 per cent (and sometimes as much as 15 per cent) of the kitchen pottery (Fulford and Peacock, forthcoming). The Carthage fabrics are divisible into ten groups, which represent at least eight distinct source areas, if allowance is made for the possibility of certain petrologically similar materials originating in the same general region. This clearly implies that hand-made wares were being widely produced and

exchanged, which is surprising for it has become almost traditional for archaeologists to regard simple unsophisticated pottery as locally made. However, it is even more striking to note that some of the groups are petrologically distinctive and must originate outside northern Tunisia. In fact these extraneous wares comprise the largest group of imported kitchen ware, so that in addition to their intrinsic interest, they are also of some relevance in assessing trade contacts.

And yet Carthage is not unique. Preliminary examination of early and late Roman material from Sabratha suggests a similar complexity, and furthermore there are records of hand-made wares from towns along the length of the Tunisian coast, from Tharros in Sardinia and from towns on the Italian mainland such as Cosa or Ostia (see below p.78). It is not unreasonable to claim that hand-made wares are much more important in the Mediterranean region than has previously been credited

Of course the existence of similar pottery has long been recognised in more remote parts of the empire such as Britain, and hand-made 'native wares' have been recorded and described from a number of places all over the country (e.g., Jobey, 1959; Kenyon, 1953; Hawkes and Hull, 1947). Precise evaluation has seldom been attempted but it is generally implied that they were made in the household to supplement requirements when wheel-made wares were too expensive or unobtainable. One writer, commenting on late Roman hand-made pots from Richborough, found it inconceivable that wheel-thrown and hand-modelled vessels were being made at the same time (Alcock, 1971:183). However, the ethnographic lesson reverses this assertion for hand-made pottery is a normal component of many contemporary ceramic assemblages and its absence is often the exceptional feature.

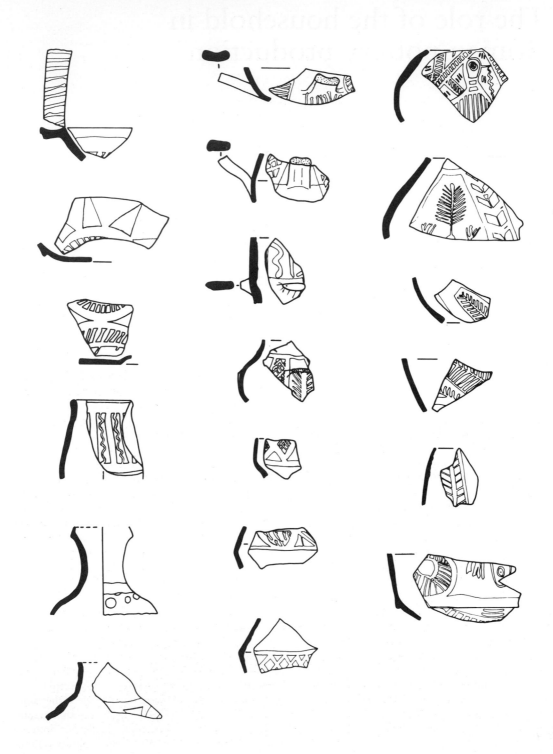

Figure 34   A selection of white or cream wares decorated with brown paint, from Vandal and Byzantine layers, Avenue Habib Bourguiba site, Carthage (From Fulford and Peacock, forthcoming.) Scale ¼.

HOUSEHOLD PRODUCTION?

Although household production has been postulated, its existence in Roman times has never been adequately demonstrated. This may prove to be very hard for it will be no easy matter to show that a ware was made on the premises where it was used. Careful typological and fabric analysis would be needed, in an attempt to differentiate individual households in the same community. The task is difficult, but it is not intractable, and already progress has been made on an analogous problem in a different part of the world. On the basis of rigorous stylistic analysis, Hill (1977) and Hardin (1977) have sought to identify the work of individual potters in the American South West, although admittedly their research was facilitated by the existence of elaborate decorative motifs.

Above all, household production must not be written off as unimportant. The survival of the Berber tradition to the present day is sufficient to suggest that it probably existed in Roman North Africa. Berber sites of the Roman period have seldom been investigated but *perhaps* contemporary designs provided the inspiration for some of the painted wheel-made wares produced in late Roman and Byzantine Tunisia (Fig. 34; Fulford and Peacock, forthcoming). The fundamental question is not whether household production existed, but how widely it was practised in the Roman empire. If it is accepted that this mode is fostered by rather special conditions, it follows that more informed discussion could be relevant in understanding matters such as the process of 'Romanisation'.

It seems probable that most of the hand-made wares isolated and described so far are the products of household industries, for in a number of cases it can be shown that they were transported some distance and presumably traded. Since general synthesis is currently impossible an attempt will be made to demonstrate and amplify this point by discussing a number of rather specific case histories.

Plate 23   Costa della Favara on the southern side of the Montagna Grande, Pantelleria, Italy. In this region gases emitted by numerous fumaroles cause decay of the rocks and form a clay which has the same mineralogical inclusions as pottery believed to have been made on the island.

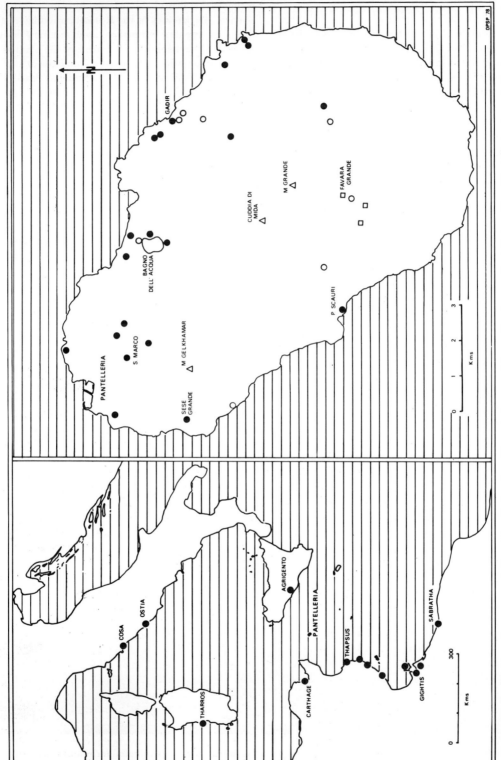

Figure 35   The distribution of pottery made from Pantellerian clay. Open circles: assemblages of pottery on Pantelleria without Pantellerian ware; squares: clay deposits.

PANTELLERIA

The suggestion that the inhabitants of the island of Pantelleria produced and exported pottery results directly from a petrological study of the hand-made wares found in the British excavations at Carthage. Although all ten fabric types contained large rock and mineral fragments, one of the commoner groups was distinguished by inclusions that were exceptionally unusual and distinctive. The thin-sections proved interesting for they were dominated by large crystals of sodic microcline (a variety of anorthoclase felspar), and by lesser quantities of the bright green mineral aegirine augite or sometimes pieces of green obsidian and lava fragments. Surprisingly, sedimentary rocks and minerals are totally lacking, which at once suggests that the pottery was imported to Carthage, for a volcanic suite such as this would be out of place in Tunisia which is a land blanketed by sedimentary rocks. Furthermore, the unusual mineralogy suggests an origin in an area of *peralkaline* volcanic rocks and these are decidedly rare in the Mediterranean region for they are only known from southwestern Sardinia and from the island of Pantelleria situated in the deep water channel separating Sicily from North Africa. Southwestern Sardinia seems an unlikely source for it is further away and the pottery in question is not common there. Moreover, the anorthoclase felspar is of a slightly different type (Johnsen, 1912). In view of the lack of alternatives, a Pantellerian source seems near proven, but this conclusion has been confirmed by further work. Firstly, more extensive thin-sectioning has revealed occasional grains of the very unusual red-brown mineral, cossyrite, for which Pantelleria is the type locality; secondly, a large fragment of green obsidian was found in a sherd of similar ware from Sabratha and this was examined chemically by Dr Warren of Bradford University who is of the opinion that it is likely to be Pantellerian. Finally, field work on the island has located clay deposits which are petrologically similar to the clay used in the pottery-making (Pl. 23; Peacock, forthcoming).

The discovery that Pantelleria was supplying pottery to Carthage is interesting, but hardly surprising for the island is only 175 km from the town and it is a natural stopping-place on the haul from Sicily to Africa. However, the wider distribution adds a new dimension, for the same ware is found over a considerable area of the Central Mediterranean stretching from Cosa and Ostia on the Italian mainland to Sabratha in Libya (Fig. 35). Doubtless the map will expand as the pottery

becomes better known. This extraordinary distribution demands an explanation and immediately it is tempting to think of the pottery as a container for more valuable produce. However the typology precludes this, for there is a predominance of open forms – platters, bowls and lids – which would be better suited as kitchen utensils rather than containers (Fig. 36). All are in a dark fabric finished with rough burnishing and they appear to have been made completely by hand, although the use of a turntable cannot be precluded. Of course simple wares such as this are difficult to date accurately, but most of those shown in Fig. 36 belong to the fifth century A.D. with the exception of the 'D'-rim bowl, which is probably late imperial. However, although common in these later levels at Carthage, Pantellerian wares have been found in a wide span of deposits ranging back to the first century A.D.

When this pottery was first encountered at Carthage it was regarded as a typical 'native ware', perhaps to be explained in terms of exchange between Carthage and the less sophisticated communities of the hinterland. This view was radically challenged when both the petrology and the distribution were studied, but it still seemed unlikely that such crude produce could be exported for its own sake to many of the most sophisticated cities of the ancient world. As an alternative it was tempting to think of the pottery as an ancillary to trade in some more valuable produce. However, the Classical literature offered little support for this theory, for to the ancient authors Cossyra was an infertile island fit only as a place of the most punitive exile (Strabo, ii, 123; Ovid, *Fasti* iii, 567); there is no evidence at all that it produced the excellent wine or capers for which it is so justly renowned today. During field survey on Pantelleria, particular attention was given to rocks which might have formed the basis of a millstone industry, but again the conclusion was negative. The basalts which outcrop in the northern part of the island were certainly worked for saddle querns during the bronze age, but the flows are so scoriaceous and dissected by jointing that it would be difficult to extract large blocks in quantity and Pantelleria could hardly have formed the basis of a viable Roman industry.

At this point the ethnographic model becomes relevant, for an infertile island where farming is difficult is exactly the environment in which household industry is liable to develop. Seen in this context the wide distribution is far from remarkable for it is precisely paralleled by the trade networks associated with the industries of Jutland or Iberia.

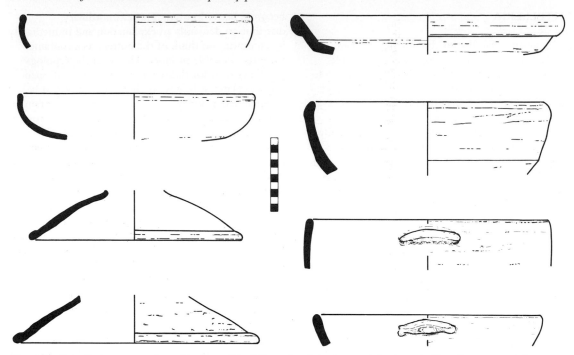

Figure 36   Pantellerian pottery from Carthage. The 'D'-rim bowl, in the top right, is probably of late imperial date, the remaining forms were common in the fifth century A.D. Scale ¼.

Doubtless sales would have been further enhanced by Pantelleria's role as a port of call. The ware need not be regarded as unacceptably crude, for like the products of present-day household industries, it was probably greatly esteemed for its resistance to thermal shock.

HAND-MADE WARES IN BRITAIN

Further potential products of household industry are known from Britain, where hand-made wares have been more intensively studied, largely because they almost invariably contain large rock and mineral inclusions which makes them an ideal subject for the petrological approach.

At the outset it seems worth distinguishing two categories. The first group comprises those wares which appear to be based upon a pre-existing iron age tradition and which were generally current in the first two centuries A.D., although some persisted much longer. The second group includes wares which appear to display no evidence of such an heritage and which seem to have been current in the later Roman period. These types both originated and thrived at a time when wheel-turned pottery was abundantly available and we may more confidently compare

them with household industry of the present day.

The problem with the former group is that the mode of production might be a continuation into the Roman period of one that was current in the iron age. Our ethnographical studies have concentrated on complex situations where a range of technical devices are known and available so that by and large the potter is able to choose the techniques best suited to his needs. Also the distribution of wares will be largely dictated by forces of supply and demand in a complex market society. However, in the pre-Roman iron age the situation could have been very different. It has been claimed that during this period the economy was 'embedded' within social relations – in other words reciprocity (gift exchange) or redistribution (from a central person or agency) could have taken the place of free market trading as a means of exchange (Hodder, 1979; Polanyi, 1957). Furthermore at this more primitive level of ceramic development the technological choice could have been less, so that if, for example, a potter failed to use the wheel it might not be for economic reasons but rather because he did not know of it. In short the clearcut relationship between mode of production, technology and marketing need not apply so rigidly as at the present day and perhaps another model might be more appropriate under these different circumstances. In view of this it seems some hand-made industries in earlier Roman Britain could owe their existence to factors which operated before the Roman Conquest, although their character may have altered in the new technical and economic climate.

Of course it would be helpful to know more of the iron age background, but an excursus into the vexed and complex question of the pre-Roman economy is hardly appropriate or feasible. Nevertheless some preliminary remarks about the iron age pottery industry are pertinent. At the outset it should be noted that iron age Britain was culturally complex and generalisations about ceramic technology are difficult. Thus, from the latter part of the first century B.C. some form of wheel seems to have been in use in the south and eastern parts of the country since the so-called 'Belgic' wares are generally described as 'wheel thrown', but these developments did not penetrate far and elsewhere pottery was produced on a turntable or with no rotary aid at all. Similarly the use of the kiln was not widespread. Woods (1974) has described some slight surface structures from the Upper Nene Valley in which 'Belgic' wares were fired just after the Roman conquest. Ephemeral traces like this have a poor chance of both preservation and discovery, and similar types may well have been used extensively in the late iron age.

Petrological study of certain classes of iron age pottery from western Britain has suggested that some of the more ornate wares were produced centrally and distributed over wide areas from *c.* 300 B.C. (Peacock, 1968; 1969b). The work has not been pursued elsewhere, but Cunliffe's (1974) 'style zones' for southern England could be a reflection of a similar pattern of production and exchange. Prior to the petrological programme it had been customary to regard iron age pottery as a household product which was seldom if ever exchanged and hence it was reasonable to use decorative styles to define specific cultures. Since the new evidence necessitated radical revision of accepted beliefs a contrasting model of specialist production and commercial marketing was tentatively postulated. However, in the intervening years iron age studies have matured and much more attention has been given to the findings of social anthropology, with a result that nowadays most prehistorians think in terms of reciprocity or redistribution as a means of primitive exchange. Unfortunately, from an archaeological point of view, free market trading for profit and redistribution from a central agency or person will produce much the same artifact distribution, so it is hard to make a firm choice between these two mechanisms on the available evidence.

There is little doubt that archaeologists have been much influenced by Polanyi's (1957a) interpretation of Aristotle's writings. He suggested that before Aristotle the economy was 'embedded' within social relations: goods were transferred by mechanisms such as reciprocity and redistribution, which differ from true marketing in the absence of a profit motive. Indeed in some cases the object may be to gain social prestige by making a loss. When exchanges are governed by the need to make a profit, there is an increase in haggling and barter and the economy begins to change to market trade which is 'disembedded' socially. Of course, even in an embedded economy long-distance exchange will still be feasible, usually by means of a special device known as the 'port of trade' (Revere, 1957). This is often situated in a politically neutral area such as a river estuary or on a tribal boundary and its purpose is to allow the high-level exchange of foods and luxuries.

According to Polanyi's reading of Aristotle, a market economy first arose in fourth-century Athens, and in view of this some archaeologists think it inherently unlikely that iron-age Britain had advanced to this level just a few centuries later (e.g. Collis, 1977; Hodder, 1979). It is clear that a great deal, perhaps far too much, has been hung upon one man's interpretation of a single, rather difficult and controversial ancient author. (See e.g. Finley (1974) and Meikle (1979) for further discussion of Aristotle on the economy.) Furthermore the veracity of Polanyi's claim has been challenged and Adams (1974) has drawn attention to evidence which demonstrates him to have been misguided in his sweeping denial of earlier market trading in the ancient civilisations of the Near East. It is also fallacious to assume that market trading is the prerogative of more sophisticated societies for it can be a feature of quite simple communities, and Harding (1967) has described pottery-trading for profit among the Sio of New Guinea.

Of course these arguments do not mean that disembedded market trading operated in iron age Britain. What it does mean is that too much has been assumed too often and we simply do not know how the economy of Britain functioned on the eve of the Roman conquest. This is particularly unfortunate in so far as it affects those pottery types which span the two periods.

One of the first types of hand-made pottery to be

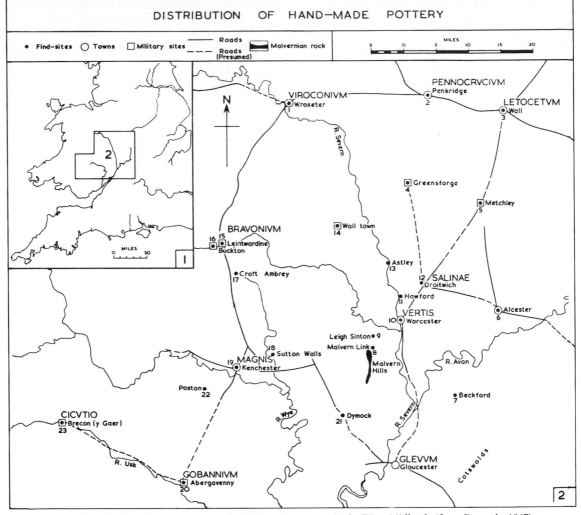

Figure 37   The distribution of Roman hand-made Malvernian pottery in the West Midlands (from Peacock, 1967).

studied in detail was that produced in the Malvern region during the first two centuries A.D. This pottery is never very common and seldom exceeds 10 per cent of an assemblage, but it is found over parts of Wales and much of the West Midlands (Fig. 37). The ware was originally thought to be locally produced on each site by the descendants of the original iron age population, but this view has been radically challenged by petrological analysis, for the included rock and mineral fragments suggest that the raw material and hence probably the pottery was derived from the area around the Malvern Hills. The forms (Fig. 38) are somewhat restricted since a majority of vessels comprise the tubby cooking pot with vertical

burnishing. They are always rather crudely made and their irregularity suggests that no turntable was employed. A good case can be made for continuity with the pre-Roman production in the area for there is correspondence in the raw materials selected and in the use of certain typological traits (Peacock, 1967).

The clay beds have not been identified with precision nor has it been established whether the inclusions are natural or deliberately added temper, but the scarcity of non-Malvernian rocks and minerals suggests that the raw materials were collected at no great distance from the hills, which in turn might imply that the potters lived on or very near to the hills. This is particularly interesting

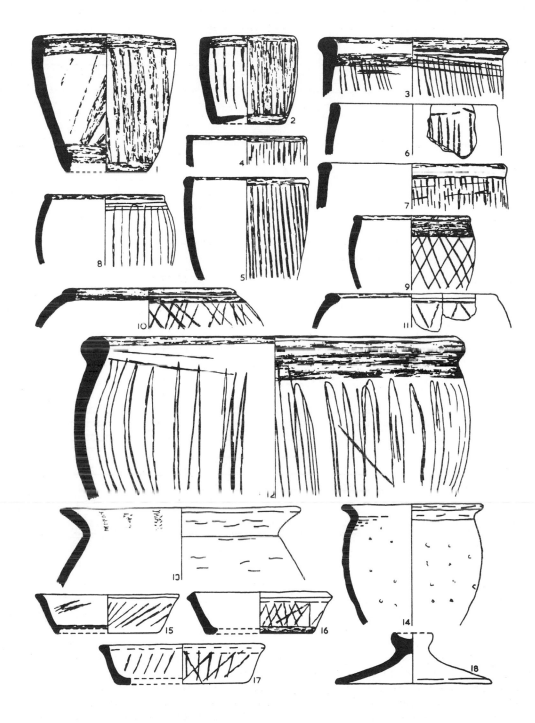

Figure 38 Characteristic forms of hand-made Malvernian pottery from Roman sites in the West Midlands (from Peacock, 1967). (Nos 1–3, 10, 12, 13 from Worcester; Nos 4, 7, 8, 9, 11, 14–18 from Astley; No. 5 from Croft Ambrey; No. 6 from Abergavenny) Scale ¼.

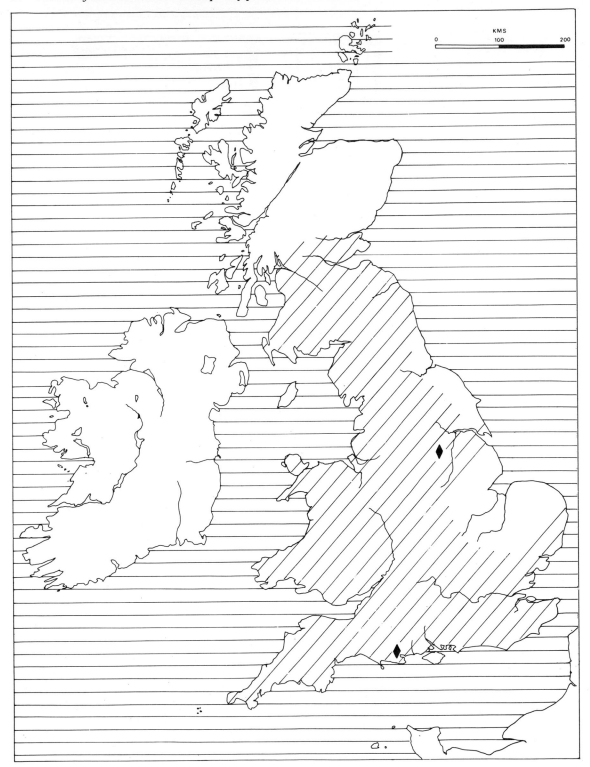

because the Malverns, dominated by bare rock and rough pasture, constitute a micro-environment where farming would be much harder than in the fertile Severn Valley to the east or in the good agricultural land of Herefordshire to the west. This is exactly the sort of place where household industry normally develops.

There are, however, other reasons for interpreting this as a household industry. The absence of the turntable suggests that pottery-making was not a primary pursuit, for it was known and used in both iron age and Roman southern Britain. Also the distribution, concentrated within a 50 km-radius of the hills, would befit a household industry rather than anything more advanced.

The Malvern pottery industry has been the subject of more detailed spatial analysis by Hodder (1974a), who has shown that there is a concentration of finds in the presumed market centres of Worcester and Kenchester, suggesting that the main towns played a major role in distribution and marketing. To some, this may seem a self-evident point that could be safely assumed, but this is emphatically not the case, for household industries distribute their wares in a number of ways and selling at markets or fairs can be of minor importance. Equally, however, the complexity of many present-day distribution systems signals the need for caution and it would be foolish to assume that Malvernian pottery was *only* sold through town markets. In fact Hodder studied the central core of the distribution and in Wales and the Welsh border land there is a wide spread of finds mainly from military sites. Later in this book it will be argued that pottery supplies to the army were largely a matter of civilian enterprise (p. 150). If this is correct, it is tempting to envisage the potter or his agent undertaking sales journeys peddling to the forts and perhaps also to the small rural settlements.

From the relatively local Malvernian products we must turn to black-burnished ware, which also has clear pre-Roman antecedents although there is little doubt that after the conquest it developed into an industry of a substantially different *genre*. Black-burnished ware is one of the commoner types of Romano-British pottery found all over the country on sites dating between *c*. A.D. 120 and the end of the Roman occupation. For many years its origin remained one of the unsolved mysteries of

Figure 39 The distribution of category 1 black-burnished ware in Britain (after Williams, 1977). The kiln area in the Wareham–Poole Harbour area on the south coast is indicated and also a probable offshoot at Rossington Bridge, Yorkshire.

Romano-British archaeology and a number of locations were suggested, including the Potteries district of Staffordshire, where modern activity would have obliterated all trace of Roman kilns! However, a major step forward came in 1963 when John Gillam showed that there were two varieties, demonstrably of different origin, which he labelled category 1 and category 2. It is category 1, vessels in a coarser fabric, made without the wheel, which are our main concern here (Pl. 16).

The main source for this variety seems to be the Wareham–Poole Harbour region of Dorset (Fig. 39). For many years local archaeologists have been discovering ash and reddened pottery, but the significance of this debris was not appreciated. However, in the late 1960s confirmation that this was pottery production waste possibly resulting from open firings came more or less simultaneously from two independent directions. Heavy mineral analysis had suggested a source somewhere in southwestern Britain, which accorded broadly with the typological evidence, since the cooking pots are very similar to those used by the Durotriges, the pre-Roman tribe centred in the Dorset area. In 1969 Raymond Farrar drew attention to some wasters from Corfe Mullen which implied that Dorset could have been a source of black-burnished ware. This was confirmed by subsequent heavy mineral work which showed that the mineral assemblage obtained from a majority of category 1 vessels corresponded exactly with that from production waste. Furthermore the same suite was obtained from pre-Roman Durotrigian vessels and from the local Tertiary sands of southern Dorset (Peacock, 1973a; Williams 1977). The general implications are now clear, and it appears that an industry with its roots in the iron age survived the Roman conquest and continued to distribute its wares locally and occasionally to more distant sites in southern England. After *c*. A.D. 120–125 the marketing arrangements were expanded and vessels were traded the length and breadth of the country as Williams (1977) has so ably demonstrated through a massive programme of heavy mineral analysis.

However, there has been no discussion of the type of industry concerned nor has anyone considered how it is possible for an iron age industry to compete with the advent of the wheel and remain buoyant until the end of the Roman occupation without technical innovation. Locally potters tried to imitate Dorset black-burnished ware on the wheel and some, such as the groups who made category 2 ware in eastern England managed to export in quantity to the lucrative military markets of the north. Why were they unable to extinguish the seemingly less efficient industry they were trying to emulate?

It is difficult to answer these questions at the moment and ideally we need a more detailed appreciation of the mode of production of Dorset black-burnished ware which might result from large-scale excavation of the production sites. For the present we do little more than hazard a few guesses based upon the only evidence available: the typology, the technological evidence of the pottery itself, the distribution pattern and the location of the industry.

Typologically (Fig. 22) black-burnished ware shows rather greater variation than the industries we have been considering, but the multiplicity of types depend on minutiae of rim design or decoration rather than a greater functional range. There are occasional jugs or pitchers but the vast majority of forms are for cooking, and when found on consumer sites they sometimes display carbonised deposits or internal scale.

We know much of the techniques of manufacture for this subject has been carefully considered by Farrar (1973). He suggests that the vessels are essentially hand-made, but the use of the turntable is implied by the precision of the cooking-pot rims and sometimes the surface finish. The turntable is probably not an innovation for there is reason to believe that it was used by the pre-Roman potters of the area. The typical Durotrigian bead-rim cooking pot (Fig. 40) is remarkably similar in both form and technique to the cooking pots recently produced on the turntable at Rakalj in the Istrian peninsula of Yugoslavia (Pl. 6). Further investigation is required, but the use of a turntable in iron age Dorset is strongly implied. Many of the later cooking pots and bowls seem to have been given a coating of white pipeclay, presumably to facilitate the burnishing. Little is known of firing methods except that there is a dearth of kilns from the production sites and it is therefore reasonable to postulate the use of bonfires as they are an efficient method of producing intensely black pottery.

The location of the industry is instructive, for today it is an area of barren heathland. There is little direct evidence of land use in Roman times, but an extensive programme of pollen analysis by Dimbleby (1962) suggests that the acid soils of many British heathlands may have begun to form in the bronze age as a result of man's assault on the landscape. Some of his evidence comes from the analysis of soils buried beneath bronze age barrows in the Wareham area, so there is a high probability that the Roman landscape was much the same as it is today. If this is

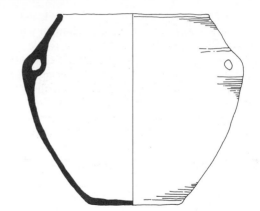

Figure 40   A typical pre-Roman countersunk-handle cooking pot used by the Durotriges. From Maiden Castle, Dorset (after Wheeler, 1943). Scale ¼.

correct, once again we are considering an industry set in an agriculturally impoverished environment.

The evidence of distribution is more complex. Up to *c*. A.D. 120 most of the pottery seems to have been consumed locally. It was certainly bought by army units stationed in Dorset and Devon and occasionally it went to more distant forts such as Usk or Richborough, but doubtless the bulk of the output was sold through the local market at Dorchester. During this period the range of forms was limited to little more than the cooking pot. The location, typology, techniques of manufacture and distribution all display the hallmarks of household industry and it is not excessive to postulate part-time domestic production possibly in the hands of women. The use of the turntable might imply rather more commercial orientation than in the Malverns.

However, from *c*. A.D. 120 onwards the picture begins to change radically for black-burnished ware becomes important and is eventually a component of almost all ceramic assemblages, whether military or civilian. At more or less the same time the range of forms increases to include bowls and dishes which were imitations of products made on the wheel elsewhere (Fig. 22). It seems that practically every household had its black-burnished 'service' in the kitchen. Clearly the potters could not have achieved this immense distribution on their own and we must now envisage the interest of the specialist dealer buying up lots and arranging for transport by road or ship. Whether the pottery was his prime interest, or whether he was drawn by some more valuable commodity such as Dorset salt or wheat from the chalk-lands, is hard to say. During this phase it is difficult to think in terms of a part-time domestic

Plate 24   A restored Dales ware jar from mid- to late third-century contexts at Doncaster, height, 25.5 cm (photo: Museum Service, Doncaster).

industry linked to agriculture. It seems more likely that work was an essential form of livelihood which would involve both men and women for as much of the year as possible. Despite the continuation of simple technology the activity must now fall within our definition of a workshop industry. Perhaps an analogy can be drawn with the pottery-making complex at Sorkun near Ankara which still produces coarse black cooking ware on a very large scale (p. 51). Although not specifically emphasised by Steele (1971) it seems that pottery-making is the major means of subsistence in the village. Perhaps in black-burnished ware we are witnessing the rise of an intensive industry of the same general type.

But why should the Dorset industry have achieved such success? Clearly part of the answer must be an intense demand engendered by a reputation for good cheap cooking wares well able to withstand thermal shock, but this hardly explains the extraordinary technical conservatism of the industry. The lack of interest in the kiln might relate to the low-grade fuel available on a sparsely wooded heathland since this could have been better suited for bonfires. On the

other hand it is difficult to appreciate why the wheel was not adopted, particularly as it was in use at nearby Corfe Mullen as early as the Claudian period (Calkin, 1935). At the moment this intriguing question is difficult to answer with certainty. Tradition may have played a major part, since potters will naturally prefer to continue in the way they were trained, but social organisation of the family or the community is another factor well illuminated by the Karia-ba-Mohammed industry at the present day (p. 26).

Another tradition perhaps of a rather similar nature is that of 'Dales ware', so called because it was once thought to have been made in the Yorkshire Dales from whence it was transported over much of northern Britain. Like black-burnished ware it was hand-made and perhaps finished on the turntable but the typology is very limited and only cooking pots (with a distinctive rim profile) are known (Pl. 24). Since no kilns have been found it could also have been fired in bonfires. Recently Loughlin (1977) has re-examined this pottery and considers it to have been made in north Lincolnshire, where it may have roots in the pre-Roman tradition. However, the characteristic cooking pot appears in the Antonine period and once established continues with little change until *c.* A.D. 375. Again it is difficult to be certain whether this was produced in a prolific household industry or something more akin to a workshop.

The marketing structure has been carefully studied by Loughlin, who considered the frequency of finds on sites of different classes. From this it would appear that road and river communications were fully exploited to distribute the goods within a 'local' market area of up to 100 km radius and not surprisingly areas of difficult access received less Dales ware. Outside this region we do not see a progressive fall-off, but rather marketing aimed at the larger permanent centres of residence from whence the ware was distributed to the surrounding countryside. This seems to imply that local needs were met by the potters themselves peddling their wares and selling through markets, while the more distant customers were served by the middleman. If this is correct, it is well paralleled in Pereruela at the present day (p. 19).

Local hand-made wares were in use during the late Roman period over much of southern England from Somerset to Kent, where they date collectively between the late third and perhaps the early fifth century A.D. (see e.g. Cunliffe, 1970; Alcock, 1971; Rahtz, 1974; Fulford, 1975a). There is no evidence

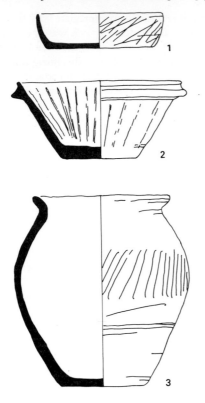

Figure 41   Wessex grog-tempered pottery from Portchester Castle, Hampshire (after Fulford, 1975a). Scale ¼.

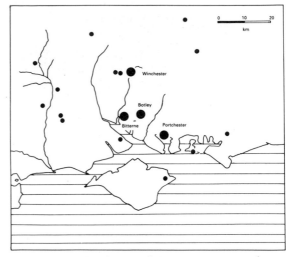

Figure 42   The distribution of Wessex grog-tempered ware. Large circles indicate sites where this pottery comprises 20 per cent or more of a total assemblage (after Fulford, 1975a).

that these traditions relate to those of the pre-Roman iron age and it is reasonable to see them as late Roman innovations, thus providing a contrast with the industries discussed above. These wares have often been regarded as charting the decay of the late Roman pottery industry so that as the products of the larger centres became scarcer and more expensive to purchase, households began to produce their own substitutes. However, this hypothesis is difficult to sustain for Fulford (1975a/b) has shown that the major producers of southern Britain did not decline during the later Roman period, but were fully active to the end of the fourth century or possibly the early fifth in some cases; it appears that the later hand-made wares are replacing nothing.

Few of these wares have been critically examined to see whether or not they were the objects of trade or home-made personal possessions, but the grog-tempered wares of Wessex are an exception. This curious type of hand-made ware occurs in a limited range of late Roman forms, principally flanged bowls, dishes and cooking pots (Fig. 41). The very coarse grey fabric contains rounded reddish particles, generally, although perhaps erroneously, termed 'grog'. The distribution, which is centred on Hampshire, is wide for so rough a product (Fig. 42).

Fulford (1975a:286) has carried out a fairly extensive programme of heavy mineral analysis which demonstrates the existence of four fabric types, each distributed widely. This immediately suggests that Wessex grog-tempered ware was produced at and distributed from a number of centres, which in turn suggests that we are considering household industry rather than household production (p. 17).

If this analysis is correct it could be that most of these late hand-made wares are the product of household industry, although there is an obvious need for this to be confirmed by rigorous typological and fabric analysis. If it is accepted that household industry is engendered by poverty, in particular harsh conditions for farming, the arrival of these wares might indicate worsening agricultural conditions for the peasant farmer during the late Roman period. Thus our ethnographical considerations have enabled us to see this pottery in a very different light: perhaps rather than heralding the end of the pottery industry it indicates difficulties in a different direction.

CONCLUSION

This discussion has centred on Britain and North Africa for here the simpler hand-made wares appropriate to household manufacture have been more intensively studied than elsewhere. There is little doubt that similar wares occur in some profusion in other parts of the Roman world. Indeed, Elizabeth Ettlinger (1977) has already drawn attention to the cooking pots of Vindonissa in Switzerland, some of which are in distinctive hand-made fabrics. It is worth remarking that these may not have been produced specifically *for* the soldiers at Vindonissa, but, like Malvernian ware, perhaps they were the product of a local household industry which sold *inter alia* to military establishments. This might explain why, for example, the Vindonissa group 1 cooking pots are also found on a number of local sites including the *vici* of Lenzburg and Kempraten, the latter over 50 km distant.

In studying hand-made wares two factors must be taken into account. Firstly, the simple typology often precludes the arguments normally based upon form so that careful fabric analysis is not a luxury but an essential part of the discussion. Secondly, many of these wares are merely a continuation of a La Tène tradition into the Roman period. It follows that a diachronic approach is desirable and this is one point where the disciplines of the prehistorian and the Romanist could be cross-fertilised to mutual benefit.

6 Workshop industries in the Roman world

Yamoun, avec son pied, imprime à l'appareil le mouvement circulaire, le mouvement des astres, le principe de toute genèse. Puis, à deux mains, il saisit la motte d'argile, comme on ferait d'un visage pour le baiser. Et soudain, que se passe-t-il? Une fleur de terre monte, monte et s'épanouit. A peine si l'homme a l'air de toucher. Il la suit dans son ascension, il la caresse, il la contient avec étonnement. Comme un dieu, Yamoun assiste à son oeuvre.

Georges Duhamel, *Le Prince Jaffar*,
p. 113

Although household pottery-making was probably more important than has been hitherto conceded, there is no doubt that the bulk of Roman pottery was a workshop product. The hallmarks of forming on the wheel and of firing in the kiln give character to Roman wares and often serve to differentiate them from those of earlier or later periods.

It is convenient to consider the subject under two headings. In this chapter we shall discuss the complexes which distributed their wares locally or at best regionally, whilst the next is reserved for the giant samian industries which often spread their wares the length and breadth of the empire. There is obviously considerable overlap and the distinction is to some extent artificial, but as we shall see, there *are* differences and in any event the division is dictated by convenience, for samian ware has been studied more intensively and from a different viewpoint.

THE INDIVIDUAL WORKSHOP

The simplest mode of production is the individual workshop, where an isolated pottery serves the community. Such establishments may be found in both urban and rural contexts, but they are more common in the countryside because a lucrative urban market is likely to promote nucleation. At present,

individual workshops are probably much more important than the scanty recorded data suggests and this could be true of much if not all of the Roman world. In Britain, for example, many Roman pottery assemblages are dominated by wheel-thrown grey wares to which it is often difficult to ascribe a source (Pl. 25). Thus, at Portchester, these comprised the largest group. As Fulford (1975a:293) remarked,

Both fine and coarse sandy fabrics are present; slipped and unslipped. Some are lighter, some darker than others, some more brown than grey; yet amongst these visually distinctive variations it is doubtful if any have significance with regard to the kiln centre that produced them, or which, if any, of the apparent variables are significant in attribution to source.

Selected sherds were subjected to heavy mineral analysis which suggested a number of different points of origin. Fulford concluded, 'It may be suggested that about 75 per cent of the grey wares comes from within a five to ten mile radius, or even less, of Portchester, while only some 25 per cent comes from further afield, say 20–30 miles, and most of that is from either the New Forest or Alice Holt centres.'

The implications are clear enough. We must envisage a scatter of small grey-ware workshops in the hinterland behind Portchester, and perhaps this pattern was repeated throughout the civil zone of the province. Certainly Portchester is not unique and the ubiquitous grey-wares are a recurring problem for the pottery worker. Hard figures are seldom recorded but Fowler's (1968) quantitative analysis of the pottery assemblage from Butcombe in Somerset leads to a strikingly similar conclusion.

Of course it would be wrong to assume that grey-wares were only the product of individual workshops or that they were not produced in nucleated concerns. However, they are *commonly* associated with the small isolated workshop and their

Plate 25 Grey-ware bowl, mid second century, from the Thames at Blackfriars, London. London Museum ac. no. 386. Height 14.5 cm.

ubiquity serves to emphasise the cumulative importance of this mode of production, at least in Britain. In other parts of the empire their place is often taken by oxidised-wares. It is difficult to appreciate why grey reduced pottery should be more prevalent in some parts of the Roman world than in others, but no one has seriously considered the matter; the choice could relate to the availability of certain types of fuel or perhaps to certain functional advantages. However, the problem is not unique to the Romanist and recurs in other periods (see e.g. Barton, 1974, for a discussion of Medieval black-wares). Recent black- or grey-wares are

encountered in Hungary (Duma, 1963) or in parts of Spain such as Quart and La Bisbal in the Costa Brava region, or Llamas de Mouro in Asturias (Llorens and Corredor, 1974). An understanding of these and other survivals might help us appreciate the logic of the choice.

A number of small Roman production sites has been discovered but unfortunately there are often interpretational difficulties. Frequently they are encountered by chance and the kiln structure alone is excavated, so that it can be very difficult to be sure that it is not part of a much larger nucleated complex. On the other hand, if a number of kilns is found it may be hard to know whether they represent a nucleation of pottery interests or a single works operating over a long period of time. The answer, of course, lies in large-scale excavation to which such humble concerns are seldom subjected.

These provisos aside, the probable sites of individual workshops are particularly well represented and recorded in Britain, Gaul, Italy and Romania (e.g. Young, 1980; Duhamel, 1973a; Cuomo di Caprio, 1972; Floca *et al.*, 1971; for gazeteers of sites). As far as can be ascertained, this type of activity does not show any chronological bias to one period or another, but the products are always similar, comprising a limited range of coarse cooking and storage vessels, which are seldom transported very far.

Perhaps the most instructive of these small workshops is that in Highgate Wood, excavated in exemplary manner by Brown and Sheldon (1975). Although situated but 10 km from London, presumably its main market, the kilns lie on a low ridge, in the countryside, away from the main roads and waterways. Excavations revealed some ten kilns together with pits, a ditch complex and two circular buildings (Fig. 19). The sequence is complex and suggests four main phases of activity spread over about a hundred years from *c.* A.D. 50–60. Despite this long time-span the evidence recovered is very slight and the debris might result from production lasting only some twenty-five weeks. Not unreasonably this led the excavators to suggest that the site was visited periodically by itinerant potters. While this is possible, and the migration of both fine-ware and mortaria potters is well attested in the Roman period, ethnography suggests an alternative more plausible solution, as it is quite normal for small isolated concerns to be operated on a part-time basis in conjunction with farming or some other activity (p. 31).

The products of the Highgate workshop are interesting. Up to *c.* A.D. 100, jars and cooking pots with a strong pre-Roman native influence were in vogue. Thereafter the output changed towards 'finer quality wares for a more selective market'. This could have been the fatal mistake which led to the demise of the pottery some sixty years later, for, as we have seen, isolated rural kilns are efficient producers of coarse ware selling cheaply to the local market but they are less suited to the production of finer pottery which tends to thrive in the larger nucleated complexes generating a more sophisticated marketing mechanism (p. 43). Perhaps the rise of fine-ware production elsewhere in the Nene Valley,

or at Colchester, made it difficult to sell Highgate ware.

Highgate is exceptionally important because it has been excavated so extensively and meticulously. However, a number of other places furnish supplementary information. The kiln site at Rowlands Castle in Sussex, located in the countryside some 13 km (8 miles) northwest of Chichester, provides another example of an isolated rural industry. The grey-ware jars, dating between the late second and perhaps the fourth centuries, are distinctive because they bear 'batch marks' incised below the rim before firing. Although nothing is known of the kiln structures, Hodder (1974a/b) has studied the distribution of this trait which clearly suggests local marketing through Chichester, for finds are virtually restricted to the predicted market area of the Roman town (Fig. 43).

It is rare to be able to study the marketing of such wares because, by and large, the distribution is so local that there are insufficient find-sites to resolve the fine detail. Thus Cunliffe (1961) excavated a late first-century kiln at Shedfield in Hampshire which was producing storage and cooking vessels, but he was unable to find parallels for the forms. The site lies in a truly rural location between the towns of Winchester, Chichester and Roman Clausentum (Bitterne), and the absence or at least scarcity of Shedfield pottery in these places presumably reflects its very local market. Similarly nothing is known of the distribution of shelly cooking pots from the isolated kiln at Greetham in Rutland (Bolton, 1968). Again wares from the second-century kiln at Sheringham in Norfolk did not reach Brancaster, 55 km (35 miles) to the west, despite a dearth of substantial settlements in the area (Howlett, 1961; information Mrs G. Andrews). Corder (1930) was unable to say much about the distribution of grey-wares from the isolated rural kilns at Throlam, operating in the third and fourth centuries, save that they did not reach York or Malton. It now appears that they were marketed almost exclusively through Brough, 15 km away (Wacher, 1969:134). Finally, the very rough wares made in the fourth century at Rettendon in Essex have been found locally at Chelmsford, Rawreth, Wickford, and Little Waltham, a total span of about 15 km (Tildesley, 1971).

This list of diminutive concerns can be extended to the Continent for similar isolated local potteries have been reported from a number of places such as Halder in Holland, Vauclair or Aux-Marais in France or Hailfingen in Germany, and the list could be

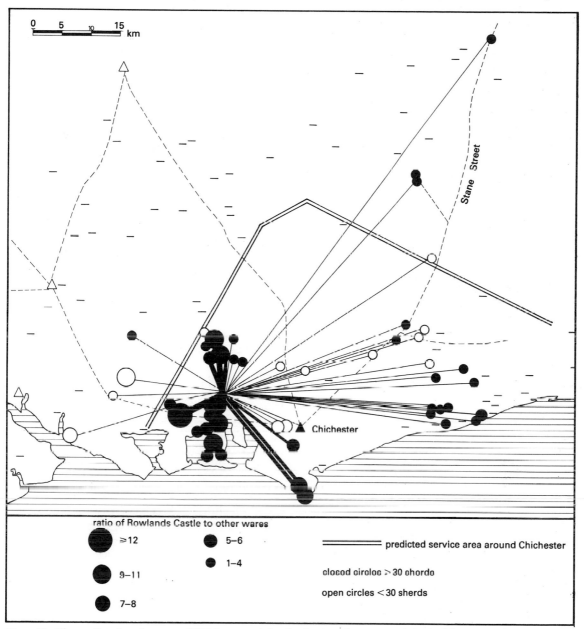

Figure 43 The predicted market area of Chichester and the distribution of pottery made in the kilns at Rowlands Castle (after Hodder, 1974b). The dashes indicate negative evidence.

extended (Willems 1977; Litt, 1969; Cartier, 1966; Stroh, 1934).

Although individual workshop industries span the entire Roman period, the earlier ones are particularly instructive because they might help in understanding the way in which this mode of production was introduced. The early wares are interesting because they nearly always display strong affinities with the local iron age pottery (e.g. Willems, 1977; Swan, 1975; Stroh, 1934, etc.). It would appear that either native potters were now using the full paraphernalia of the workshop or that trained personnel were trying to serve local tastes. If native iron age potters adopted new technology, the reasons for and mechanisms of change are intriguing if enigmatic. Of course, the overall introduction of the wheel presents

Plate 26   Black-burnished ware category 2 cooking pot and dish, second century, from London. London Museum ac. nos. 2873 and 19803, heights 14.5 and 6 cm.

no difficulty for in the ultimate iron age it was used in southern and eastern England as well as on the Continent. However, the extensive use of the kiln is another matter. Although kilns were used in the La Tène period on the Continent they are rare and in England the only potential iron age examples (p. 81) are prefabricated surface structures, markedly different from the ones commonly adopted by the early Roman workshop potters. There is thus a hiatus which demands an explanation. At present there seem to be three possible reasons for this change in firing practice.

1. Perhaps a changing pattern of land use deprived potters of the plentiful supplies of cheap fuel required for open bonfire firing. Small quantities of higher grade fuel would necessitate the use of a kiln.
2. Perhaps a changed social order meant fewer personnel available to assist with the labour-intensive process of fuel gathering for bonfire firing. Pottery-making became an individual rather than a communal activity.
3. Perhaps many of the potters worked for a while around military garrisons and learnt new methods from other camp-followers before returning to the countryside.

It is hard to choose between these possibilities, but some evidence can be adduced in support of the third (see pp. 98 and 150).

The question of land ownership is another intractable problem. At the moment there is little evidence to suggest that many of these kilns were operated as part of the villa economy (p. 132). However, someone must have owned the land on which they were built and if it was not the potter himself he would doubtless have been subject to some form of control, if only fiscal, which was certainly the case in the Medieval period (Le Patourel, 1968). On balance the concept of tenant potter-farmer seems most attractive, for it is one that is well supported from ethnography.

Some small workshops appear to display anomalies, and indeed one of the advantages of the ethnoarchaeological approach is that irregularities are brought into sharp relief. For example, the kiln at Halder in the Netherlands was producing black Terra-Nigra-like wares, exhibiting a strong pre-Roman native tradition, as one might expect for the period *c.* A.D. 65–80. The same kiln may have been used for firing mortaria bearing the stamp ADIVTOR, and Willems (1977) suggests that the site could have been a branch of the potter's main works at Bavay or perhaps Amay in Belgium. However, it is curious to find mortaria being made in an isolated workshop. Ethnographical observations suggest that such specialisation would be abnormal and indeed the bulk of the Roman evidence from northwestern Europe shows that mortaria were, above all, the products of nucleated industries, while in Italy they

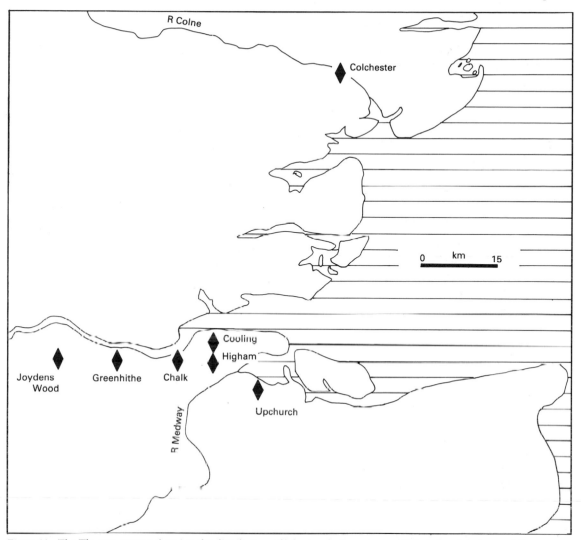

Figure 44 The Thames estuary showing the distribution of kilns producing category 2 black-burnished ware (after Williams, 1977, with the addition of a recent discovery at Higham).

were often made on estates (p. 130).

Since the Halder kiln produced but twenty-two rim fragments, none of them true wasters, it might be doubted whether they were made in the kiln, and clearly fabric analysis is required before the argument can be taken further. If it can be established that they were kiln products it might be possible to make further deductions about the nature and setting of the industry.

A rather similar problem arises with the mortaria produced at Wilderspool in northwestern Britain. The site, lying near the river Mersey, seems to be situated away from the main centres of civilian or military occupation and yet its mortaria were distributed widely throughout the northwest (Hartley and Webster, 1973). In this case the three kilns discovered by May earlier this century are clearly part of a larger complex, linked to a settlement, the nature of which is only gradually becoming clearer (cf. Frere, 1977:385). Here the anomaly is probably an illusion occasioned by a lack of fieldwork.

However, Roman Britain does present a phenomenon which is hard to parallel at the present day, although this probably reflects the need for more detailed ethnographical observation and evaluation. It is seen best along the estuary of the river Thames, where a scatter of widely separated small kilns seem to have been making imitations of

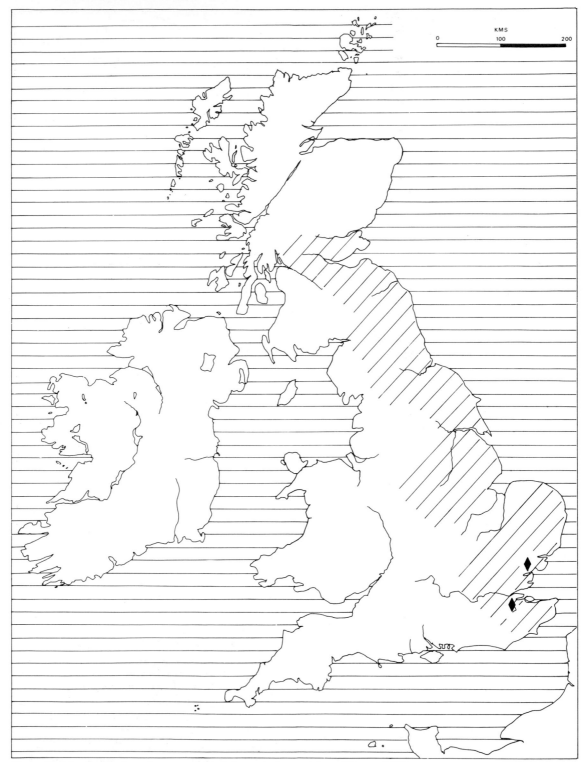

Figure 45 The distribution of category 2 black-burnished ware (after Williams, 1977).

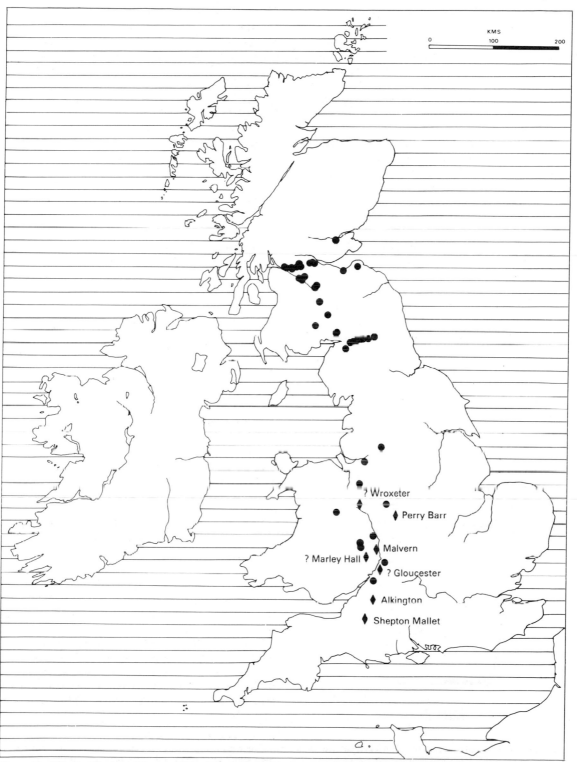

Figure 46 The distribution of Severn Valley kilns and ware in the second century (after Webster, 1976, 1977). I am indebted to Roberta Tomber for information about the possible kiln site at Marley Hall. Not all find-sites in the West Midlands are indicated.

Dorset black-burnished ware, using the wheel (Fig. 22 and Pl. 26). This variety (category 2) was recognised as a distinct entity long before its origin in eastern England had been ascertained (Gillam, 1963). At present, six possible kiln sites are known along the north Kentish coast and additionally there is evidence for production at Colchester (Fig. 44). Since both fabric and the range of forms are fairly uniform it can be difficult to distinguish the products of individual potteries, but heavy mineral analysis has provided a key to characterisation (Williams, 1977). Remarkably, it appears that material from the smaller centres, as well as Colchester, was reaching the northern military market (Fig. 45). This industry is thus something of a paradox, for small scattered rural potteries seem to be behaving as though they were one nucleated concern. They are linked by typology and fabric as well as by common long-distance markets.

The same phenomenon is encountered in the west Midlands, where small kilns, situated along the Severn Valley, were making a number of characteristic forms in a distinctive orange-buff fabric. The known production sites stretch from Shepton Mallet and Alkington in the south to Malvern and Perry Barr in the north, while further kilns are postulated at Wroxeter, Cirencester and Gloucester (Webster, 1976; here Fig. 46). Some of these kilns, such as Alkington, were making nothing but Severn Valley ware but others such as Malvern or Perry Barr also produced grey-wares. The close similarity in fabric between these centres can be readily explained by the geology, for all seem to have exploited the ubiquitous Keuper Marl. However, the typological links, particularly well displayed in the necked jars or tankards, are striking (Fig. 47). The product distribution is also interesting for Severn Valley ware is not only very common in the west Midlands, but in the second century it is also found in northwestern Britain on Hadrian's Wall and on the Antonine wall. It has yet to be ascertained whether material from the rural as well as the putative urban potteries was the object of long-distance trade, but in view of category 2 black-burnished ware, shared markets are a distinct possibility.

Again, Todd (1968) has suggested that the distinctively burnished grey-wares, common in the east Midlands during the third and fourth centuries, was produced at a number of typologically linked kilns. These seem to have been concentrated along the Trent Valley from Torksey to Meering near Newark, with outliers at Swanpool, near Lincoln, and possibly Ancaster.

It is worth noting that all these wares, Severn Valley, black-burnished 2 and East Midlands Grey were produced along river valleys, each of them dominated by a major waterway. Perhaps the existence of suitable clays enabled potters to produce a desirable product, which could then be collected by a middleman, because of a ready means of access and distribution. In effect, the waterway shortens the distance between potters so that in some respects they act as a rural nucleated concern, as well as continuing to operate as an individual workshop in their own right.

Webster's (1976) comments on the possible origins of Severn Valley ware are instructive. The earliest pottery seems to have been produced *c.* A.D. 55–70 in the lower Severn Valley by civilian potters catering for a predominantly military market. They were of diverse origins, some probably of Belgic origin, some from Durotrigia, some probably from the vici around military camps on the Continent. They each brought their own styles with them and learnt new ones at their new centres where they produced pots in local materials and,

Figure 47 Severn Valley ware. No. 1, necked jar with wide mouth, mid second–late third century, No. 2, tankard, second to early third century (after Webster, 1976). Scale ¼.

0 cm 4

perhaps under the influence of the demands of the military market, developed a remarkably uniform series of forms and a fairly standard fabric.

During the second century there seems to have been a gradual migration of potters northwards into new territories, where similar clays are to be found. Unfortunately this attractive hypothesis is supported by little firm kiln evidence from the crucial southern part of the area, but it accords well with what we know of military production (p. 150), and provides an illustration of one way in which rural workshops might originate.

URBAN NUCLEATED INDUSTRIES

Although individual workshops can occur in an urban or suburban environment they are *par excellence* a feature of the countryside. If a town possessed the necessary resources of clay, fuel and available space it would generally attract a number of potters, as did many of the more important military establishments. The concentration of wealth in a town would be an important factor in the multiplication of potteries, but the more sophisticated urban way of life would demand a greater range of vessels which would in turn attract a wider spectrum of competent specialists. However, the town's role as a market centre would be of utmost importance because visiting middlemen would provide facilities for a much wider product distribution so that higher output and profits could be sustained. The urban potter is in the happy position of being able to make direct retail or wholesale transactions more or less at will.

For these reasons, urban potteries produce a much greater variety of wares than the individual workshop and these generally travel much further. While the town may obtain some of its everyday cooking-wares from the surrounding countryside, there is often still room for further production on the spot. In addition we must anticipate the manufacture of lamps, mortaria, colour-coated vessels or even samian ware in this more sophisticated and demanding environment.

Unfortunately relatively few urban potteries have been thoroughly investigated for it is often a considerable task which must be tackled piecemeal over many years. Nevertheless an impression of the very wide product range can be gained by consulting some of the better documented pottery-producing towns such as Colchester, Cologne, Bavay, Trier, Lincoln or the Nene Valley around the town of

Durobrivae. (For examples and further references see e.g. Hull, 1963; La Baume, 1959; Jolin, 1959; Wightman, 1970; Thompson, 1958; Webster, 1944; Corder, 1950; Hartley, 1960; Wild, 1974, etc.)

Of course not every town had its own pottery but clearly many of the major ones did. In central France, for example, Ferdière (1975) documents production at Chartres, Bourges, Tours, Orleans and many smaller settlements as well. The same pattern certainly applies to the civil zone of Britain, but there are nevertheless many major towns which, so far, have produced no evidence of potteries. The factors affecting whether or not a town would develop a local ceramic industry are interesting but complex. Suitable clays must be available, the land use around the town must be of a type which produces useful fuel or which does not obliterate naturally available supplies, there must be access to land suitable for pottery-making and there must be a source of skilled manpower. The latter could be crucial and it seems that the development of a nucleated urban industry might be greatly favoured by the presence of a pre-existing industry whether it be of military or pre-Roman origin.

In Roman times, kilns were very rarely built within the urban complex. At Cologne the first-century groups of the Lungengasse and Neumarkt areas appear to have been situated within the walls but they probably pre-date the establishment of the *Colonia* and are generally considered to mark the outer limits of the earlier Oppidum Ubiorum (Lung, 1959; La Baume, 1958, 1959). On the other hand, the potters' quarter at Augst dating between the mid first and mid second centuries A.D. may well have lain on the periphery but within the urban complex (Swoboda, 1971) and this type of location has a much earlier antecedent in Classical Corinth (Stillwell, 1948).

However, there is no doubt that a majority of kilns were placed extramurally. Many examples have been published in the literature and we need but cite a handful of the better documented: Romula in Romania (Popilian, 1976), Chartres, Tours and Orleans in France (Ferdière, 1975), Colchester and Durobrivae in Britain (Hull, 1963; Wild, 1974; Artis, 1828). Study of these and many other examples suggests that the detailed arrangement is often far from random. While isolated kilns are found almost anywhere the clusters are often aligned along a major route out of town. In some cases this might be determined by natural constraints such as the presence of a river or the sea or by the location of clay deposits. However, there are obvious

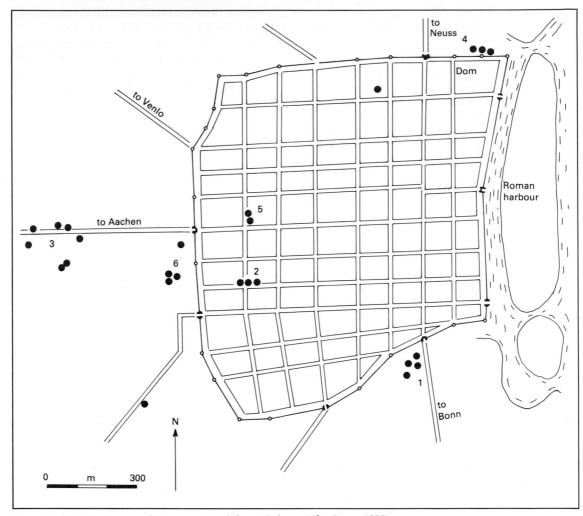

Figure 48   The distribution of Roman pottery kilns at Cologne (after Lung, 1959).

commercial advantages in being visible from the main road and in many cases this could have been an important factor.

Unfortunately few towns provide an opportunity to synthesise the development of an urban industry, for the area occupied by urban potteries is often vast and well beyond the scope of a single excavation. More often than not the record has accumulated slowly and includes a disproportionate number of chance and ill-recorded discoveries, so that dating becomes a problem. However, Cologne is an exception and furnishes a relatively clear chronological picture. During the first century kilns seem to have been located immediately outside the walls of Oppidum Ubiorum (Fig. 48, groups 1, 2, 4, 5). They produced a wide range of pottery including

cooking wares, white clay colour-coat and lamps. However, they were soon overtaken by the development of the Colony and in the second and third centuries the wider spread along the Aachener Strasse develops (Fig. 48, groups 3 and 6). In this later period the range of products includes cups, handled jugs, plates, mica-dusted wares, theatrical masks and green glazed terracottas. There seems to be a greater range of products with more emphasis on luxury than kitchen wares but the differences with the earlier period are slight and difficult to assess without quantitative data. The new location is interesting for it implies that land was still available for potting within a few hundred metres of the town wall.

Unfortunately patterns are hard to substantiate

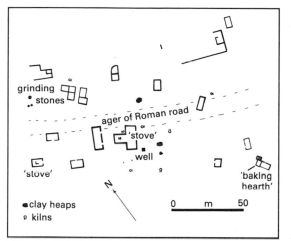

Figure 49 The scatter of kilns and probable workshops along the Ermine Street outside Durobrivae (Water Newton) (after Artis, 1828).

elsewhere. At Colchester, for example, chronological analysis suggests a rather random development, but the dating is not really close enough to be sure that no patterning is present. It worth noting that Hartley (1960:9) has suggested that the dated kilns at Durobrivae were located progressively further from the town wall with the passage of time (cf. Fig. 49).

However, some of the urban potteries in Roman Britain contrast with those of the present day for they display a much more extended distribution than is

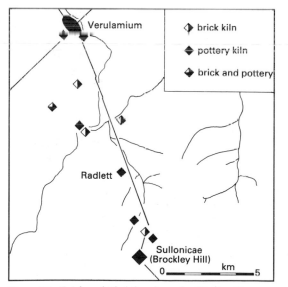

Figure 50 Brick and tile kilns along the Watling Street south of Verulamium (St Albans) (after Saunders and Havercroft, 1977).

usually encountered. Verulamium is a good example for the kilns have been found stretching some 12 km southwards along Watling Street (Fig. 50; Saunders and Havercroft, 1977). The products do *not* get more rural with increasing distance from the town for mortarium kilns with a wide product distribution have been found at Radlett and Brockley Hill (e.g. Castle, 1972; Hartley, 1973). All the kilns seem to comprise a single complex for which Verulamium was the major market and distribution centre.

It is hard to account for this wide spread of sites. One possible explanation might be that the pattern is based on an earlier distribution of estate kilns or perhaps individual workshops which, because of market possibilities, turned to producing more widely sought Romanised wares. However, perhaps the diaspora had more to do with land use and the location of good clays. There is evidence from both the study of mortarium stamps and spectrographic analysis of the clays that one mortarium maker G. ATTIVS MARINVS moved from Colchester to Radlett before migrating to Hartshill in the Midlands (Hartley and Richards, 1965). Presumably he chose the site because of its resources or because there was nowhere else available nearer town. The same may have applied to the potter who made mortaria and colour-coated pottery at South Carlton, 6 km north of Lincoln (Webster, 1944). Despite the distance he must be regarded as part of the Lincoln urban complex, but here we are admittedly entering a grey area between individual and nucleated concerns.

The marketing of urban wares is an interesting matter, but unfortunately one upon which little progress has been made. We must expect wares to travel differentially, with the more specialised ones finding sales in distant markets. This may well be the case, but it is hard to substantiate and at present there is even a little contradictory evidence. Thus, Colchester samian ware which one might expect to be widely distributed, is confined to the southern part of East Anglia (Hartley, 1970). On the other hand Williams (1977:177) has shown by heavy mineral analysis that the coarse grey-burnished ware made in the Lincoln racecourse kiln reached Leicester, some 80 km (50 miles) distant (cf. Corder, 1950).

At present stamped mortaria seem to offer the best hope of evaluating marketing. Figure 51 is based upon Hartley's (1973) assessment of the distribution of mortaria made in Colchester during the period A.D. 140–200. There is a very clear concentration of products over wide areas of East Anglia and Kent and considerable quantities in the northern military zone. It is clear that the potter is now relying on the

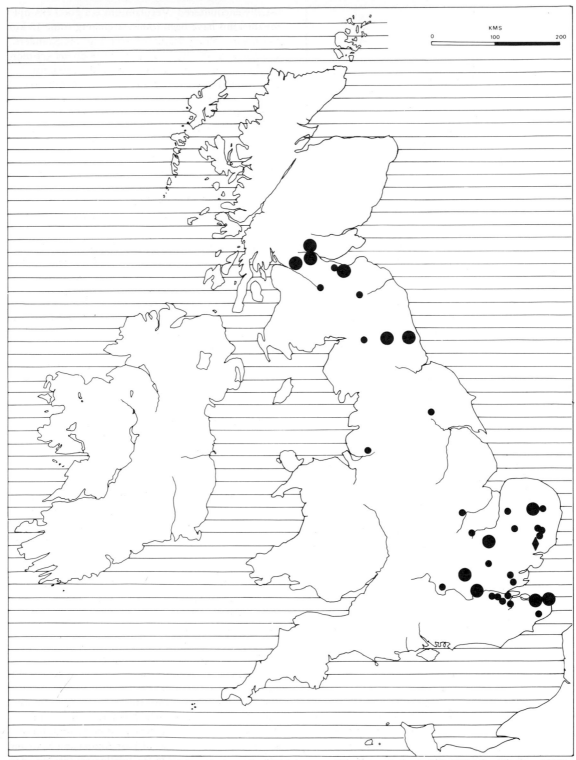

Figure 51   The distribution of stamped mortaria made at Colchester within the period A.D. 140–200 (after Hartley, 1973).
Large circles indicate two or more finds.

middleman. It is not extravagant to see two groups of *negotiatores* at work, the one supplying wider markets in the southeast, the other specialising in the northern military market. It is interesting to note that category 2 black-burnished ware, some of which was made at Colchester, displays a remarkably similar distribution. Perhaps it achieved this, not for its own sake, but because mortaria were demanded by the troops in the north and it was able to travel on the same commercial current. This could explain why it overtook its rival on northern sites, Dorset black-burnished ware, for a short time from the early Antonine period (see p. 96; Williams, 1977:table 3; Gillam, 1973:56).

NUCLEATED INDUSTRIES IN THE COUNTRYSIDE

Nucleated rural industries are to be seen throughout the Roman world. However, they have been most intensively studied in Britain and hence it is here that the burden of this discussion must rest. As at the present day, these industries produced a wide range of wares, but generally there is a specialised product which is widely distributed and which presumably provided the main source of income.

In Britain it is now possible to see the introduction of rural industries against the developing pattern of ceramic production as a whole. This topic has already been discussed by Fulford (1977b), from whence a full bibliography may be obtained, but the evidence is here interpreted in a slightly different way because of our new viewpoint. Broadly, the picture appears as follows (Figs 52–3). In the late first and second centuries urban potteries seem to have been particularly important. Many of the major towns seem to have possessed kilns active during this period including Colchester, Durobrivae, Lincoln, Mancetter, Verulamium, Gloucester and Mildenhall. Additionally, the military activity at Caerleon, Holt and York may have differed but little. There was also considerable activity in the Cantley-Rossington Bridge area of Yorkshire, which could relate to the fort at Doncaster (Buckland *et al.*, 1980).

During this period there seem to have been few major rural industries apart from black-burnished production in Dorset and the Thames estuary, both of which are special cases (pp. 85 and 95). Nucleated complexes in the countryside are thus hard to find, but Brampton in Norfolk could be an exception, although unfortunately it has been little explored.

However, magnetic survey suggests that there are about 150 kilns in the group and they could have been active in the second and third centuries. Among the products are flagons, amphorae and mortaria, the latter apparently exported to east Yorkshire and beyond (Knowles, 1977; Hartley, 1973:43).

The third century seems to have been a period of radical change and the pattern of production in the later Roman period is very different. Of the urban potteries only Mancetter and Durobrivae continued to export their wares widely. However, the pottery industry as a whole did not decline, but rather expanded as large rural centres of production developed. The most important of these was Oxford with its widely distributed colour-coat and parchment wares, followed by the New Forest which dominated Wessex with its colour-coat, Hadham in East Anglia and Crambeck in Yorkshire which supplied much of the north. Grey-wares alone were produced at Alice Holt in Surrey and in the Derbyshire ware complex at Hazelwood and Holbrook: both were marketed very widely.

In essence, then, later Roman Britain witnesses a move in the major pottery centres from the towns into the countryside, a process which culminates in the fourth century. This transformation can be explained in a number of ways, none of which is entirely satisfactory, although each has merits. The depletion of urban clay deposits is one possibility, although improbable, as pottery-making requires very little raw material. Equally, exhausted fuel supplies, although a popular explanation of change in the ceramic industry, is unlikely to be significant, for at the present day industries invariably develop a symbiotic relationship with their environment (p. 25). Alternatively rising urban costs may have led to a search for more favourable locations in the countryside. Fulford (1975b:130) has suggested that the pressure of maintaining urban facilities, with its inevitable rise in taxation, caused the wealthy to invest in large country estates, and there is no doubt that the late Roman period is clearly one of rising rural prosperity. This view is also supported by Young (1973:108; 1977a) who attributed rural ceramic complexes to the entrepreneurial interests of landowners. Clearly the potters are unlikely to have owned land, and some sort of relationship must have existed (p. 94). However, the case may have been somewhat overstated for the pottery industry demands very little cash investment and today the returns are not particularly high, so it is more likely that potters were tolerated by landowners rather than a significant source of income. In any case it is

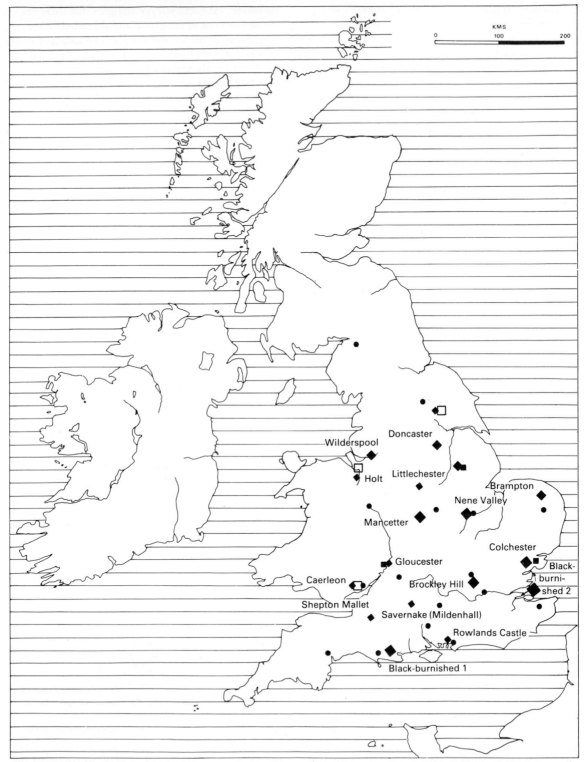

Figure 52   The distribution of major kiln groups in late first- and second-century Britain (after Fulford, 1977b). Diamonds indicate kilns, dots Cantonal capitals, squares *Colonia*, and open squares Legionary fortresses.

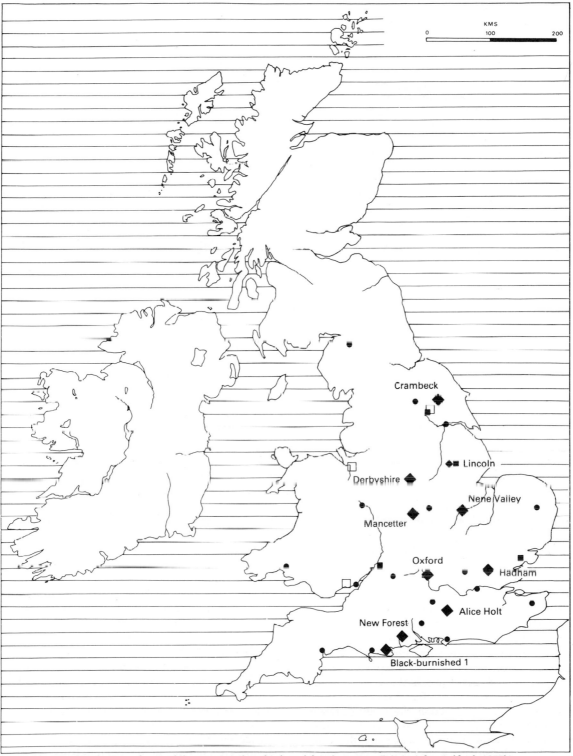

Figure 53 The distribution of major kiln groups in late third- and fourth-century Britain (after Fulford, 1977b). Symbols as Fig. 52.

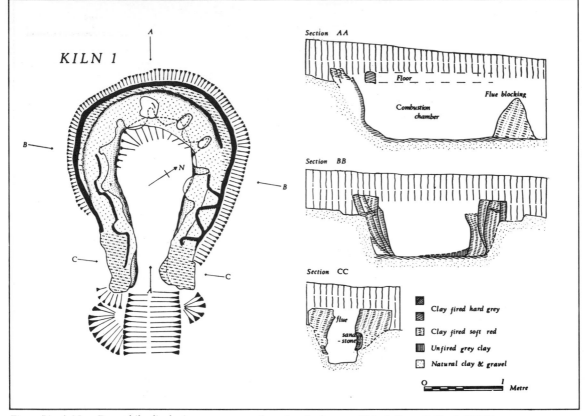

Figure 54　A New Forest kiln displaying a sequence of repairs. Amberwood kiln 1 (from Fulford, 1975b).

difficult to demonstrate a relationship between pottery-making and estate economy (p. 132). On the other hand the impetus for establishing rural industries could have come from the potter himself rather than the landowner and Fulford (1975b:7) has suggested that rural industries may have been exempt from certain taxation such as the *Collatio lustralis* of Valentinian.

It is probably wrong to consider the industry in isolation for pottery-making and farming are often intimately linked. If we accept the concept of a symbiotic relationship, it follows that a change in the pattern of nature of land exploitation will affect the pottery industry, either through supplies of fuel or through a depletion of available manpower. Thus if there was a profound change in the type of farming practised around towns, with perhaps greater emphasis on grain production, this might be reason enough for potters to migrate elsewhere to a more favourable location. Full consideration of the matter would take the discussion well beyond the scope of this book, but it is worth noting that there are

indications of agricultural reorganisation and of the greater intrusion of farming into town life in late Roman Britain (cf. Applebaum, 1972).

Finally we must consider the question of marketing. Today the middleman is an essential ingredient in the success of a rural complex and this must have been the case in the Roman world also. Indeed rural developments would have been impossible unless there was a sophisticated network of *negotiatores* willing to travel into the countryside to make wholesale purchases. Thus, in addition to the factors reviewed above, exploitation of rural resources would require a certain level of market organisation.

The rise of rural industries is thus a complex matter which cannot be satisfactorily resolved and it may be that there is no simple answer, for the factors could have differed from one centre to another.

The rural industries of Roman Britain varied considerably, as they do at the present day. Fortunately a number of monographs have recently appeared and we are particularly well informed about

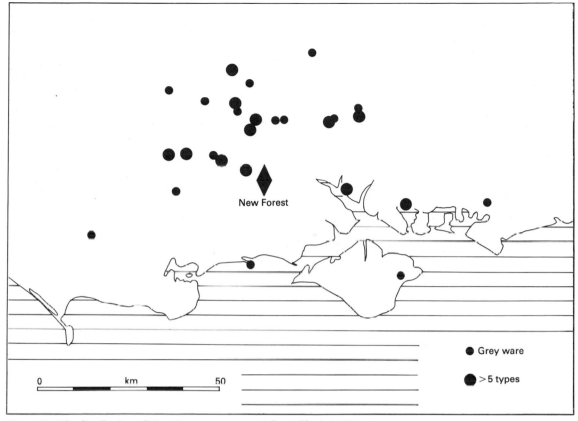

New Forest

● Grey ware

◕ >5 types

0   km   50

Figure 55   The distribution of New Forest grey-wares (after Fulford, 1975b).

the industries of the New Forest (Fulford, 1975b), the Oxford region (Young, 1977a) and that of Alice Holt, near Farnham (Lyne and Jefferies, 1979). These three centres show appreciable differences and it is instructive to compare and contrast them.

The New Forest kilns are located in an infertile area of heathland east of the Hampshire Avon. They occupy an area where farming is difficult and this could have been a factor in the choice of site. The kilns are spread over an area of about 20 square km and occur in clusters of three or more. Excavation has concentrated on the kiln structures and there is little firm evidence for workshops or drying sheds. The kilns are small, without a central floor support, and many of them show an unusual feature for they have clearly been repaired a number of times by plastering the walls with clay before use (Fig. 54). The products which date *c*. A.D. 270–400, comprise colour-coated beakers, bowls, flagons and mortaria, white parchment wares with red painted ornament on a white ground, together with beakers, bowls, dishes and jars in grey-ware. The distribution is interesting for the fine-wares are spread over an arc of *c*. 80 km radius, but one type of beaker, which often occurs in quantity, has a range of over 100 km. This contrasts with the grey-wares which seldom travel more than 35 km from the kiln (Fig. 55).

The New Forest industry appears to have been of a fairly rudimentary nature. The patching of the kilns and the lack of substantial workshops implies part-time seasonal activity, perhaps operated by potter-farmers somewhat akin to William Smith of Farnham (p. 38). Perhaps, like William Smith, the potters did much of their own marketing through local country fairs and the urban markets in the *Civitas* capitals of Winchester and Dorchester. However, the differential distribution of the wares is intriguing and could indicate that the potters were marketing their coarser wares locally while the middleman was purchasing consignments of the more exotic products for sale further afield. If we assume that producers and consumers would each travel 15–25 km to a market, the products would achieve a span of 30–40 km which corresponds

Plate 27　Oxford red colour-coat bowl with white painted decoration. Young, 1977a, form C77, *c.* A.D. 340–400. Found in Mark Lane, London. London Museum, height 10 cm.

almost exactly with the grey-ware distributions (cf. p. 156). The fine-ware travels up to twice this distance, so either the potters made longer journeys with selected more valuable wares or the selection was made at the pottery by the middleman. It is difficult to choose between these possibilities and, of course, there is no reason why both mechanisms could not have operated simultaneously.

The Oxford potteries were of a different *genre*. Situated in the country between the Roman towns of Alchester and Dorchester-on-Thames, they occupy a fertile region where pottery-making had a long history throughout the Roman period and perhaps back into the pre-Roman iron age. During the period *c.* A.D. 240–300 the area became immensely important and this position was sustained throughout the fourth century. The kilns were spread over some 50 sq km and a number have now been excavated. In addition, workshop structures, clay mixing tanks and various pits have been recognised. Particularly significant are the 'T'-shaped driers believed to have been used for pottery (p. 66 and Fig. 28), for these suggest an attempt to prolong the working season. The kilns are small, but it is remarkable that seasonal patching, so well displayed in the New Forest, is not

recorded. Overall, it would appear that we are considering a much more sophisticated industry, operating for a longer season each year.

The products are closely similar to those of the New Forest – colour-coated flagons, beakers, mortaria and bowls (Pl. 27), white-ware mortaria and parchment wares, in addition to grey-ware jars and cooking pots. The distribution is striking for while the grey-wares were marketed locally, some of the colour-coated vessels are found in profusion throughout southern England and comprise a major type southeast of a line from the Humber to the Severn, with some material reaching Scotland or the Continent. The role of the middleman is beyond question and we can confidently assert that without the attentions of the *negotiatores* the Oxford potteries could not have achieved their pre-eminence (Fig. 56).

The Alice Holt potteries situated 65 km (40 miles) southeast of London provide a further contrast. They are situated in an area of poorly drained gley soil unfit for agricultural use and now dominated by woodland. Most of the kilns are found tightly concentrated in an area of about 4 square km, but there are outliers 7 km to the northwest near

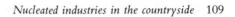

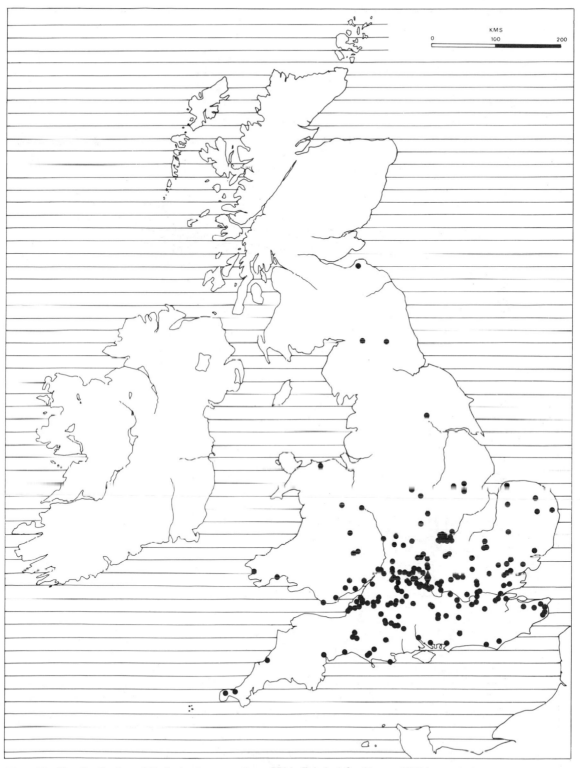

Figure 56 The distribution of Oxford colour-coat form C51 in Britain (after Young, 1977a).

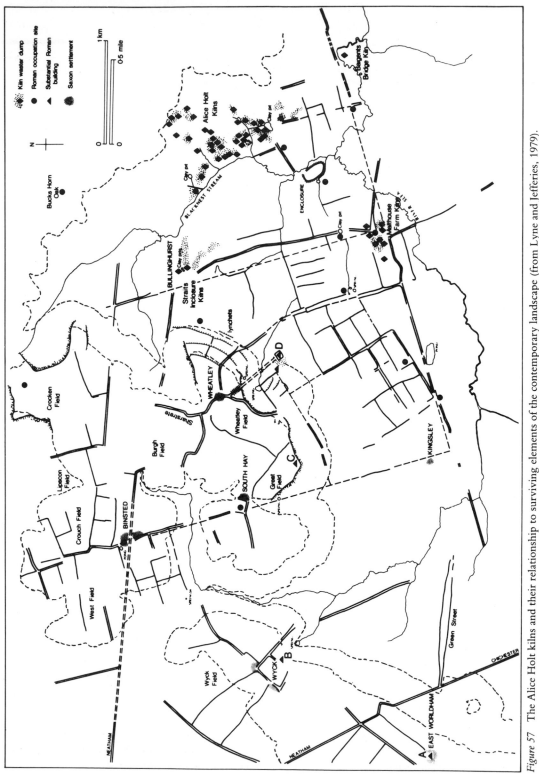

Figure 57   The Alice Holt kilns and their relationship to surviving elements of the contemporary landscape (from Lyne and Jefferies, 1979).

Plate 28   Alice Holt grey-ware jar from Old Ford, Bow, London. Late Roman. London Museum, height 31 cm.

Farnham and Tilford. The complex has a long life from the late first to the fourth or possibly even the early fifth century, but it is not until the late third or early fourth century that it became important.

There has been comparatively little excavation, but a few kiln sites have been explored and it is suggested that some comprised turf-built surface clamps while others are of an unusual double flue variety possibly domed with turves (Lyne and Jefferies, 1979:17–18).

However, the lack of excavation has been compensated by thorough field survey and systematic sampling of the waste heaps. This work has revealed details such as water channels and clay pits as well as the relationship of tracks and field systems (Fig. 57). The potteries seem to occupy the less desirable land on which it was not profitable to lay out fields.

However, the most extraordinary feature of this industry is its products, which are exclusively

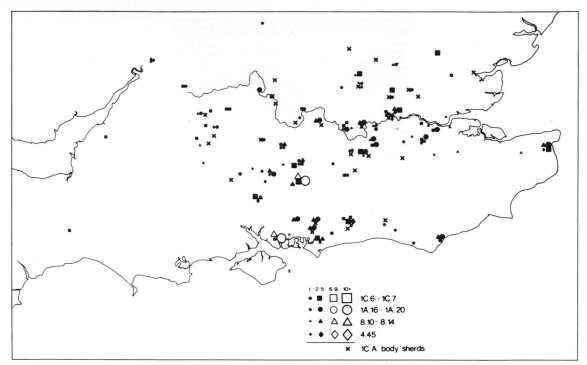

Figure 58　The distribution in Britain of Alice Holt grey-ware storage jars (class 1), flagons (class 8) and bead-rimmed jars (class 4), during the period *c.* A.D. 350–420 (from Lyne and Jefferies, 1979).

grey-wares, sometimes bearing a white slip. Cooking pots, lids and jugs are present but the main speciality seems to be storage vessels (Pl. 28). This large nucleated complex is thus producing ware that we would expect to be associated with the individual workshop and its manufacture at Alice Holt is something of a paradox.

The distribution of products highlights the problem because it is extraordinarily broad for a ware of this class. Up to about A.D. 270 the ware is distributed locally as befits a grey-ware, and a radius of *c.* 50 km would encompass practically all known finds. In the later third century the pattern changes and by the late fourth century Alice Holt ware is found all over southern England and on the Continent (Fig. 58). It is clear that marketing has changed and the pattern of selling at local markets and fairs has now been enhanced by the intervention of *negotiatores*. But why should they take an interest in common coarse wares which must have sold very cheaply and generated minimum profit? Much of the transport must have been by road which was notoriously costly (p. 159) and this alone would have made resale difficult.

At first sight Alice Holt is an anomaly which

accords with neither common sense nor ethnographic observation. One explanation might be that wide distributions were achieved because of a lack of competition from small local workshops, but this argument can be discounted in view of Fulford's observations on the grey-ware fabrics of Portchester (p. 90). However, it is interesting to observe that the most widely distributed types are the storage vessels, which one would normally expect to be produced very locally. However, if they were containers for a more valuable commodity the wide distribution can be seen in a more comprehensible light, a possibility grasped by Lyne and Jefferies who postulated transport of a liquid commodity, perhaps even wine. However, once the traffic had been established there is no reason why part of the load could not comprise grey cooking wares which it might not normally be economical to trade very far. Lyne and Jefferies (1979:57) sum up the situation admirably:

The Alice Holt industry, however, although it did not concern itself with the mass production of kitchen wares, distributed its best and most distinctive products as commodity packaging. As such the cost of production and transport was no problem, being easily covered by the value of the contents, which may well have been enough to cover part or all of the transport costs of cooking pots etc. placed on the same cart or in the same boat.

The three examples briefly summarised above serve to illustrate different facets of large-scale rural production: each case is individual and yet in some measure conforms to the rules. There is little point in discussing the Continental evidence for at present there is a lack of detailed studies. Nevertheless, it would be wrong to give the impression that rural nucleation is an exclusively British phenomenon, for analogous industries have been recorded in Belgium, in the Bois de Flinès and at Vervoz-Clavier, in France at Vrigny or at Butovo and Hotnitsa in Bulgaria, to cite a few better known examples (Amand, 1971; Willems, 1969; Ferdière, 1975; Soultov, 1976). However, on the Continent samian ware was *par excellence* the product of both rural and urban nucleated complexes and this is the subject of the next chapter.

7 The giant fine-ware producers

Your honours have seen such dishes, they are not China dishes, but very good dishes.

William Shakespeare, *Measure for Measure*, Act 2, Scene 1, 96–7

The production of red-gloss table ware was one of the more important facets of the Roman ceramic industry. Great quantities were used throughout the Roman empire and it was traded far beyond the imperial frontiers to southern India, Africa and well into barbarian Russia (Wheeler, 1946; Kropotkin, 1970:16). Today these wares are known by a variety of names such as Arretine, samian (the equivalent of china), *terra sigillata* or simply red-slip. However, they comprise a single tradition of fine-ware manufacture which takes slightly different expression in the multifarious workshops spread throughout the Roman world. Today this pottery is of unrivalled importance to the archaeologist, for it has been the subject of many years of patient scholarship, inspired by its elaborate decoration and a wealth of potters' stamps; wares can thus be more accurately dated than any other type of pottery. Also workshops can be pinpointed with some precision, affording considerable scope for the study of trade, although this aspect has been little exploited, largely because of the overwhelming quantity of material (Pl. 29).

Evidently this ware was also important in the ancient world for it is one of the few classes of ceramics directly mentioned in the literature. Pliny's (*Naturalis historiae* xxxv, 160) celebrated passage is worth quoting.

The majority of mankind employs earthenware receptacles for this purpose [i.e. burial]. Among the table services samian pottery is still spoken highly of; this reputation is also retained by Arezzo in Italy, and merely for cups by Sorrento, Asti, Pollenza, and by Saguntum in Spain, and Pergamum in Asia, Also Tralles and Modena in Italy have their respective products, since even this brings the nations fame.

There are difficulties with this paragraph as some of the places Pliny mentions have yielded no traces of production, while other known centres seem to have escaped notice, but for the first time we are considering a ceramic industry worthy of a passing note from a Classical author. We must resist the temptation to go further and suggest that red-gloss production was of major economic importance: Pliny has singled out a ceramic curiosity and that is all.

Since red-gloss pottery is generally the product of large nucleated complexes, both urban and rural, this chapter should be read in conjunction with the previous one. Although New Forest and Oxford products are not usually classed as samian there is little doubt that the potters would have considered themselves part of the same tradition. There is a measure of overlap, but the deductions we can make are markedly different.

ORIGINS OF THE INDUSTRY

Roman red-gloss pottery must be seen against the broader backcloth of the Classical fine-ware tradition of which it is an essential component. During the Greek bronze age a technique was evolved which enabled pots to be decorated with a lustrous black slip. In the subsequent Archaic and Classical periods this was brought to perfection and the masterpieces of the Greek vase painters rest in large measure upon an ability to manipulate materials so that the painted parts of the vessel would turn black on firing, while the unpainted, reserved parts, would remain red.

During the subsequent Hellenistic period, artistic achievement declined and the upper end of the ceramic spectrum was held by mould-made imitations of metal vessels decorated with a minimum of painted vegetable ornament. This

Plate 29   Samian bowl from King William Street, London. Dragendorff form 29, from La Graufesenque, Neronian. Stamped OF FELCIS, mould signed Mod[estus]. London Museum ac. no. A 22709, diam. 24.5 cm.

period witnesses a step towards mass-production and doubtless it was in response to changed marketing conditions, as the city state gave way to larger political and economic units.

By about the middle of the second century B.C., for reasons at present obscure, red-gloss pottery was produced in the region of Asia Minor around Pergamum. Technically the difference is a minor one, but nevertheless it is here that we find the earliest antecedents of the Roman fine-pottery tradition.

In Italy, ceramic development during the fourth to first centuries B.C. followed a remarkably similar course. The painted vases of Magna Graecia gave way to styles such as 'Gnathian' or 'Calene' ware, both of which are black-gloss pottery interpretations of themes better suited to a metallic medium. There is little doubt that Campania became one of the more important centres of Italian black-gloss pottery, but although the best pieces bear elaborate moulded decoration, the bulk of the production, even at Cales, was of plain wares as Woolley (1911) long ago demonstrated. This 'Campanian' ware, as it is sometimes called, was traded and widely imitated in the western Mediterranean and it plays much the same role in the last three centuries B.C. as samian does in the first three A.D.

Much of the best black-gloss of this period may originate in Campania as Lamboglia (1952) suggested, but it was certainly made in the northern part of Italy as Morel (1963, 1965) has convincingly

claimed. It would appear that by the first century B.C. many an Italian town had workshops producing black-gloss in the Greek tradition and there is some evidence to suggest that Arezzo, the most celebrated centre for red-gloss, was among them (Morel, 1963; Comfort, 1940:189). The change to red-gloss seems to have taken place quite suddenly around 30 B.C. As in Asia Minor the reasons for, or advantages of, this new fashion are far from clear. It has been plausibly suggested that it relates to a migration of workers from the east, for the signatures which appear in the earliest Arretine stamps suggest that the industry could have been founded by a freedman of *M. Perennius Tigranus*, whose cognomen is oriental. From the outset he seems to have employed Greek workers who were allowed to stamp their names on moulds along with the firm's name (Oxé, 1933). The earliest signatures which appear in the Rhineland are those of *Pilemo* and *Pylades* which must therefore post-date Drusus' campaign of 15–11 B.C. However, two other names are mentioned on this early Arretine, viz., *Cerdo* and *Nicephorus*, but as their works are not found on the Rhenish forts they must have been active before *c*. 15 B.C. On the other hand the works of all the potters are stylistically similar and cannot be separated by any great lapse in time so that *c*. 30–25 B.C. seems a good estimate for the first works of *Cerdo* and perhaps the beginning of the Arretine industry (Pryce, 1942; Oxé, 1933).

The suggestion that red-gloss was brought by a

Figure 59   Crater of the form Dragendorff 11 (from Oswald and Pryce, 1920).

migration of potters from the east is both convenient and attractive, for it would provide a mechanism for introducing new technology and it would also account for the strong eastern influence displayed by the typology. The typical Arretine crater, Dragendorff 11 (Fig. 59) is little more than a Megarian bowl to which a pedestal has been added, and the latter were a characteristic product of many eastern workshops during the second and first centuries B.C. It is hardly surprising therefore that many scholars have postulated a westward movement of eastern personnel. Oxé (1933) and more recently Pucci (1973:268) have favoured a trade in eastern slaves trained in ceramic techniques, perhaps following the fall of Alexandria in 30 B.C.

Unfortunately this hypothesis cannot be accepted without reservation, on several counts. Firstly, as Westermann (1955:92) reminded us, it was fashionable to give western slaves Greek names, so that the stamps need not furnish information on the origin of the potters. Secondly, Megarian bowls were not exclusively produced in the east and a number have been found with Latin signatures suggesting an Italian origin. Furthermore, as Goudineau (1968:341) has shown, Arretine plates form part of a typological sequence developed from indigenous pre-Arretine traditions, albeit with some oriental influence. Perhaps it is also significant that only a few years later other types of Italian ceramics show evidence of hellenisation. Thus from *c.* 16 B.C., if not before, the typical Italian wine container, Dressel form 1, is replaced by another amphora imitating those of the island of Kos (Dressel 2–4). Presumably it was becoming fashionable to drink Greek-style wine and

growers required the appropriate container (Peacock, 1971). In fact all the new elements of the Arretine industry could have been present in Italy before *c.* 30 B.C. with the exception of the red-gloss which presents no technical difficulty. Seen in this light, the Arretine phenomenon could equally well result from a growing awareness of the east and an indigenous attempt to follow fashion.

Whatever its origin, one of the marked features of Arretine ware is its commercial success. Few types of pottery travelled so far and in such profusion, for the distribution stretches from Britain to India (Wheeler, 1946). There is little doubt that this achievement was due in large measure to the improved trading conditions created when Augustus organised the empire and it is perhaps no coincidence that the date suggested for the beginning of the industry is almost the same as that of the battle of Actium in 31 B.C.

Arretine or its late Italian derivatives, which show a reflux of Gaulish influences, continued until around A.D. 60–70 but little was traded north of the Alps after about A.D. 40 (cf. Comfort, 1936; Stenico, 1959). In its heyday Arretine was immensely popular and it is hardly surprising that similar ware was produced at places other than Arezzo. Long ago Bruzza (1875) published a collection from Pozzuoli which included moulds and wasters clearly suggesting manufacture in the area. There is also some evidence for workshops at Luni, in the Po Valley and in the area around Rome as characteristic vessels seem to be concentrated in all these places.

Most intriguing of all are the activities of *Cn Ateius* whose main workshop underlies the modern city of Arezzo (Maetzke, 1959). Chemical analysis of his wares and moulds suggests that he also made pottery at Pisa as well as Lyons and La Graufesenque near Millau in France (Picon and Garnier, 1974; Williams and Dannell, 1978). The significance of the workshop excavated at La Muette near Lyons has been made clear by this scientific work and very recently debris of that predicted at La Graufesenque has come to light in excavations (information M. A. Vernhet). The origin of the Rutenian industry thus becomes a degree clearer and it is interesting to note that other Gaulish potters considered themselves to be making Arretine ware; thus from La Graufesenque we have the stamp SCOTTIVS FE/ARETINV, while Lezoux has produced DVRA/F ARE.

The origin of the Gaulish samian industry as a whole is a complex question involving the interaction of multifarious centres through the transmission of ideas and the movement of personnel. The spread of the tradition from Italy to southern, central and

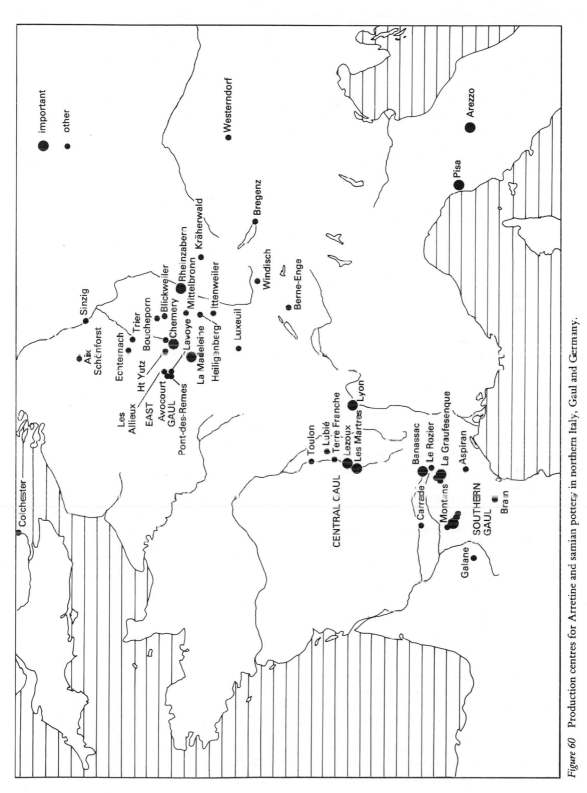

Figure 60   Production centres for Arretine and samian pottery in northern Italy, Gaul and Germany.

eastern Gaul has long been the subject of research and a sequence of 'influences' has been established (Fig. 60). However, the nature of these connections has become clearer in recent years, largely because of rigorous attention to die links between the stamps used in different places. Hartley (1977) has reviewed some of the salient points in a masterly article upon which much of the following discussion rests.

Although the direct influence of Arretine on southern Gaul has long been suspected, this is now proven in view of the results of fabric analysis and the *Ateius* discoveries at La Graufesenque. However, the relationship is probably not a simple one and there is reason to suspect that ideas may have been transmitted via the workshop at Lyons which ceased production by about A.D. 25. Before *c.* A.D. 20 the potters at La Graufesenque were using pale non-calcareous pastes which did not fuse in firing. As Bulmer (1980:14) has suggested this could imply that they were local Rutenian people, brought up in native, rather than Italian, potting traditions. However, after *c.* A.D. 20 technique was greatly improved and it is really from this date onwards that the centre begins to develop. It is tempting to see *Ateius* as the agent of change, transferring his allegiance from Lyons to La Graufesenque. The other great southern Gaulish producer, Montans, whose kilns have for long been considered the earliest in the area, may also have been the subject of Italian influences, whether of a direct or indirect nature, but this has yet to be established. There was certainly some interaction between La Graufesenque and Montans and between La Graufesenque and minor potteries in the area such as Aspiran and Le Rozier; Hartley suggests the latter were branch works. Little is known of Banassac, but there are clear die links, possibly indicating the transference of personnel from La Graufesenque.

In central Gaul the industry at Lezoux has a long history. The earliest ware is often rather crude and contains large flecks of mica: Boon (1967) has aptly called it 'a coarse ware of high quality', although as Dannell (1971) has stressed, better quality ware was also produced. Since the typology suggests Italian influence and since Lezoux samian seems to have been grafted upon a pre-existing La Tène tradition, there is every reason to regard this ware as a precocious attempt by indigenous potters to imitate the fashionable red-wares. The samian industry at Lezoux is now believed to have begun as early as *c.* A.D. 10–20 (Boon 1967:30) and since Lyons is but 100 km to the east perhaps it provided a spur for these developments, if not technical knowledge and

certain skilled personnel. Later there is clear evidence of impetus from southern Gaul for at least two pre-Flavian potters, *Il(l)iomarus* i and *Manertus* moved from La Graufesenque to Lezoux.

By about A.D. 100 a new centre was established at Les-Martres-de-Veyre in the Auvergne, a short distance south of Lezoux. Since this seems to have taken over some of the markets of La Graufesenque, it is tempting to suggest that it was founded by a group of potters migrating northwards to enhance sales. However, although certain Les Martres names can be matched at La Graufesenque, they are all common ones, and in addition it is difficult to establish stylistic links between the two centres. Thus the origin of Les Martres remains somewhat enigmatic. On the other hand its demise is rather better documented, for it seems that around A.D. 120 there was a mass migration to Lezoux attested by names and dies common to both places. Thereafter Les Martres declined until its extinction in *c.* A.D. 160.

Lezoux certainly had connections with the smaller potteries further north. Either branch workshops were established, or at least moulds were supplied to Lubié, Toulon-sur-Allier and Vichy (see below p. 124). However, Lezoux also had a strong influence in east Gaul. Some potters moved to Faulquemont-Chémery perhaps via Boucheporn by A.D. 70, if not before. *Rutan*, one of the earliest potters at Boucheporn, probably came from Lezoux, and he together with another potter *Canaus* may have been responsible for grafting samian production onto a pre-existing gallo–belgic tradition (Hatt, 1979).

The east Gaulish potter or potters *Saturninus* and *Satto* are thought by some to have originated in Lezoux, but Hatt (1958) has argued cogently for Les Martres. They had a complex career for their works are found in the Flavian period at Boucheporn and later at Chémery, then Blickweiler, finishing around A.D. 150–75 at Mittelbronn (Lutz, 1970).

In the second century, centres such as La Madeleine near Nancy continue to show strong central Gaulish influences.

Thus the movement of potters from central Gaul began as early as the first century and this was a major factor in the spread of the industry. The migration of early southern Gaulish potters is not precluded, but is harder to demonstrate. Of course the east Gaulish industry is very complex and other factors are certainly involved. In addition the complexity is compounded by the frequency with which potters moved around in the east-Gaulish-Trans-Rhenish zone. Sometimes they migrated from one established works to another, in other cases they may have founded a new industry which was sometimes superimposed upon a local coarse-ware tradition. This seems to be true of the great centre at Rheinzabern which possessed a coarse-ware industry later enhanced by a migration of samian potters from Heiligenberg and Ittenweiler (Ritterling, 1927). At Lavoye in the Argonne an earlier industry seems to have benefited from an influx of samian workers originating from La Madeleine.

Hartley gives some instructive examples of potters' movements, based upon a careful study of dies. Thus the stamps of *Cintunagus* suggest migration from Chémery to Lavoye, then to Haut Yutz, Heiligenberg-Ittenweiler and finally to Rheinzabern. The second-century potter *Lupica* appears to have started work at La Madeleine before moving to Sinzig and Colchester. Some potters seem to have gone far to the east before returning to the Rhineland. Thus, *Domitianus* worked at Heiligenberg, Kräherwald and Waiblingen in Swabia before ending up back at Rheinzabern, while *Marinus* iii had a similar career: Heiligenberg, Ittenweiler, Kräherwald, Waiblingen and Rheinzabern. These few examples suffice to demonstrate the complexity of the industry and the close connections between centres.

From this brief discussion it should be evident that the study of the western sigillata tradition is well advanced. Elsewhere in the Roman world origins are more difficult to assess as stylistic analysis is in its infancy and the excavation of production sites is badly needed. One might expect the later eastern sigillata wares to owe much to Hellenistic Pergamene ware, but the true situation appears to be much more complex, since there are imitations of Arretine forms and even the use of Latin stamps. It is not impossible that much impetus may have derived from an *eastwards* migration of potters working in Italy (cf. Hayes, 1972:10).

The origin of the north African red-slip industry is also somewhat obscure. At present it is possible to do little more than point to imports of south Gaulish samian in Tunisia and eastern Algeria and to note that some of the earliest African red-slip seems to be imitating the latest Gaulish and Italian products found on African sites (Guery, 1980; Hayes, 1972:15).

The origin of centres of Arretine and samian production is clearly far from simple for it involves a complex relationship between indigenous traditions and migrating potters with new ideas, but the general outline is beginning to emerge.

LOCATION OF THE INDUSTRIES

One of the curious features of the sigillata industries is the extraordinary location of some of the major producers. Arezzo is a prime example: its wares were distributed throughout and far beyond the empire and yet at the centre of this diaspora is an Umbrian town, situated some 250 km by mountain road north of Rome. The river Arno on which it lies is hardly navigable, while the nearest seaport is some 150 km distant across the rugged mountains of Tuscany. Similarly, La Graufesenque served Gaul, Britain and much of the western empire and yet the potteries were in the small Roman town of Condatomagus lying in the heart of the wild Cevennes massif. Export to the Mediterranean would involve an expensive mountainous haul over the Causses, while the northern markets were blocked by the Massif Central.

The central Gaulish industries make more sense as they lie on the northern fringe of the Massif Central and are connected via the river Allier to the Loire, one of the main waterways of France, but they are hardly in a commercially strategic central place. The east Gaulish potteries alone seem to be sensibly located within their relatively limited distribution area.

Of course the production of samian pottery is to some extent determined by natural constraints because a clay with rather special firing properties is essential (p. 62). Nevertheless, this factor has perhaps been overestimated for there are a remarkable number of places able to produce samian. In any case this argument does not explain why Arezzo maintained its supremacy despite competition from Pisa and Pozzuoli on the coast. The latter was certainly dominant in the eastern Mediterranean but in theory it should have eclipsed all other centres, for at the time it was the great port of Rome.

The siting of these industries remains something of a paradox and here we can do no more than consider some of the parameters to be evaluated in future discussion and research. Terra sigillata is *par excellence* the product of nucleated industries where the making and selling of pottery are characteristically separate activities. This explains why production can arise in a spot far from the beaten track and if there are no competitors in more favourable locations the industry might develop and thrive. However, this is at best a partial answer for the middleman would surely favour Pozzuoli or Pisa rather than Arezzo as a point of purchase.

The location of these giant producers of the Roman

period is remarkably similar to that of the present-day Potteries in Staffordshire, which, with their worldwide exports, rank among the largest ceramic industries in existence. And yet the Potteries are more than 50 km (30 miles) from the sea and cut off from markets in the north and east by the Pennine Ridge, which has always been difficult to cross. Even more extraordinary is the lack of suitable clay, for nowadays it is imported from Devon and Cornwall and the only real asset of the area is an abundance of coal for firings. In fact the industry owes its position to geological and historical circumstance rather than present-day conditions. It has been argued that pottery-making developed in pre-industrial Staffordshire because of poor farming potential (Hollowood, 1940; above p. 25). This would have generated a reserve of skilled manpower with few distractions other than potting, and this resource alone could have accounted for the prolific development of the industry in the eighteenth century. It is not enough to view an industry in purely geographical terms, for the historical perspective can be essential in appreciating location. If this is accepted it follows that Arezzo's lead over its competitors could be due to the strength and nature of the pre-existing traditions of which we know virtually nothing.

It is interesting to note that certain Gaulish samian potteries seem to have been founded in places where a non-sigillata industry was already established. We have already mentioned Lezoux, Rheinzabern, Lavoye and Boucheporn, but doubtless future discoveries will expand and amplify the list.

Finally it is worth noting that the Arretine potteries seem to comprise urban rather than rural complexes, thus conforming with the little we know of workshop location in the Greek and Hellenistic worlds. At Arezzo most of the potteries may lie beneath the modern and Medieval town (Stenico, 1958). Further potteries have come to light at Ponte a Buriano near the river Arno, where *C. Tellius* had his works, while there is a further outlying complex at Cincelli some 10 km distant which has yielded the stamps of *C. Cispius* and particularly *P. Cornelius*. However, Cincelli can hardly be regarded as rural for *C. Tellius* also had a workshop there, clearly showing the connection between the two areas. Again, the potteries at La Graufesenque may comprise an urban complex and it is interesting to note that recent excavation on the 10-hectare site has revealed sophisticated structures including roads, temples and houses (Vernhet, 1979).

On the other hand the Roman town at Lezoux

could have been small and insignificant in comparison with the outstanding importance of the potteries (Fabre, 1935), and it might have been a consequence rather than a *raison d'être*. Similarly many east Gaulish workshops were located in the country – Boucheporn, Blickweiler, Faulquemont-Chémery, the Argonne, La Madeleine etc. Only in rare cases, such as Trier, is the industry established unequivocally in an urban environment (Huld-Zetsche, 1972).

THE ORGANISATION OF THE ARRETINE INDUSTRY

Much of our knowledge of industrial organisation stems from the study of potters' stamps and since Arretine and Gaulish samian stamps are somewhat different it is convenient to consider each separately.

Arretine stamps, in their earliest and most informative stage, bear the name of the works owner followed by that of one of his slaves, a status generally indicated by the use of the genitive case. Occasionally the servile status is directly mentioned in the stamp as in *Surus Sari L(uci) s(ervus)*. These stamps are thus important documents in the history of slavery, for not only do they indicate that a slave economy was operative in the ceramic industry of the first century B.C., but they also furnish information about the status of slaves in society, for a man whose name appears alongside that of his master was probably a valued and respected artist in his own right.

Goudineau (1968:352) and Comfort (1940) have drawn attention to the changing forms of Arretine stamp (Fig. 61). The earliest platters of large dimensions bear multiple radially arranged stamps, while smaller vessels have but a single centrally placed stamp. About 15–10 B.C. multiple stamps give way to the exclusive use of a single impression in a rectangular frame. From about A.D. 15 there was a further radical change and late Arretine stamps are totally different: they are composed of abbreviations rather than names and the frame takes the form of a human footprint, usually the right one. The reason for the adoption of these *in planta pedis* stamps is interesting if obscure. Goudineau suggests that the elimination of multiple stamping is a logical simplification of the process, but that the excessively abbreviated *in planta pedis* variety cannot be explained in this way. He suggests that the marks of this later period may have served another purpose, namely that of distinguishing the genuine products of Arezzo

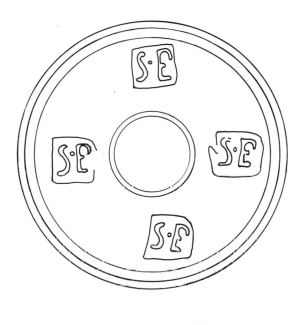

Figure 61 Arretine stamps (after Oxé and Comfort, 1968). Scale ½.

from those of the numerous competitors who were springing up; the stamps would thus be a sort of 'made in Arezzo' trademark. However, this explanation is unconvincing because *in planta pedis* marks were by no means the monopoly of Arezzo and were widely used in central and southern Italy (Pucci, 1973:274).

Study of the stamps listed in the great *Corpus Vasorum Arretinorum* (Oxé and Comfort, 1968) suggest the existence of numerous separate firms at Arezzo. There are about ninety recorded but some allowance has to be made for small firms as yet undiscovered. Naturally they are not all contemporary and at best the figure can be taken as an indication of the very large size of the complex. There can be little doubt that there was a measure of co-operation and co-ordination between workshops for this is both a characteristic and a benefit of nucleation. However, Goudineau (1968:350) envisages a considerable degree of co-operation. He was particularly impressed by the standardised forms and fabrics, which display little variation between workshops and postulated some form of central office controlling the product. Perhaps installations such as tanks for clay levigation, or the kilns, were also used communally. This co-operation could work

in a number of ways. Firstly, the industry could have been united by a co-operative liaison between proprietors so that the entire process from clay extraction to levigation and firing could have been undertaken communally or by a relatively small number of groups. Alternatively, there may have been three groups of specialists each dealing with one of these activities. Thirdly, a compromise is possible, with certain larger firms acting as self-contained units, able to help the smaller producers with some of the processes. The last two hypotheses are particularly attractive as they can be substantiated to a degree, from the ethnographical record.

However, as Pucci (1973) was at pains to stress, the theory of a co-operative venture is without proof. There is no literary or epigraphic mention of a *collegium* of clay-workers in Arretium, nor do the stamps suggest much co-operation between firms. There are occasional examples of the transfer of slaves from one master to another as between *P. Cornelius* and *C. Tellius* or between *C. Volusenus* and *L. Titius* but there are only about six recorded instances of this. If firms were operating on a co-operative basis, one might expect this phenomenon to be much less common or perhaps so common that it was unworthy of mention. The separate nature of the enterprises is clearly indicated in one case for the establishments of *Rasinus* and *C. Memmius* were merged for a time, producing the stamp *Rasini Memmi*. Later, presumably when the association ended, one of the names (usually that of *Memmius*) was deliberately erased from the stamp (Pucci, 1973:273). There are of course other examples of stamps bearing the names of two or more proprietors, but in nine cases the names appear to belong to the same family and only four link unrelated names. Thus the majority of associations seem to imply family businesses.

Furthermore the archaeological structures from Arezzo suggest a number of discrete units. The workshop of *Ateius*, for example, appears to have been a self-contained entity (Maetzke, 1959). The great levigation tanks of *M. Perennius* (p. 54) and his kiln, possibly situated under the church of S. Maria in Gradi, could be typical of the installations possessed by most works.

Finally, there is no reason to accept that the standardisation in fabric and form need imply co-operation. The characteristic Arretine paste could be due to geologically homogeneous clay beds, while typological standardisation is not the monopoly of Arezzo. As Pucci (1973:272) has argued, African sigillata shows a similar morphological homogeneity despite production in widely separated centres where co-operation would have been impossible.

Pucci's own approach to the industrial structure of Arretium is particularly instructive. He attempted to estimate the size of the workshops by counting the number of slaves associated with a given master, using the *Corpus Vasorum Arretinorum* as his guide. At the top of the list is *Rasinus* with no fewer than sixty slaves, at the bottom *C.* and *L. Avillius* who have but one, while *Perennius* is about in the middle with thirteen. Relatively few firms have more than twenty slaves, many have between ten and twenty and even more have less than ten. It is salutary to note that of the five hundred slave names known, only about forty were engaged in the production of decorated vessels. Of course these figures cannot be used as an absolute guide to size because we do not know how many slaves were employed at any one time; *Rasinus*, for example, is unlikely to have had sixty slaves working at once. On the other hand, only the key men would have been recorded and they must have been supported by numerous unnamed ancillary workers engaged in the menial tasks of clay extraction and preparation as well as firing.

What we can say is that the upper end of the industry seems to have been divided into very large units and the levigation tanks of *Perennius*, which held 10,000 gallons, seem entirely in keeping (p. 54). In large establishments some degree of specialisation is inevitable and this is illustrated by the limited numbers engaged in making decorated ware. Furthermore the slaves seem to have been owned by a master who was not engaged in the day-to-day work, for if so he would surely be unlikely to give his slaves' names such prominence. The composition of Arretine stamps seems to accord well with the concept of a proprietor with his skilled foreman or artists.

These characteristics serve to differentiate the larger Arretine establishments from the normal workshop, but if we have read the evidence correctly, the traits illustrate almost perfectly the 'manufactory' as defined in Chapters 2 and 3 (p. 9). This was precisely the conclusion reached by Pucci from a Marxist viewpoint. The existence of this somewhat complex mode of production in the Roman ceramic industry is unexpected and at first sight surprising, but nevertheless it does provide a context for the very wide distribution of Arretine ware. Furthermore the spawning of branch works can be seen in perspective; a normal workshop might have to curtail its activities if skilled personnel went elsewhere, but this need not be the case when working on the scale of the manufactory.

Although the existence of manufactories seems well attested, it must be stressed that most of the establishments at Arezzo might fall within the workshop mode of production. Furthermore, although as Pucci has demonstrated there is little direct evidence for co-operation, it was almost inevitably present and it is the level at which it operated that remains to be established by careful observation and excavation.

THE ORGANISATION OF THE GAULISH SAMIAN INDUSTRY

The stamps on Gaulish samian ware have long been the subject of detailed study but the common potters' marks are much simpler and less informative than those on early Arretine. They generally take the form of a name followed by F, FE, FEC (*fecit* – made by), M, MA (*manu* – by the hand of) or OF (*officina* – workshop) (Fig. 62). They are usually to be found in the centre of the base and occur most frequently on the less common plain forms but are sometimes found on decorated forms and on the rare undecorated types. It has been suggested that their purpose was to differentiate the work of various potters making the same form (Johns, 1971:16). The problem of unravelling industrial organisation is much more difficult and it is necessary to consider fragments of evidence derived from a number of different sources. We will commence by discussing the question of slave labour, after which we shall consider the size of the individual units and this will be followed by an evaluation of the degree of specialisation and co-operation within the industry. Finally we shall attempt to assess the evidence in the light of models derived from a more recent period.

With one exception (Hartley, 1977:153), slaves are not attested on samian stamps and there is a case for assuming that the workers were free. This difficult question was long ago evaluated by Grenier (1938) who drew attention to circumstantial evidence which furnishes some clues. For example, the cemeteries at Lezoux and Rheinzabern, presumably consisting largely of potters' graves, suggest a uniform distribution of modest riches rather than a highly stratified society. Similarly buildings at Lezoux and Faulquemont-Chémery, which may have belonged to potters, would have afforded comfort rather than luxury. On the other hand, a unique *graffito* from La Graufesenque mentions a team of slaves engaged in various tasks (Marichal, 1971:No. 25b). However, they may have been ancillary workers rather than

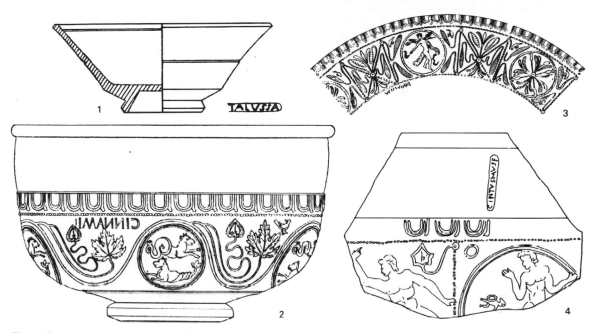

Figure 62 Samian stamps. No. 1, potter's stamp; No. 2, advertisement stamp; No. 3, mould-maker's stamp (from Oswald and Pryce, 1920); No. 4, bowl finisher's stamp (after Knorr, 1952). Various scales.

potters and perhaps even a temporary addition to the workforce. It seems that slavery may not have been the rule in Gaul and at best slaves appear to have played a more menial role than at Arezzo.

The sheer quantity of stamps bearing different potters' names is a clear witness to the very large size of the industry as a whole, and similarly there is no doubt that the main producing centres such as La Graufesenque, Lezoux or Rheinzabern had very considerable potters' quarters. However, this does not tell us the size of the individual production units. Some idea of the size of central Gaulish establishments is provided by *Cinnamus*, the largest of the Lezoux firms. Seven potters' names are associated with his bowls, suggesting that they were his workers, although they could have been independent craftsmen purchasing moulds (Stanfield and Simpson, 1958). However, whatever the interpretation, it is instructive to compare this limited number of 'associates' with the large number of slaves connected with many of the Arretine firms.

The problem of size can also be tackled by considering excavated remains, but unfortunately many sigillata production sites have been inadequately excavated and others remain unpublished largely because of the problems of processing the prodigious quantities of pottery recovered. In consequence there are few places where it is possible to study relationships between structures. The meticulous excavations at Trier (Huld-Zetsche, 1972) have revealed kilns, buildings and other structures, but the excavated area is too small to get much idea of workshop arrangement. Over 200 kilns are known from Lezoux, but records are poor and attempts to distinguish groups have been fraught with difficulty. Grenier (1938) quotes Héron de Villefosse: 'In 1882 Plicque discovered numerous vestiges of the *officina Liberti*. In this factory and in the immediate environs he had recognised eight kilns of which three belonged to the *officina Primi* . . . near to it was found a kiln of Plautinus.' This gives the impression of a scatter of small workshops, whereas one might have expected an important potter like *Libertus* to have possessed fairly substantial installations.

One of the best impressions of a samian workshop is provided by Ludowici's (1905) work at Rheinzabern, for all its shortcomings. The suite of installations attributed to *Comitialis* are particularly instructive (Fig. 63) since, even allowing for partial recovery of the evidence, the size and number of structures points to a small workshop rather than a manufactory. At present, then, the emerging picture seems to be one of remarkably small establishments, though this could change as more adequate information becomes available.

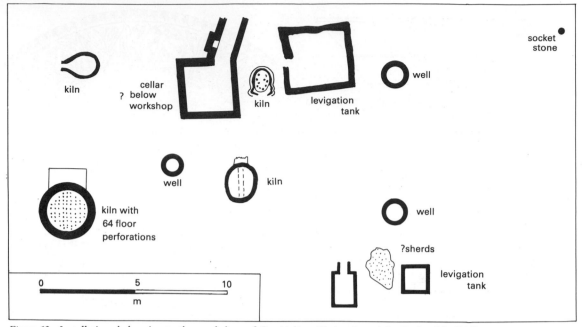

Figure 63   Installations belonging to the workshop of *Comitialis* at Rheinzabern (after Ludowici, 1905).

Potters' stamps remain a valuable source of information on industrial organisation. Everywhere potters' marks are very common: they are the stamps of the men who made the vessel or of the proprietor, although in small firms these are likely to be one and the same man. Other types of stamp have been recognised on figured samian ware (Fig. 62). Firstly the large prominent stamps among the decoration, such as those of *Cinnamus* of Lezoux, are regarded as deliberate advertisements included at the behest of the works' proprietor. A second type of mark is that of the mould-maker whose name usually appears in cursive script below the decoration. A third category of worker is the bowl finisher, the man who trimmed the rim and added the footstand when the vessel was removed from the mould. His mark appears on the plain rim band of Dragendorff forms 30 or 37. In addition the making of *poinçons* seems to have been a specialised business and these are sometimes signed. Thus the graffito *Marinus* appears on a *poinçon* used by the firm of *Ateius*.

It is clearly important to keep these distinctions firmly in mind, for while all operations may have been carried out by a single potter in one workshop, this is not necessarily the case. As Hofmann (1971), Johns (1963) and Hartley (1966) have stressed, this point has been too often neglected in the past resulting in a confusion of different potters' styles.

Johns (1963) cites some instructive examples. Thus the southern Gaulish potter *Masclus* placed his stamp within the base of his bowls, but also signed among the decoration, suggesting a small firm which was responsible for all operations. On the other hand the east Gaulish bowl-finisher *Lutaeus*, who worked at Heiligenberg and Rheinzabern, placed his stamp on the rims of at least three proprietors, *Reginus, Satto* and *Ianus*, suggesting that either he was an independent craftsman unattached to any particular workshop or that he obtained moulds from the larger firms.

Hartley (1966) has further discussed the sale of moulds and cites as examples a mould by *Attianus* of Lezoux and bowls in a local fabric taken from a mould of *Tetturo* of Lezoux, both found in a workshop at Toulon-sur-Allier. It is often difficult to distinguish true sales from the establishment of branch workshops and hence the bowls stamped CINNAMIOF from Vichy could either indicate purchase from Lezoux or the establishment of an outlying branch of the *Cinnamus* firm. Clearly rigorous scientific investigation of mould fabrics might supply a clue, but even so a large firm might concentrate its mould-making activities in one place from whence they would be distributed. However, Hartley gives some examples where the sale of moulds is virtually proven. *Reburrus* of Lezoux, for

Plate 30   Graffito from La Graufesenque. Hermet, 1923, no. 2. Collection Hermet, Musée Fenaille, Rodez, Aveyron (Photo courtesy M. A. Vernet and L. Balsan).

example, cut his own name *after firing*, in the moulds of the *Casuris* workshop and, again, the cursive signature of *Secundus* almost certainly cut after firing appears below decoration in the style of *Quintillianus*.

Of course it is very difficult to be sure that a signature was cut after firing when examining bowls made from these moulds and there is a strong possibility of confusion between mould makers and mould purchasers. In such cases a great deal of very careful stylistic and epigraphic study is required before the vessel can be interpreted. In general the alternatives have been inadequately considered and although the buying and selling of moulds can be established the extent of this practice is hard to evaluate.

The problem is well illustrated by the potteries in the Argonne region of eastern Gaul, where the workshops are spread over a wide area 40 km from north to south and 20 km from east to west, comprising the forest of Hesse and the Biesme valley (Chenet, 1927; Chenet and Gaudron, 1955). Many sites have produced the same stamps and the same decorative *poinçons*, and so, not unreasonably, Chenet

regarded them as one and the same establishment or at least a sort of industrial syndicate. However, this is not necessarily the case for the movement of potters between workshops is well attested (p. 119). In addition the purchase of moulds and *poinçons* from the larger firms with specialist departments or from specialist craftsmen adds further complexity.

The stamps on decorated samian suggest a degree of specialisation at least in the larger workshops and perhaps considerable interaction between production units. However, further light on the way the industry was organised is furnished by a remarkable series of tally lists recovered from La Graufesenque (Pl. 30). They comprise graffiti inscribed on waste sherds, but their interpretation is difficult because they are written in vulgar Latin or Celtic. It is hardly surprising that they have been the subject of scholarly debate for nearly sixty years, since the definitive publication by Hermet (1923).

Hartley (1970:237) has drawn attention to twenty lists inscribed on the bases of dishes bearing the stamp CASTI or OF CASTI (i.e. the workshop of *Castius*). These record a total of 409,315 vessels made by thirty-four workmen. At first sight this could be taken to indicate that *Castius* owned a manufactory employing thirty-four workmen, but this hypothesis will not sustain detailed analysis.

The tally-lists from La Graufesenque display a consistent arrangement. When complete, they begin with a heading which always takes the form of the celtic word *tuθos* followed by a number from one to nine. The core consists of a list arranged in four columns. Each line begins with the name of a potter, usually known from stamps on other vessels. This is followed by an indication of vessel types and then the size and number of pieces. Finally, at the bottom is the total number of vessels, which can range up to 30,000.

Various hypotheses have been advanced to explain these lists. Some have regarded them as accounts enabling the foreman to check the output of potters under him, while others have interpreted them as lists of vessels in export consignments. A third view suggests that they catalogue the contents of kilns before or after firing and this is now generally accepted as it is supported by supplementary evidence. The key to interpretation is obviously the heading containing the difficult Celtic word *tuθos*. Duval and Marichal have advanced substantial arguments that this can be translated as 'kiln' (Duval, 1967; Duval and Marichal, 1966). Furthermore their suggestion is confirmed by a 'vertical' analysis of the lists, for they often comprise two parts, one listing large vessels in dozens or hundreds, the other listing smaller ones in thousands. If this is correct it suggests that firing was done communally at La Graufesenque by specialised kiln operatives, and we can envisage large kilns attached to the bigger works or working independently of numerous small concerns. Recently a large kiln, which may have been used for this purpose, has been excavated (information M.A. Vernhet) and perhaps investigation of the surrounding terrain will indicate whether it was part of a large ceramic production complex or an isolated structure unconnected with clay preparation and forming.

Similar tally lists have been recorded elsewhere. They are known from Arezzo and Orta in Italy (Comfort, 1940:191) as well as Montans, Blickweiler and Rheinzabern (Oxé, 1925). If they are truly analogous, their discovery implies communal firings at other places, but the lists are strikingly few in comparison with the wealth of evidence from La Graufesenque and perhaps the dearth implies that such firings were the exception rather than the rule. On the other hand groups of wasters from Les-Martres-de-Veyre contain vessels from several potters welded together by the heat of the kiln (Johns, 1977; Rogers, 1977).

Fabre (1935:109) postulated communal firings at Lezoux because there appear to be two types of kiln: large rectangular ones which he presumed to be used for biscuit firing and small circular ones for producing the gloss finish. However, his hypothesis is without proof and it is more probable that the rectangular kilns were for bricks rather than pottery. It may be significant that very little gloss pottery is associated with them and Lezoux has failed to produce a single tally list, despite extensive explorations in the nineteenth century.

Although communal firings seem well attested at least at La Graufesenque, there is little indication of the degree of co-operation between potters in the forming and decorating of vessels. However, Knorr (1919, 1952) long ago noted that southern Gaulish samian was characterised by a *mélange* of decorative motifs, so that it is difficult to distinguish the work of individual potters by their ornamental style. This is very curious and stands in complete contrast to central and eastern Gaulish samian where the styles of different firms are very distinct (Stanfield and Simpson, 1958:xxxv). This could indicate radically different modes of production, with, on the one hand, potters grouped into large communal manufactories, while on the other small discrete workshops were the rule. However, this is far from proven because the differences could result from the way in which the moulds were produced. If their manufacture was a centralised activity by specialists, perhaps executing orders for other potters, this might lead to stylistic homogeneity, while discrete workshops responsible for their own requirements might explain distinct decorative differences between potters.

It is now time to draw together these disparate fragments of evidence, although even tentative conclusions must be somewhat hazardous. In sum, the main points appear as follows. Communal firings seem to be established for La Graufesenque and possibly for Les-Martres-de-Veyre, but elsewhere the evidence is slight. The homogeneity of style at La Graufesenque could indicate a similar association during the early stages of manufacture, but equally this trait could be explained in terms of centralised mould manufacture. In central and eastern Gaul the evidence currently available points to a plethora of small workshops and even the largest seem to be very modest in comparison with those of Arezzo. There seems to be some degree of specialisation with workers responsible for particular parts of the process. Many of these small workshops seem to be linked in some way. Correspondence in dies in some cases indicates movement of personnel, in others it is better explained by the transference of moulds. However, despite this fragmentation into small units the industry as a whole achieves a very wide market for its product, not unlike that of the factory mode of production at the present day.

The question we must now face is a very difficult one, for we must begin to consider the type of economic structure which would contain these observations. The crux of the matter seems to be the nature of the connection between workshops, which is unfortunately difficult to evaluate archaeologically. There seem to be three levels at which interaction can take place though all could, and probably did, operate at one and the same time. Firstly, workshops can interact at a purely commercial basis, in the buying and selling of moulds for example. Secondly, personnel could be peripatetic free agents, migrating from one place of employment to another in search of new opportunities, and thirdly, a more rigid structure is possible, perhaps akin to the 'dispersed manufactory's discussed above (p. 10). With regard to the first of these possibilities, there seems no doubt that equipment was bought and sold, but the extent of the practice is unknown. With regard to the second and third, the migrational tendency of samian potters is well attested, but it is far from clear whether they were acting as free agents or subject to superior control. It is instructive to illustrate the problem with an example from a more recent period of history.

In 1773 an English journeyman potter, William Ellis of Hanley, toured America in search of work (Bivins, 1972:25). His precise itinerary is not recorded, but we know from the records of the Moravians in North Carolina that he stayed for a while at Salem, working with the community's cantankerous but skilled master potter Gottfried Aust. The liaison was particularly beneficial to Aust for he had been attempting to make 'Queensware', a high-fired earthenware made in the large potteries of Leeds, Liverpool, Derby and Staffordshire, but popular throughout the English-speaking world. The *Aufseher Collegium*, the ruling body of the Moravians, noted that Ellis 'understands how to glaze and burn Queens Ware, so that the Collegium approves Br. Aust's suggestion, which is, that a kiln, suitable for burning such ware, be built on the lot . . . which adjoins Aust's'. Ellis was to receive 'food and clothing and a douceur for

his work, and we will learn all we can about glazing, of which Br. Aust already has some knowledge'. Excavations on the site suggest that the venture was a success for the Queensware ascribed to this period is of good quality and virtually identical to the English product. What is more, Ellis, seems to have brought some tools with him for characteristic decorative motifs are faithfully reproduced.

The relevance of this to samian is obvious, for if we lacked the historical records and merely looked at the typology of the pottery, it would be tempting to suggest that Wedgwood or one of the other English factories had a minor branch in America. However, the Salem industry is unconnected economically with the parent factories and by analogy a similar mechanism could account for the links between samian workshops.

On the other hand the same typological effect might result from a series of workshops linked to form a dispersed manufactory. This much tighter and controlled structure would undoubtedly involve the setting of standards and the supply of the equipment necessary in their execution. It might also provide a context for the movement of personnel whether for private or commercial reasons. Of course there is nothing startlingly new in this concept because archaeologists have for many years been talking of 'branch factories' operating within the samian industry.

It is, however, in marketing that these two mechanisms may display considerable differences. A peripatetic potter grafted onto an indigenous industry is likely to inherit the established marketing system, and may achieve little more than a local distribution for his fine-wares, at least during the initial stages. Doubtless this is the context in which many of the small east Gaulish works should be seen. It is only if there is a mass migration to a single spot, that the industry will be large enough to attract the middleman and hence achieve a wide distribution: Rheinzabern could be a good illustration.

On the other hand the dispersed manufactory would be backed by a sophisticated marketing system. It would not matter that a potter was working in the backwoods away from the main routes and conurbations, for he would be part of a much bigger system capable of buying and distributing his produce widely. It is interesting to note that central and southern Gaulish wares are commonly found in quantity far away from their point of production and few wares travel further. Yet in central Gaul at least they seem to be the product of very small units; this would be entirely feasible within the contexts of the dispersed manufactory.

In this discussion I have endeavoured to amplify and formalise suggestions that are both known and accepted by samian scholars. However, I have not furnished specific illustrative examples because this demands verification that is not at present available. Thus it is tempting to regard the potteries using *Cinnamus* moulds as part of a single dispersed establishment. However, before it is possible to sustain this claim a rigorous programme of fabric analysis would be required on both moulds and products. It would also be necessary to compare the distribution networks of the different branches for they should coincide if this hypothesis is correct. A model has been proposed and it now requires careful testing.

8 The role of the estate in Roman brick and pottery production

Am I to follow the books of the Sasernae, father and son in thinking that the proper working of potteries [figlinae] has more to do with agriculture than the working of silver and other mines which are doubtless to be met with on some land? Potteries [figlinae] however have nothing to do with farming any more than stone or sand quarries, though we need not on that account neglect to work them and reap the profit from them on land where they can be conveniently worked.

Varro, *de r.r.*, 1. 2. 22–3. Trans. Ll. Storr-Best, *Varro on Farming*, 17.

There is no doubt of the importance of the estate in the Roman economy. Most real wealth was generated by land ownership, the acquisition of which was one of the best investments a man could make. It was not uncommon to find a patrician holding several substantial properties in Italy or other parts of the Roman empire: the younger Pliny, for example, had one block of land near Lake Como and another in Umbria, inherited from his relatives. Some estates were very large indeed and employed thousands of slaves, but it is difficult to estimate accurately the optimum or usual size (cf. Duncan-Jones, 1974:323).

There is no doubt that an estate, particularly a large latifundium would attract a good deal of ancillary industry and Varro (*de r.r.*, i.22.1) offers the sound advice that everything possible should be made on the spot. As Righini (1971) has stressed, ancillary industries were probably a common part of the villa economy. The production of dolia is specifically mentioned by Varro and thus this rare documentary reference provides a clear indication that certain ceramic products could be made on estates. Callendar (1965:xxv) reasonably infers that amphorae might sometimes have been among them. However, it is not clear whether Varro is advocating an ideal or recounting general practice and the passage quoted at

the head of this chapter is equally enigmatic; the task of evaluating the importance of estate production rests firmly with the archaeologist. There are two lines of approach. Firstly, the study of kiln location might reveal examples demonstrably situated within estate boundaries, and secondly, more precise indications might be expected when stamps specifically mention that the product was made on a particular person's estate. In both cases the evidence must be evaluated with caution for even if it can be shown that ceramics were produced on an estate, it might still be difficult to discern the relationship between owner and producer. The latter could be employed by the former, but equally he might be an independent tenant paying rent. However, despite this problem the subject is worth pursuing and it is possible to cite a number of examples where firm indications emerge. In the majority of cases we are concerned with bricks and 'brickyard pottery' (p. 69) and only rarely is it possible to suggest that normal pottery was produced in this way.

KILN LOCATION

In a number of cases kilns have been found on or very near villa sites and in some instances the relationship is close, immediately suggesting that the kiln was an integral part of the villa economy. The clearest example of this was excavated in 1957 at Mürlenbach near Trier where a brick-kiln was enclosed in a square annex which was both aligned and connected with a range of villa buildings (Fig. 64; Reusch, 1958). In this case it is inconceivable that the kiln was operated independently under lease and there is every reason to suppose that its main function was to serve the estate. A rather similar connection was revealed at Eccles in Britain

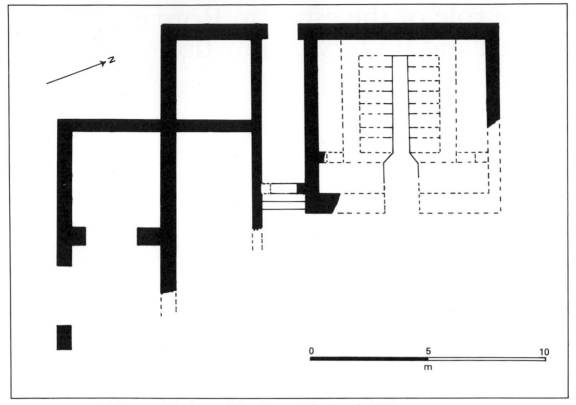

Figure 64   The brick kiln at Mürlenbach, near Trier, Germany (after Reusch, 1958).

(Detsicas, 1967). Although the brick-kiln was not part of the main villa complex it was found inside and aligned with a wall which was probably a boundary around the core of the property.

Unfortunately these examples are the exception rather than the rule and in other cases the association is much looser – all that can be said is that the kilns are situated near a villa. This appears to be the case at Hoheneck and at Bedburg-Garsdorf in Germany where kilns were found within *c.* 200 m of presumed villa buildings (Paret, 1911; Piepers, 1971). On similar grounds estate production has been postulated at Ashtead and at Wykehurst in Surrey (Lowther, 1948; Cunliffe, 1973; Goodchild, 1937).

Several authors have mentioned the possibility of pottery being produced on estates but only rarely have kilns been found near villas. Among the notable exceptions are the Evelette villa, southwest of Liège in Belgium, and Bedburg-Garsdorf, which had two pottery ovens in addition to the brick-kiln already mentioned (Willems, 1966; Piepers, 1971). At Aspiran in the south of France a complex of thirteen kilns making samian ware and amphorae seems to

have been associated with traces of a villa-like building (Genty, 1975, 1980).

However, a most spectacular example of a villa and associated pottery kiln was discovered by Goodchild (1951) at Aïn Scersciara on the Tarhuna Plateau of Tripolitania in Libya. An unexcavated villa probably located under a conspicuous mound seems to have been connected via an elaborate portico with a waterfall where there may have been a shrine or nymphaeum. Only 100 m north of the waterfall were two large circular pottery kilns. Goodchild did not record the nature of the products but later investigation by Paul Arthur suggests that Tripolitanian amphorae may have been important. In Italy amphorae have been found on production sites at Mondragone and Albinia apparently associated with brick-making debris, mortaria and other coarse pottery (Peacock, 1977d; Hartley, 1973). The addition of clay baths, sarcophagi and dolia completes the typical range of Roman brickyard pottery, any of which might be estate-made. Aïn Scersciara is important as it provides the first firm indication that amphora production was part of the villa economy at least in North Africa, which accords with epigraphic evidence, for Manacorda (1977) has argued that Tripolitanian amphorae were produced on the estates of such noted men as *Caius Fulvius Plautianus*, Praetorian Prefect under *Septimus Severus*.

Although we do not have abundant evidence, there are grounds for suggesting that ceramics were produced on Roman estates – but the extent to which this was practised is not entirely clear. Our Ashburnham model leads us to anticipate some trade within the immediate surroundings and hence it is reasonable to predict that not every estate would have its own kilns, but that some would be supplied by their neighbours or from other more commercialised enterprises.

Unfortunately negative evidence is unreliable and in most cases the lack of an excavated kiln structure on a villa estate could indicate the need for more excavation as readily as a real absence. Some clues might be expected from patterns of product distribution but, alas, we know all too little about the movement of the bricks and tiles with which the industry is largely concerned. Petrological and other scientific methods offer considerable hope for the future, but their potential has been little explored. If we wish to understand the distribution we must at present restrict ourselves to the bricks and tiles which bear civilian stamps, but here difficulties arise, for the practice was rare and unfortunately few stamps can be assigned to their kiln with precision. Nevertheless, there are a few instructive exceptions.

Special prominence must be given to the recent discovery of a tile-kiln at Hermalle-sous-Huy near Liège which was used by a tiler who stamped his work QVA (Delarue, 1974). Six stamps were found amongst the production waste, leaving little doubt that the source has been correctly identified and at the same time emphasising that only a small proportion of the produce would have borne this mark. It is not clear whether or not this was an estate kiln, but the distribution of QVA marks is interesting: they are found on nine sites within a 40 km radius, three of which are the local villas of Amay, Warzée and St Georges. This at once suggests that these estates were not making their own bricks and tiles but were importing from other local sources including the Hermalle-sous-Huy kiln.

In Britain no kiln using civilian stamps has yet been excavated and the practice was very rare except in the Cirencester region (McWhirr and Viner, 1978). Here it is interesting to note that individual stamp types are generally found on a variety of sites ranging from towns to villas, and some of the latter (e.g.

Figure 65   Relief pattern flue tile (Lowther, 1948, group 1, 'W-chevron') (from Walters, 1905).

Hucclecote or Lillyhon) have produced three or four different marks. Again the pattern suggests that estate production was localised rather than a widespread phenomenon.

The villa on Ashtead Common in Surrey produced evidence of associated brickmaking and it is thought to have been the centre of an industry making elaborately impressed relief-pattern flue tiles (Lowther, 1948; here Fig. 65). The dies range from simple chevron designs to delightful florid or dog and stag patterns (Pl.31). They were applied to the wet surface with a roller and probably served as keying for plaster, although, if so, it is difficult to see why the designs needed to be so elaborate. The distribution of these *tubuli* is quite remarkable for although there is a concentration of finds in Surrey, the same dies occur over very wide areas and are found as far away as Leicester or Margidunum in Nottinghamshire. The find-sites include villas, towns and other settlements. At its zenith it is clearly much more than an estate industry, although it probably began as one. Lowther suggested that journeymen from Ashtead made tiles at these more distant locations taking their roller stamps with them, a proposition which gains support from ethnographic comparisons (p. 38), but it could be tested quite

Plate 31   Fragment of relief pattern flue tile from Ashtead, Surrey. Dog and stag pattern. London Museum, height 17 cm.

easily by fabric analysis. A preliminary attempt gives grounds for optimism (Johnston and Williams, 1979).

These few examples suffice to suggest that in northwestern Europe at least it was not the rule for each estate to be self-sufficient in bricks and tiles, but instead most consumers bought either from neighbouring villas which may have originally established kilns to meet their own needs, or from purely commercial enterprises. Pottery production is even rarer and seldom seems to have been part of the villa economy. This conclusion is remarkably similar to that reached by Ferdière (1975) after careful consideration of kiln location over a wide area of central France. He suggested that, on the whole, ceramic production was dissociated from the economy of the countryside, for within his area he could point to only one possible and one very doubtful example of an estate tilery. If this is correct we must envisage a natural tendency for production to become increasingly centred on the commercial market rather than the estate so that there will be a transformation from estate production to what we have called the 'workshop' (p. 9). This seems to have happened in nineteenth-century Sweden (Bruno, 1954), and it may also have happened on a considerable scale around Rome in the first two centuries A.D. as we shall see in the following section.

THE BRICK STAMPS OF ROME

In Italy, particularly in the area around Rome, bricks of certain periods commonly bear stamps and these are usually much more informative than the simple formulae which typify the general run of Roman brick stamps. It is not surprising that they have been the subject of intensive epigraphic study for nearly four hundred years with landmarks by such eminent scholars as Dressel (1891) and Bloch (1947), a tradition now continued by the Finnish Institute in Rome with notable publications by Tapio Helen (1975) and Margareta Steinby (1975).

Roman brick stamps are elaborate and are often composed of several lines arranged in a circular or crescent-shaped frame (Fig. 66). In ideal cases they may record a wealth of information as the following example demonstrates

EX. PR. M.A.V. OFFIC ANNI ZOS FIG
CERM PONT ET ACIL   [CIL 248]

ex praedis M. Anni Veri, [ex] officina Anni Zosimi, [ex] figlinis Cermanianis [?]; Pontiano et A[t]iliano consulibus

We learn that the brick was made on the estate of *M. Annius Verus* by *Annius Zosimus* in the *figlinia* of *Cermanianus* during the consulship of *Pontianus* and *Atilianus*. Not only is the brick accurately dated but we also have information about the way in which the industry was organised. This possibility was grasped long ago by Dressel, Bloch and other eminent workers. Their findings are conveniently summarised by Loane (1938) or Frank (1940) who present a vivid picture of the developing industry and of the notable people involved in it. Although fired roof-tiles had a long history in the Mediterranean area, brick only became popular as a building material after the great Neronian fire of Rome when the inadequacy of tufa was clearly demonstrated, because of its inability to

Figure 66   Brick stamp, probably from Rome (from Walters, 1905).

withstand the effects of heat. Large quantities of brick were preferred in the rebuilding and local estates, hitherto equipped with small-scale brickworks, rose to meet the demand. As this was regarded as good estate management rather than an industrial activity many patrician families were able to exploit this source of wealth without loss of status and it is suggested that the Antonine dynasty rose to prosperity and power on the basis of a fortune made in the brick industry. During the second century the Emperor's share of production grew steadily until by the time of the Severi it was virtually an Imperial monopoly.

Unfortunately, this coherent and attractive story has taken some hard knocks in a recent reassessment by Helen (1975). He suggests that the stamps should be read in a rather different way, leading to a radically modified picture of industrial organisation. At the heart of the problem is the meaning of the word *figlinae* and the relationship between the estate owner (*dominus praediorum*) and the brickmaker or *officinator*. The conventional interpretation has been that *figlinae* translates as 'brickworks' while the *dominus* is the owner of the concern employing the *officinator* as his subservient works foreman. However, Dr Helen suggests that the word *figlinae* is a general term meaning 'clay area' and he convincingly reasons that this makes better sense in the context of many stamps. For example, it overcomes the problem of *figlinae Marcianae* which seems to have been owned by three *domini* at the same time. It would be curious to think of a brickworks owned co-operatively by three families, but the problem would be resolved if *figlinae Marcianae* referred to a clay area which passed through three adjacent estates. Dr Helen also critically appraises the relationship of *dominus* and *officinator*, concluding that in a majority of cases there is no reason to suppose that the latter is legally subservient to the former. Some *officinatores* are women and many are of high rank. It thus seems unlikely that they are slaves or work's foremen and it is more probable that they are in many cases the owners and entrepreneurs of the brick industry, albeit paying dues to the *dominus*. The emphasis is thus moved away from the landowner and we can no longer assume that he was the prime mover or even the main beneficiary in the remarkable development of the Roman brick industry.

However, there is one problem still outstanding, for first-century brick stamps are different to second-century ones and we must consider why this is so.

On second-century stamps many well-known people, including the Emperor himself, are mentioned as *domini*. In the first century there is frequently no mention of the *dominus* and those that do appear are generally unknown and do not figure in the political history of the period. Helen considers it unlikely that there was a radical change in the way the industry was organised, and sees the contrast as resulting from a changing pattern of land ownership. There was a tendency for land to concentrate into the hands of a few wealthy people and of course the Emperor was one of the chief beneficiaries. Thus we are not witnessing a concentration of the brick industry under Imperial leadership as Frank thought, but rather developments in land acquisition and inheritance.

This hypothesis certainly explains why so many famous names are found in second-century brick stamps but it does not explain why the landowner is so seldom mentioned in the first century, and this remains an unsolved problem. However, here our ethnographical considerations are pertinent for they suggest a possible solution. If we take nineteenth-century Sweden as our model, it seems entirely feasible that a thriving industry of scattered individual units might have its origin in estate production (Bruno, 1954). Perhaps what we are witnessing in first- and second-century Rome is the gradual commercialisation and hiving-off of economically self-sufficient units from a pattern of estate production. During the first century the brickworks were still tied to the estate or at least the memory of estate production was not far away. A *dominus* making bricks essentially for his own use would not need to have his name inscribed as this would be redundant information, but he might like to know from which of his several kilns a batch of material came so that he could keep a check on quality. However, when the works were in the hands of independent entrepreneurs and bricks were being made for the market rather than for internal consumption, it might be commercially valuable to mention upon whose estate they were produced. 'Our bricks are good enough for the Emperor himself' the *dominus* inscription might proclaim.

Another problem which has yet to be satisfactorily resolved is the reason for the sporadic incorporation of a date in the stamp. A law of Utica in North Africa required bricks to be matured for five years before use but this must refer to mud bricks, for while these require maturing fired brick does not. At present it is difficult to account satisfactorily for dates, though of course they are of utmost value in dating Roman buildings.

The brick stamps of Rome give us a unique opportunity to examine the working and development of an important facies of the industry. As a next step it would be useful to compare successive distribution patterns, but before such a study will reap its full reward it is necessary to learn more about the location of the brick-making *praedia*. At the moment we know remarkably little and it is hoped that the mineralogical studies in hand at the Finnish Institute will furnish some sure indications. In the meantime we can but review the little information available.

THE LOCATION OF ESTATES

Despite the wealth of brick stamps from Rome, very few can be assigned with accuracy to their point of origin. Fortunately there are a number of exceptions which are worth examining. For example, reference to the *figlinae subortanea* must mean the *figlinae* below Orta or Horta, a name which survives today in the present-day place name of Orte, a town situated 80 km north of Rome. Convincing though complex arguments can be advanced for placing the important *figlinae Caepionianae* in the same general area (Helen, 1975:87). It is surprising to discover that material was coming from so far away, but doubtless the market

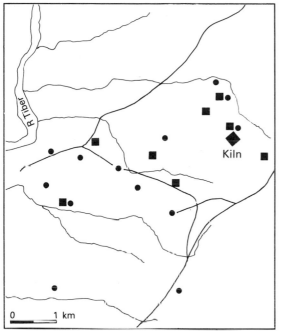

Figure 67 Part of the *ager eretanus*, showing the kiln and brick stamp distribution of Q. *Sulpicus Sabinus* (squares) (after Ogilvie, 1965). Circles, other 1st cent. stamps.

possibilities of the principal city of the empire and the existence of cheap transport via the Tiber made such a distant location viable.

Another brickyard placed with some certainty is that of Q. *Sulpicus Sabinus* who was working in the first half of the first century A.D. His stamps are known from the Via Tiburtina, Cures and perhaps the Palatine Hill where a similar although not identical stamp has been recovered (Ogilvie, 1965). However, the remaining ten finds come from a small part of the

ager eretanus, about 30 km northeast of Rome. The find-spots cluster in a limited area, about 4 km by 2 km bounded by roads, within which evidence of a kiln has been found (Fig. 67). It is tempting to regard this distribution as approximately delineating the extent of a single estate. Certainly the pattern fits our Ashburnham model and lends weight to the proposition that brickworks might have been more orientated towards the estate in the first century.

A rather similar approach has been adopted by Adamasteanu (1955, 1960) in a search for the *latifundia Calvisiana*, one of the many very large estates in Sicily. The place name *Calvisianis* is mentioned in the Antonine Itinerary and it must evidently lie somewhere in the eastern part of the plain of Gela. A number of sites in the area have produced tiles stamped CAL or CALVI and it is likely they are products of the estate kilns. They probably do indicate roughly where the *latifundia* is to be found, but as Wilson (1979) has warned, the evidence must be used with care, and because of the possibility of commercial sales, we cannot uncritically use stamps as an accurate guide to the mapping of estate boundaries nor can we use concentrations of finds as a guide to the whereabouts of the core of the estate.

One of the recurrent themes of this book is that all ceramics, no matter how humble, have something to tell us about the past. From this brief sketch it should be evident that common brick and tile, although too long neglected, could provide a wealth of interesting data. Full application of the modern tools of scientific fabric analysis will be needed if we are to fully exploit the possibilities and to progress beyond the relatively few stamped examples, for the typology of bricks and tiles promises little.

9 Ceramic production by official organisations

The Legion has carpenters, masons, wagon makers, smiths, painters and other artisans on hand for the construction of the barracks and winter quarters or repairing damaged machines, wooden towers and other equipment for . . . siege and defence; . . . they also have workshops for shields, cuirasses and bows, arrows, missiles, nets and all types of weapons . . . . They are especially concerned that whatever seems necessary for the army should never be lacking in camp . . . . The officer in charge is the prefect of the workmen.

Vegetius, *de re militari*, 2.11

The production of building materials, and to some extent pottery, by official bodies is an important facet of the Roman ceramic industry. Unfortunately it is one upon which ethnography is scarcely helpful for it provides but few instructive insights. In general both questions and answers must be generated by the ancient material alone.

It is not surprising that building materials (which can be of strategic value) figure much more prominently than the rather trivial production of pottery, and it is predictable that military forces should be particularly involved in this activity. There is some evidence for the production of bricks and tiles by municipal and state authorities but these are of little account when compared with the prolific activities of the army and navy. It is thus appropriate to emphasise military production and to concentrate firstly on brick- and tile-making before investigating the more ambiguous evidence for the involvement of armed forces in pottery production.

MILITARY CERAMICS

During the initial phase of conquest an army can have few ceramic needs. Cooking and eating utensils will be of metal and for these we have both the evidence from military sites and that from illustrations in Trajan's column in Rome. Additionally forts would be of wood rather than stone. During the consolidation phase we can expect a change: bases will be rebuilt in more durable materials and the extensive use of pottery becomes feasible. At this somewhat delicate stage it is perhaps desirable that an army should maintain its hold on brick-making for strategic reasons and because of the heavy demand military building would incur. Even if civilian sources existed they might not be geared to withstand the inevitable strain. Pottery is quite another matter, and it is reasonable to predict that supplies from civilian sources would be preferred, if the available vessels were of a range and quality to sustain a Mediterranean way of life.

In the third, defensive, phase we can expect a different picture, for civilian and military population are working together towards a common end and hence major contributions by civilians should be the rule. Military ceramics are of wide interest because they are likely to reflect social and economic interaction between soldier and civilian. For this reason we cannot study military production in isolation and we must consider the broader problem of ceramic supplies to the army as a whole.

Army involvement in making bricks and tiles is well documented because the custom of stamping the products with the name of the unit involved in their manufacture was widespread. Unfortunately this very convenient trait was not introduced until the mid first century A.D. and appears to have been adopted at different times in various parts of the Roman world. In Pannonia stamps first appear at the end of the first century, in Dalmatia they are Vespasianic or later, while in Rhaetia they are found in the early second century (Spitzlberger, 1968). In the Rhineland the earliest (unstamped) tiles appear to be those from Haltern, while elsewhere in Germany

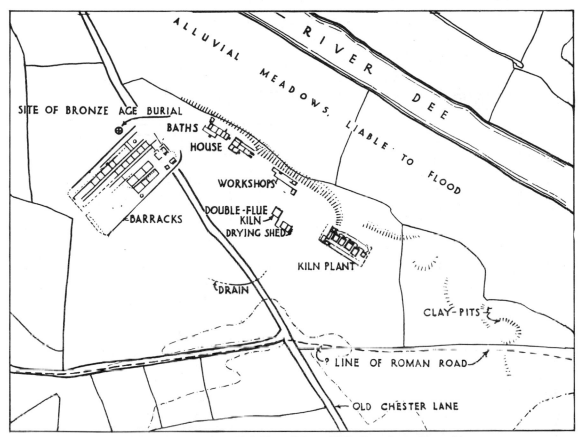

Figure 68 General plan of the military works at Holt (from Grimes, 1930). Barracks are 56 m wide.

further unstamped examples have been found in Tiberian levels, but they are always scarce and it is not until after A.D. 40 that brick comes into general use (e.g. Müller, 1979:13). It used to be asserted that the earliest stamp was one of the second Legion which was stationed at Strasbourg in A.D. 43 before being moved to the theatre of action in Britain (e.g. Szilágyi, 1972). However, this is a handwritten inscription (reading LEC II) and the earliest true stamps now appear to be those of the *Legio IV Macedonica* which arrived at Mainz around A.D. 43–45. In Britain stamping does not appear before the second century but there is evidence of earlier unstamped brick production at Exeter (Bidwell and Boon, 1976; McWhirr, 1979c).

The appearance of stamping raises the interesting question of its purpose. One possibility is that it was a means of registering output, and it might be suggested that perhaps every hundredth brick received a stamp. This hypothesis is difficult to accept because such a form of registration would also

be required by private brickworks who did not generally stamp, and in any case Brodribb (1979) has shown that even military bricks bear other marks, best interpreted as a system of tallying. Szilágyi (1972) mentions the interesting idea that bricks might have been subject to some form of taxation and a military stamp was needed to indicate exemption. However, such taxes could operate on a wide basis and might not account for the appearance of stamps at different times in various parts of the empire. Perhaps it is more likely that stamping was introduced for the same reason that modern Governments mark their property – to deter pilfering and unofficial distribution. In a newly conquered territory such measures might be unnecessary until military production reached a high level and until there was possible confusion with recently established private works. Alternatively, in some cases the risk of loss might increase when bricks had to be transported from their place of manufacture. Thus, perhaps bricks remained unstamped at Exeter because

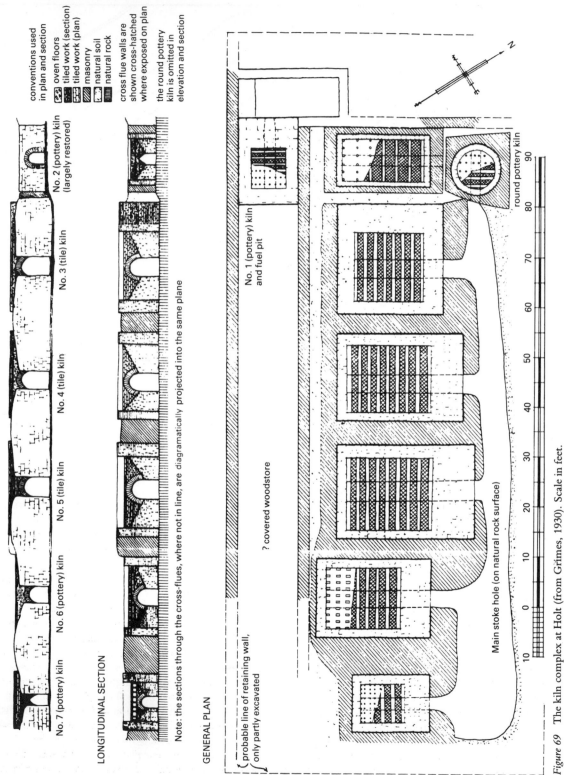

ELEVATION

No. 7 (pottery) kiln   No. 6 (pottery) kiln   No. 5 (tile) kiln   No. 4 (tile) kiln   No. 3 (tile) kiln   No. 2 (pottery) kiln (largely restored)

LONGITUDINAL SECTION

Note: the sections through the cross-flues, where not in line, are diagramatically projected into the same plane

GENERAL PLAN

conventions used in plan and section
oven floors
tiled work (section)
tiled work (plan)
masonry
natural soil
natural rock

cross flue walls are shown cross-hatched where exposed on plan

the round pottery kiln is omitted in elevation and section

No. 1 (pottery) kiln and fuel pit

? covered woodstore

probable line of retaining wall, only partly excavated

Main stoke hole (on natural rock surface)

round pottery kiln

Figure 69 The kiln complex at Holt (from Grimes, 1930). Scale in feet.

they were destined for the fort alone and not for use on other installations as well.

Unfortunately our knowledge of the actual techniques and organisation of military brickworks is slight because the evidence is weighted heavily towards the stamps themselves; the sites of some military brickyards are known but few have been fully excavated. One exception is the works depot at Holt in North Wales, which was established on the banks of the river Dee primarily to supply building materials for the fortress of the twentieth Legion at Chester some 15 km (9 miles) downstream. Fortunately Grimes's (1930) exemplary publication compensates in some measure for the shortcomings of the early twentieth-century excavation. The conditions of discovery make it difficult to assess the working life of Holt with certainty but it may have been active from the late first century through to the third and perhaps even fourth century. However, although the stratigraphy is not clear the general plan is instructive (Fig. 68). The northernmost part of the site is clearly residential; excavations revealed the remains of a dwelling house with a hypocaust, a bath house, and a substantial area of barracks which might have accommodated about two centuries. This is particularly interesting because it suggests a minimum size for the workforce which clearly involved a considerable number of soldiers.

To the southeast of the residential quarter were the workshops – the more ephemeral traces of walled pits, floors and foundations are not marked on the plan, but the small workshop with a hypocausted drying room at one end is particularly noteworthy (marked 'drying shed' on Fig. 68; see Fig. 28). To the southeast again was the main kiln plant. This remarkable structure consisted of a battery of one round and some seven rectangular kilns with perhaps a covered woodstore behind. The two smallest kilns may have been for pottery rather than bricks and their position suggests that they could have been somewhat later insertions (Fig. 69). Whether or not all the brick kilns were in use at one time is not clear but the variations in size and alignment imply a gradual expansion of plant capacity.

The general arrangement, so well displayed at Holt, seems to be paralleled by other military brickworks on the Continent. Recent excavations at Dormagen in Germany have revealed part of the brickworks of the *Legio I Minervia* (Müller, 1979). It is suggested that the yard supplied unstamped material to the Legion's fortress at Cologne followed by expansion when the unit moved to Bonn shortly after A.D. 40, but stamping did not commence until

around the middle of the first century. Activity seems to have been relatively shortlived for the works did not function when *Legio XXI rapax* was garrisoned at Bonn betweeen A.D. 71–83. At first sight (Fig. 70) the works appear to have been more randomly arranged than at Holt, but there is a cluster of three kilns which seem to be aligned with a large wooden structure 39 m long and 10 m wide, perhaps best regarded as a drying shed. No residential accommodation has been found, but the workers were probably garrisoned in the auxiliary fortress situated less than 1 km to the north.

One of the best-known military works is that of Holdeurn, near Nijmegen, in Holland, published in some detail by Holwerda and Braat (1946). The pre-war excavations yielded a wealth of structural evidence representing a considerable period of activity within the first three centuries A.D. Unfortunately, although the published plans are detailed and helpful, the work suffers from a dearth of sections making it difficult to assess sequences and contemporaneity. A detailed critique would be out of place and here we must be content with an outline sketch.

The excavations were concentrated in two areas about 100 m apart. The southernmost area produced the remains of a complex building while the northern site was dominated by a series of kilns used for both pottery and brick manufacture (Fig. 71). Kilns A, H, I and J were apparently used for pottery while B, C, D, E, F and G were for bricks and tiles. The earliest pottery kilns are the small rectangular structures H and I, which produced local gallo-belgic wares of a type used by the tenth Legion garrisoned at Nijmegen from A.D. 70–105. Other pottery kilns (not marked on Fig. 71) are thought to have existed to the east of the main block and diminishing quantities of pottery may have been produced up to the second half of the second century. That this was legionary activity is suggested by a pottery *poincon* reading LXGPF (*Legio X gemina pia fidelis*).

Among the brick kilns, G appears to be earliest and was built with material stamped by the *Exercitus Germanicus Inferior* established a little before A.D. 180. Its construction was followed by C and B. Pottery kiln A may be broadly contemporary with B; the former can be precisely dated because its building materials have consular dates. The stamps read *Sub Jul Cos* and *Sub Jun Macri Cos*; i.e. *Sub Didio Juliano Consulare* and *Sub Junio Macri Consulare* which suggests a date around A.D. 180 as we know from other sources that Didius Julianus was consul in A.D. 175 and legate in A.D. 180 or 181. Pottery kiln J is

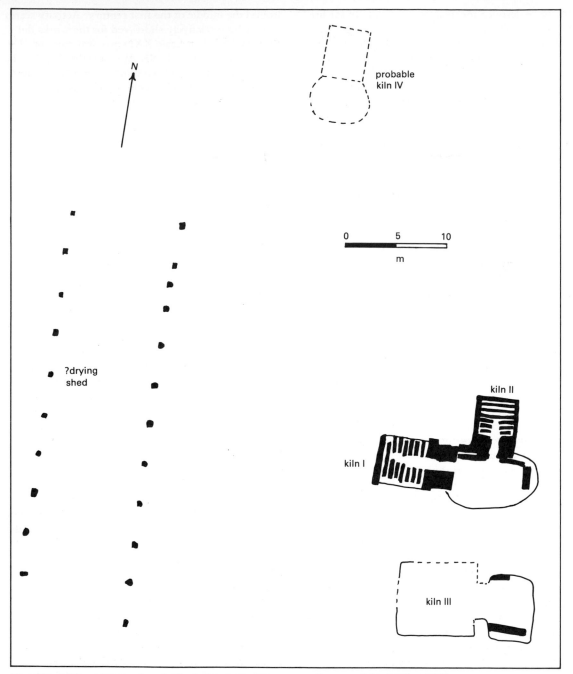

Figure 70   Military kilns and probable drying shed at Dormagen, Germany (after Müller, 1979).

ascribed to the same period. The date of kiln E is uncertain but D was constructed with the bricks bearing the stamp *Ex Ger Inf* and additionally those of *Legio I* or *XXX* some of which bear the word *Anto* (*niniana*) dating them to the reigns of Caracalla and Elagabalus (A.D. 211–22). F is more difficult to date, but it could have been relatively late, for the flue was blocked with bricks bearing late stamps of *Legio XXX*.

Holdeurn is thus complex but because of the

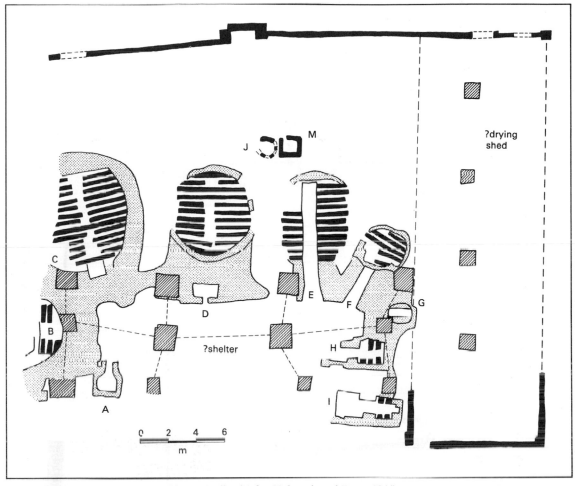

Figure 71 The kiln complex at Holdeurn, Holland (after Holwerda and Braat, 1946).

wealth of stamps it provides a unique opportunity to study the development of a kiln plant. We can assume that some kilns would have had a considerable life and that many would have been in use contemporaneously. The related orientation of A, B, C, D, E, and F suggests this, and the remains of brick pillar bases implies that the stoke holes may have been covered by a common roof (Fig. 71). If this is correct we are witnessing a marked expansion in production capacity and hence perhaps demand for brick and tile during the late second and early third centuries.

Other structures shown on Fig. 71 include a stone-lined levigation tank (M) near kiln J and a large rectangular building *c.* 27 m × 9 m. Traces of the latter are decidedly ephemeral but if correctly delineated it is similar in size to the building at

Dormagen and could also have been a drying shed.

The main works building to the south is shown in Fig. 72 and it comprises four ranges around a central open courtyard. It seems to have been constructed by the tenth Legion between A.D. 89 and 96 and later refurbished by the *Exercitus Germanicus*. The large structure C in the northeastern corner was probably constructed at this time and has been interpreted as a place for storing prepared clay prior to use. However, its curious relationship with a conduit could indicate that it functioned as a place when clay was levigated or mixed.

After the destruction of building H, perhaps in the early third century, building B, residential accommodation, was constructed over the remains. The curious structure H remains enigmatic.

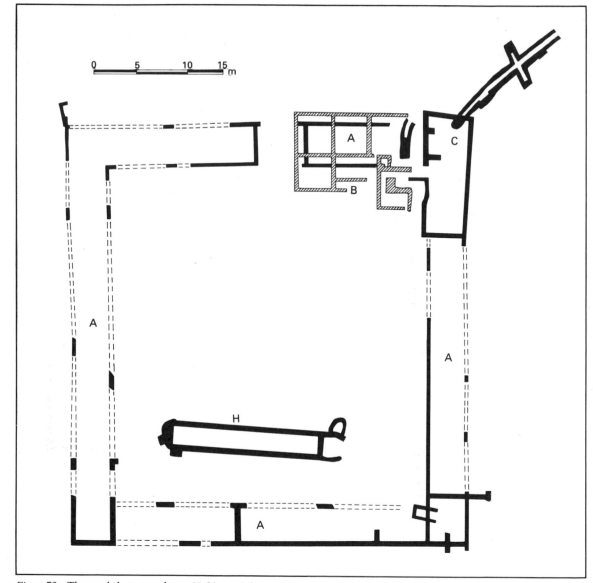

Figure 72 The workshop complex at Holdeurn (after Holwerda and Braat, 1946).

Although the three sites discussed are superficially different they have a number of features in common. In particular, all three have batteries of kilns and evidence for drying sheds, which suggests an attempt to maximise output during the brick-making season. In this respect legionary brickworks stand in marked contrast to civilian kilns which frequently turn up in ones or twos. Today most brickworks have multiple kilns so that some can be loaded while others cool.

A number of brickworks within or outside auxiliary forts have also been investigated and these are generally classed as military. Unfortunately in most cases the excavated evidence consists of little more than kiln structures and it is impossible to amplify the above discussion. In Britain auxiliary works have been postulated from eight sites, the majority of which are of early second-century date. In three cases, Brampton, Muncaster and South Shields (which is exceptionally late), two or more kilns have been discovered, but in the remainder only an isolated structure has been recorded (cf. McWhirr, 1979b).

Unfortunately, but not surprisingly, we know all too little about clay-working, as opposed to firing, methods (cf. P1.15). Some sort of wooden moulding frame would be required but none has survived and even stamp dies are remarkably scarce (e.g. Morgan, 1979). The latter must have been commonly of wood, sometimes with metal or even leather letters attached, for *poinçons* of pottery or made entirely of metal have been rarely recorded (Szilágyi, 1972).

While military stamps give clear evidence that bricks were made under military supervision they do not tell us how the industry was organised. It is plausible to envisage work by soldiers or alternatively by slaves and civilian conscripts working under their *aegis*, although the large barrack block at Holt suggests that not all soldiers could have been supervisors. However, a couple of graffiti furnish more precise indications on this matter. One from Holt reads: *Iulius Aventinus milis.*

While it does not state that soldiers were involved in clay-working clearly Julius Aventinus, a soldier, was near enough to a newly formed tile to inscribe his name on it. However, even more telling is an extensive inscription on an altar from Dobreta in Dacia (Macrea, 1947):

Avrelivs Me / rcvrivs milis c [ohor]/
tis p[rimae] sagitt [ariorum] in / figlinis
magis / ter super m / ilites 1x scripsit /
Avrelivs lvlianvs / milis co [ho] rtis primae

Thus Aurelius Mercurius appears to be the master clay-worker in charge of 60 soldiers. It is interesting to note that another *magister figulorum* also appears at Holdeurn. If the Dobreta inscription is a true reflection of the general situation it suggests that military brickworks must have been managed in a sophisticated way perhaps with intense specialisation within rather large units of soldiers. Military production was probably more reminiscent of the manufactory than the common rural brickworks which employ but small groups of workers under the master. It is against this background that we must view the inclusion of the master's name on Legionary stamps. Not infrequently stamps take the form LXVLSN, i.e. Legio XV followed by LSN presumably the initials of the *magister figulorum* (von Petrikovits, 1950).

However, the situation is by no means simple, for an interesting stamp has been recovered from Gellep near Krefeld which von Petrikovits (1954) reads as follows (Fig. 73):

S[. . .] Ces [. . .] in Kan[abis] L[egionis?]
[I M[inerviae]?], / coh[ortis]II
varc[ianorum] c[ivium] R[omanorum].

Figure 73 Brick stamp from Gellep near Krefeld, Germany (after von Petrikovits, 1954).

The formula mentioning both the worker (S . . . Ces . . .) and the place of manufacture (the *vicus canabarum* perhaps of the first Legion Minervia) is a characteristic of civil stamps. Thus perhaps S . . . C . . . was a civilian rather than a soldier making bricks for the army. Von Petrikovits uses this as an argument for dating the tile to the fourth century when the army used material from both civil and military sources.

While on the subject of personnel it is perhaps worth recalling the little evidence bearing on the *per capita* output which, it appears, could have been around 220 tiles a day. Thus from Holdeurn we have the graffito:

Kal ivnis qvartvs laterclos N CCXIIII
['Quartus made 214 tiles on the first of June.']

A number of similar graffiti are known from various parts of the Roman world and all are in broad agreement suggesting a normal output of around 220 tiles per day. Dates are also recorded elsewhere and they are concentrated in the months of June to October suggesting that this was the main production season (Spitzlberger, 1968).

From this brief examination of factors operating within production units we must turn to the broader issue of the relationship between works depot and fort, which must inevitably involve discussion of brick-stamp distribution and the question of interpretation.

Firstly it seems worth pointing out that some legionary brickworks produced for more than one unit (cf. von Petrikovits, 1950; Holwerda and Braat, 1946). This practice might explain an otherwise obscure memorandum on a tile from Hesse (Walters, 1905:388):

Stratura tertia laterculi capitulares num leg XXII
['In the third layer large tiles of the number of the twenty-second legion.']

The question of the significance of military stamps has been under review since the last century. The earlier view shared by such eminent authorities as Meyer and Mommensen was that the occurrence of a

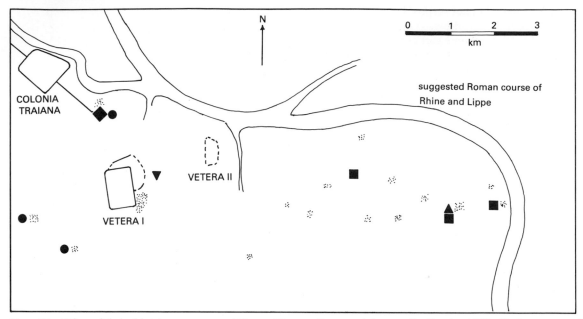

Figure 74   Military kiln and brick stamps around Vetera, Xanten, Germany (after von Petrikovits, 1959). Circles, stamps of the thirtieth legion; squares, the twenty-second legion; triangle, the fifth legion; and inverted triangle the sixteenth legion. Areas of Roman settlement are stippled. Stamps from the fortresses not shown.

military stamp will indicate the presence of the named troops on that spot (Szilágyi, 1972). Even when the material is obviously re-used in a private structure, it is reasonable to maintain this position because second-hand brick is unlikely to be moved very far from the place where it was originally employed. Ritterling was rather more cautious in view of the wide distribution of certain legionary stamps but he suggested that the stamps of cohorts could be used in this way. Although there are exceptions it is certainly true that in most cases cohort stamps are only found on a single site.

A significantly new consideration was introduced by Staehelin (1948) in his discussion of the Vindonissa Legionary stamps. He pointed out that many were found on estates around the fortress and he suggested that they were received by private landowners in exchange for supplies of corn and other essential commodities.

A rather similar interpretation has been adopted in the Rhineland. Von Petrikovits (1959) has used the spread of legionary stamps around the fortress of Vetera at Xanten as a partial guide to the *territorium legionis* on which were located farms supplying the needs of the legion (Fig. 74). The same situation may have existed at, for example, Neuss, but unfortunately extensive robbing of the many estates around the fortress could account for the dearth of

stamped bricks. Of course the precise status of these *villae rusticae* around fortresses is hard to evaluate. It seems likely that they were privately owned, but such an area might be particularly favoured for settlement by army veterans with close military affiliations (von Petrikovits 1960:65). We may thus be looking at a special case and it would be rash to assume that army bricks were *normally* sold to the private sector in exchange for goods supplied. On the other hand, Mócsy (1953) has drawn attention to the essentially pre-Roman nature of the population living within *territoria* in Pannonia and clearly the situation may have varied from fort to fort.

Rather more difficult to understand are a number of buildings in Slovakia and Moravia which contain tiles of *Legio XV Apollinaris* (Mócsy, 1974). These *villae rusticae* could have had some economic connection with the army but it seems more plausible to accept the view that they were built by Roman troops for co-operative barbarian chiefs after Trajan's treaties with the Germans.

In sum, there is very little evidence for transference of military bricks and tiles to the private sector and in the few cases cited above good economic or strategic explanations are not hard to find. We must conclude that the early writers on the subject were essentially right: military stamps will indicate military activity or interest, although few would nowadays postulate

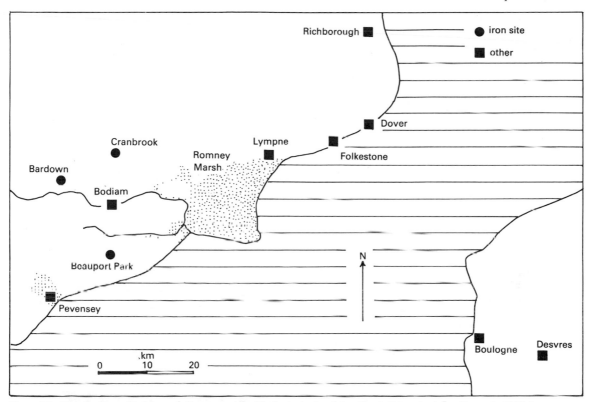

Figure 75 Distribution of bricks and tiles stamped with the insignia of the *Classis Britannica* (after Peacock, 1977c).

the existence of a garrison on the basis of a stamp. This is more or less the position reached by von Gonzenbach (1963) when she reassessed finds of stamps used by legions based at Vindonissa in Switzerland. She recognised two contrasting facets of the distribution. Firstly there is the concentration of finds on estates in the central Aargau region, noted by Staehelin and interpreted as the supply zone of the fortress. However, there is a further spread of stamps for which this explanation is patently untenable. They come from a wide area much of which would be unsuitable for agriculture and are commonly found at key points on the road network, on operational bases on the Rhine, near bridges, on lake harbour sites or even on the high Alpine passes. A strategic interpretation seems the only realistic possibility. At once the rôle of Vindonissa can be seen in perspective for here we have an illustration of the important part played by the fortress in securing the routes by which goods would be transferred from Italy onwards towards operational bases on the Rhine.

The long-distance transport of military bricks and tiles is relatively uncommon, but has been well documented along the Rhine (von Petrikovits, 1950). Stamps of the fifth and fifteenth Legions based at Xanten have not only been found around the fortress, but are known from Neuss, Krefeld, Cologne, Bonn, Remagen, Koblenz and Bingen, a span of some 200 km. Brickworks certainly existed in the middle Rhineland but it was found necessary to supplement building projects with supplies from the Lower Rhenish area. Similarly the works depot at Holdeurn not only supplied materials to Nijmegen but also to the whole lower Rhenish area, and bricks of the tenth Legion travelled to Neuss far upstream. In contrast, it is interesting to note that there is comparatively little evidence for the movement of material downstream from the middle and lower Rhineland. At first sight this is curious, for we might anticipate use of the strong Rhine current to distribute materials, but paradoxically heavy goods seem to have been moved in the most difficult direction. One explanation could be that the Rhine was used as a major axis for transporting food and other goods from the Mediterranean lands, a view supported by the study of amphorae and other vessels, for these show a predilection for the Rhône–Rhine route (Peacock, 1978; Greene, 1978). Barges travelling downstream would have discharged their cargo by the time they reached the lower Rhine and might require ballast for the return journey. In the absence of anything more suitable bricks might well have served. This hypothesis would readily explain why the movement of bricks upstream was so popular, but perhaps we can take the argument a step further and also infer strong army involvement in movement of all types of goods down the river (see p. 158).

If this interpretation is correct it could also explain the somewhat curious distribution of the bricks of the *Classis Britannica*, the fleet of Roman Britain (Peacock, 1977c). Bricks stamped with the initials of the fleet (CLBR) are known from nine sites around the shores of Sussex and Kent and from two localities in the Boulogne region of France (Figs 75–76).

Petrological study has demonstrated the existence of two fabrics, one of which is believed to originate in the central Weald of England, the other near Boulogne. The British fabric comprises about a third of all stamped material from Boulogne but very few Boulogne stamps have been recorded from Britain and there are but a few pieces from Dover. Again this could mean that cross-channel ships had more spare capacity when travelling from Britain to the Continent than vice versa. If so this implies that the fleet played an important role in importing goods from Gaul to Britain. Although Cleere (1974) has shown the fleet was deeply involved in the extraction of Wealden iron, there might thus be little case for supposing that much of this found its way to the Continent.

The bricks of the *Classis Britannica* serve to illustrate another rather interesting point. The ceramic materials used in the construction of fleet structures in perhaps the first to the mid third centuries are very uniform and distinctive. The later shore forts in the same area, Pevensey, Lympne, Dover and Richborough, are of quite different, unstamped, materials; there is much greater variety of fabrics and a dominant new fabric type appears. Yet as Frere (1967:221) has stressed the fleet must have continued to exist into this period. The simplest explanation could be that in the late Roman period the fleet took on a defensive role and was supplied with materials by civilian sources. Perhaps Sandgate Castle provides a good analogy for the way in which military needs of the shore fort system were met (p. 50).

From brick and tile we must now turn to the more

Figure 76   Typical stamps of the *Classis Britannica* (after Peacock, 1977c). Scale ½.

difficult problem of military pottery production. That legionary and auxiliary troops made pottery is beyond question, and it is merely the extent of this activity that is still in doubt. A legionary fortress would have extensive requirements which might warrant the use of military personnel to satisfy its everyday needs. On the other hand it could and did attract ancillary civilians who might be engaged in supplying or even producing wares specifically for military consumption. Under such circumstances military and civilian production could look remarkably similar from an archaeological point of view and this may be one of the reasons why so much confusion has beset the use of the term 'legionary' ware. However, from an *economic* viewpoint the contrast is total for on the one hand we have an embedded system of relevance only to the army, on the other a stimulus which could eventually lead to external commercial development. The task is difficult, but discrimination between the two situations is vital.

Unequivocal evidence for army pottery production is scarce. However, at both Holt and Holdeurn, small kilns supposedly for pottery are closely associated with the main brick-firing plant and they seem to be part of the military installation. Greene (1977) has taken the matter further and drawn attention to the presence of the exotic techniques such as lead glazing, the use of red paint or mica-dusting, which give character to the so-called legionary assemblages, setting them apart from the general run of indigenous ceramics. At Holt and Vindonissa such influences seem to derive ultimately from the Eastern provinces and Greene tentatively suggests that foreign slave labour may have been employed in military potteries, although whether they were of *directly* eastern origin is a debatable point (cf. Ettlinger, 1951).

However, kilns are not the only firm evidence of legionary pottery-making for in some cases wares were stamped. Although seldom encountered, military pottery stamps are known from Nijmegen, Vindonissa, Brigetio, Cannstatt and Aquincum (Bonis, 1977; Dickinson and Hartley, 1971:132). The list is not long but the range of stamped products is wide including a lamp, imitation samian, mortaria and coarse-wares. These scattered and isolated instances are important as they firmly indicate a widespread military involvement in pottery-making, although they are decidedly rare. Either we must assume that the legions were scarcely interested in pottery-making or that they seldom marked their wares.

The archaeological literature reveals many cases of

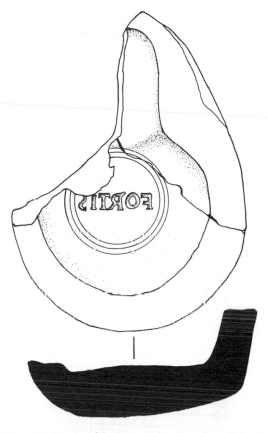

Figure 77   Mould of the lamp-maker *Fortis* from Brigetio, Hungary (after Bonis, 1977). Scale ½.

pottery kilns found outside both legionary and auxiliary forts of widely varying dates. They are very common and it will suffice to mention but some of the better documented such as Haltern, Neuss, Xanten, Cologne, Dangstetten in Germany, or Brigetio and Aquincum in Hungary (see e.g. von Schurbein, 1974; Steiren, 1952; Vegas, 1964; Hagen, 1912; La Baume, 1972; Fingerlin, 1971; Bonis, 1977; Szentléleky, 1959). In Britain Swan (1975) has argued that the Savernake kilns in north Wiltshire may have originally served a military base at Mildenhall, while kilns at Hardingstone in Northamptonshire may have served a suspected fort at nearby Irchester (Woods, 1969). At Muncaster and Brampton pottery as well as bricks seem to have been produced (see p. 142).

Almost everywhere these extra-mural kilns seem to have been concerned with the production of coarse-wares but some produced exotica such as lamps, relief wares, or imitation samian. In practically every case the problem is the same: were

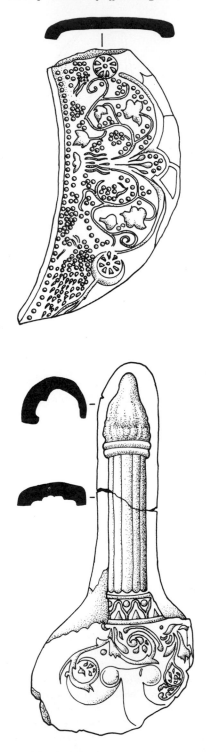

Figure 78 Pottery moulds for making ceramic imitations of metal prototypes. (from Brigetio, after Bonis, 1977). Scale ½.

these kilns operated by soldiers or civilian camp-followers? Few indications are available, but some sites such as Brigetio furnish food for thought. Among the very rich and exotic assemblage from the potters' quarter are a number of moulds for making the so-called factory lamps (Fig. 77). These have the name of the firm clearly marked on the base and among those recorded is FORTIS, perhaps the most prolific of all the manufacturers working in the late first century (Bonis, 1977; Szentléleky, 1969). Fortis is believed to have been based at Modena in northern Italy but he may have had branch works in the north and was certainly widely imitated, which is not surprising for it is a simple matter to copy a lamp by impressing the original into a matrix. The moulds from Brigetio could indicate imitation as readily as the establishment of a civilian branch works. This certainly appears to have been the case in the Danubian limes in Bulgaria where both imported and local imitations of north Italian lamps have been recognised (Čičikova, 1974). However, an army which took such care to mark its own brick products, and sometimes its pottery, is perhaps unlikely to have been content with another name on its lamps, and so this could be an indication that civilians were at work. However, Brigetio has produced ceramic imitations of metal artifacts (Fig. 78) and these are a feature of military assemblages elsewhere, at for example Aquincum, Noviomagus, Mogontiacum, Saalburg and Vindonissa. In addition Brigetio is one of the few places to yield a legionary pottery stamp. The evidence thus is confused and appears to point in two directions at once.

A similar paradox arises from the examination of coarse-wares. It is reasonable to postulate that everyday cooking pots will be made in the potter's customary way. They should thus serve as an indication of his origins and we might anticipate a soldier from abroad to produce rather different styles from the indigenous and presumably civilian potter. On this basis the potters are overwhelmingly civilians, for the cooking wares are normally closely linked to those of the province where they are found. An excellent example of this has been recorded from the pre-Tiberian kiln complex near the fort of Mainz-Weisenau where many of the products relate to the local late La Tène series (von Pfeffer, 1977).

It would be inappropriate to list all the evidence – accruing from study of pottery assemblages as well as kiln debris – which point to a strong native element in military pottery production; but this does seem to apply at least to Spain, to wide areas of southern and central Germany and in lowland Britain (Greene,

1979b; Darling, 1977; Webster, 1973). The exception is northern Germany where Greene (1979b) has suggested pottery-making seems to derive more directly from the Italian tradition.

However, even within the zone of native influence there are problems. Holdeurn for example has yielded a pottery *poinçon* of the tenth legion reading LXGPF (*Legio X geminia pia fidelis*) suggesting military activity at more or less the same time as some of the earlier pottery kilns were producing gallo-belgic-type wares for use in the Nijmegen fortress. It thus appears that a thoroughly military-looking complex was producing the local pre-Roman pottery. Again Holt appears to be a military complex *par excellence*, but it has nevertheless produced a mortarium die bearing the personal, and possibly civilian, name, *Julius Victor* (Grimes, 1930:131).

A similar range of conflicting evidence surrounds the use of the term 'legionary' ware in Britain. At Caerleon, for example, certain sherds bear names cut before firing, which are Roman rather than native in character and would be entirely appropriate to a legionary soldier. On the other hand, mortaria in the same fabric are widely distributed and occur on civil as well as military sites suggesting that they were civilian products (Boon, 1966). Furthermore at York 'legionary' ware has been found as wasters associated with stamped tiles of the ninth Legion and yet production seems to have continued after the Legion left (as it may have done at Caerleon), implying strong civilian interests (Perrin, 1977).

The emerging picture is not a simple one but our perspective will become a little clearer when we consider the probable ceramic supply mechanisms operating within the army. A short excursion on the means by which the army procured its pottery is pertinent.

It has often been asserted that the army usually obtained its pottery through special orders or contracts placed with dealers or directly with the producers (e.g. Webster, 1973:162; Frere, 1967:161; Richmond, 1955:167). Hartley (1973:41) has drawn attention to some interesting documentary evidence which refers to military orders for other commodities:

That it was possible for authorities to issue contracts to manufacturers for supplies to the army is evident from Berlin Papyrus 1, 564 (Lewis and Rheinhold, 1955, 515; an authorization and advance payment made by the Praefect of Egypt to the weavers of the village of Philadelphia for the provision of one belted tunic, four Syrian cloaks and one blanket to the armies in Cappadocia), and is implied by ILS 4751. One might *a priori* expect the army to buy in bulk

direct from manufacturers, but the quantities involved in the Berlin Papyrus are pitifully small and it is evident that since contracts were used for such small-scale supplies, they would all the more have been essential for bulk supply. However, it seems at least as likely that the army authorities would deal with negotiatores as direct with potters or the owners of potteries.

Contracts for pottery are difficult to demonstrate with certainty, but it has been suggested that the Romano-British black-burnished industry may have achieved its dominant place because of the stimulus of army orders (e.g. Peacock, 1973a:64). Similarly, small quantities of Severn Valley ware from a sector of Hadrian's Wall have been explained in terms of a minor contract (cf. Middleton, 1979; Webster, 1972). The model is useful and in many ways attractive, but unfortunately it has been assumed rather than tested or critically evaluated.

Contract ordering could operate on a provincial, regional or unit basis and we might expect a decreasing degree of uniformity between assemblages depending upon the level at which the system was working. If all the forts in an area were supplied centrally we would expect near total correspondence between sites, while if individual units did their own ordering we might expect a difference between sites, but in each case the pottery assemblage might derive from a limited number of sources. As Breeze (1977) has pointed out this is demonstrably not the case among certain forts in Northern Britain, which show a marked ceramic variation between one another and a considerable variety within each site. This is particularly evident when we study one particular class of vessel such as mortaria. At Bearsden, for example (occupied from c. A.D. 148–58), they derive from Mancetter and Hartshill, northwest England and possibly from a local source in Scotland (Breeze, 1977). The same is true for other sites and other classes of vessel and the observed data contrast with what we might expect from a sophisticated system of contracts. On the other hand the existence of pottery stores at for example Inchtuthil, suggests a degree of central administration with perhaps the quartermaster buying essential equipment for resale to the soldiers. Breeze reconciles these apparently conflicting views by suggesting that wares might have been purchased centrally from shops in the vicus or from visiting traders, and of course soldiers were always at liberty to supplement their individual requirements from the same source. It is difficult to better this perceptive hypothesis and it could well be that the private trader, local or long-distance, rather than the military contract is our key to understanding army pottery. In this respect it is interesting to note that Young (1977b) could see no evidence for special arrangements in the supply of Oxfordshire ware to the army. On the other hand, in an important study of pottery from early military sites in western Britain, Darling (1977) has stressed the similarity of supplies to legionary fortresses and other forts, well exemplified by corresponding assemblages from Exeter, Waddon Hill, Hod Hill and Lake Farm. In addition, she emphasises the strong ceramic connection between the two auxiliary forts of Gloucester Kingsholm and Cirencester. Thus, the possibility of army ceramic contracts is by no means precluded and much more careful statistical work is required in different parts of the Roman world before any generalisations will emerge.

However, these somewhat inconclusive considerations are important, because if pottery really was, on occasions, procured in a *laissez faire* manner the same could apply to the establishment of kilns near forts. Perhaps the army merely needed to establish itself and market forces would do the rest. Of course the entrepreneurs could include natives capable of making cooking wares as well as workers from other provinces following the army to provide table-ware, lamps and other requirements of civilised life. This minimal view of army involvement has the great merit that it accounts for the variability and complexity of military assemblages and at the same time explains the great scarcity of legionary pottery stamps. On the other hand the army certainly did undertake its own production, even if only on a small scale and in parts of the empire where local sources were inadequate or where civilian potters had failed to accumulate in sufficient numbers. However, paradoxes we noted from Brigetio and Holdeurn, Caerleon and York might be explained by assuming that the army merely acted as a catalyst, encouraging civilian production either by co-operation or coercion. Perhaps legionary potteries can be conceived as a complex and variable liaison between soldiers and civilians at times sharing facilities. If this is accepted it is not improbable that the migrants who worked at, for example, Holt and Vindonissa, were civilian camp-followers afforded hospitality by the army.

Perhaps this somewhat loose relationship is reflected in the well-known passage written by Vegetius in the fourth or fifth century A.D. and quoted at the head of this chapter. Important activities seem to have been in the hands of soldiers directed by the *praefectus fabrum* (cf. Sander, 1962), and it is hardly surprising that there is evidence suggesting that brick-making was organised in this way. Perhaps more ephemeral pursuits, pottery-making among them, were left to the civilian camp-followers, albeit with encouragement and perhaps even facilities provided by the *praefectus fabrum.*

If this is a correct evaluation of the relationship between soldier and civilian we are perhaps coming near to understanding one mechanism by which Mediterranean pottery techniques were transmitted to the Barbarian world after conquest (p. 94).

MUNICIPAL AND STATE PRODUCTION

There is very little evidence for the production of pottery by organisations other than the army, and municipal or state activity seems to be largely restricted to brick and tile manufacture. Even so the evidence is sparse.

Perhaps the best example of the products of a town brickworks is afforded by the RPG stamps from Gloucester. There can be little doubt that the initials can be expanded as *Rei Publicae Glevensium*, an interpretation reinforced by the occasional inclusion of a magistrate's name in the stamp. As far as we can see the works seem to have been established *c.* A.D. 110–25. The products appear to have a very narrow distribution for the 260 samples recovered all come from the *colonia* of Glevum and a limited area around

Figure 79   Tegula from London bearing the stamp PP BR LON (from Walters, 1905).

it which should correspond to the *territorium* (cf. McWhirr and Viner, 1978).

The numerous stamps from London with the formula PP BR LON can be expanded to read *P. Provinciae Britannia Londini* (Fig. 79). These have long been regarded as products of 'the Roman equivalent of the Office of Works . . . used for various buildings of an official character' (Wheeler, 1930:50). Again the distribution is very tight for such stamps have not been found outside London.

In the same vein, the stamps from Rome indicate official control of the brick industry at least by the time of Diocletian: no doubt reorganisation was dictated by both the economic reforms and building requirements of the period (Block, 1947).

The evidence from stamps is important because it indicates that officially owned brickworks were created to meet urban needs at different periods. It is quite possible that this mode of production was more extensive than appears at present, as it is only visible where stamping was the rule. It is hard to find examples of municipal works producing unstamped bricks, but *perhaps* the cluster of kilns discovered during road-building outside Cazeres was a town works of the same type (Manière, 1971).

Imperial stamps are fairly widely distributed. For example, Wilkes (1979) has shown that bricks and tiles bearing imperial stamps were imported to the coastal cities of Dalmatia and the immediate hinterland from the time of Augustus or Tiberius at least until the reign of Vespasian. The kilns have not been excavated but are thought to have lain in northeastern Italy on the coast of Aemilia and in the vicinity of Aquileia at the head of the Adriatic. Until more is known of the location of these kilns it will be difficult to assess the underlying organisation, but one explanation could be that bricks were produced as part of the economy of Imperial estates. It is difficult to prove this at present but amphorae from certain areas sometimes bear imperial stamps and since these vessels are on occasions demonstrably the products of estate brickyards (see p. 130), this hypothesis is strengthened (Callender, 1965:267).

10 Pottery and the Roman economy

Remarks made by Plato, Aristotle, Cicero or Seneca, revealing as they may be of the moralists' and philosophers' attitudes towards the crafts and manual workers, do not necessarily tell the whole story. Their bias is clear: the question is to what extent other sections of society subscribed to it.

Alison Burford (1972:25).

Much of this book is devoted to the production of ceramics and so far comparatively little has been said about trade and marketing. This is the other side of the matter and must inevitably take the debate into the much wider field of Roman economics. Before venturing specific comments on the way in which pottery could have been distributed and sold, we must consider more general themes. It is important to assess the likely place of Roman pottery-making in the Roman economy and to discuss the way in which pottery can further our understanding of economic matters. The subject has broad ramifications for many books have been, and doubtless will be, written about the ancient economy; here we can do no more than review certain aspects pertinent to our main theme.

PRINCIPLES AND APPROACHES

The classical economy can be approached in two ways. Firstly, the general framework and sometimes more specific aspects can be established by evaluating written sources, which may include both surviving texts and epigraphic references. Alternatively the problem can be tackled by examining and interpreting the material manifestations of economic activity, such as settlement patterns, floral and faunal remains or artifact distributions. Both are perfectly valid lines of enquiry and ideally any synthesis should take into account all forms of evidence.

Unfortunately this is scarcely practicable and in fact most of our knowledge of general matters stems from the study of literary sources, since sophisticated archaeological analysis is only just beginning. There is thus an inescapable gulf between the economic historian and the archaeologist, but hopefully the future will see a more balanced and integrated approach, even if the current academic scene is less than encouraging.

The classical authors have long been studied by scholars searching for economic content in a body of literature that is largely of political or philosophical intent. In recent years a number of important works by Finley (1973, 1965) and Jones (1974; 1964) provide a view of the emerging picture. The Romans, it appears, lived in a world with little conception of even rudimentary economic theory as we know it today, with only a slight interest in technological development, and then certainly not as a direct means of achieving economic growth, but theirs was a world which laid great store by agriculturally derived wealth. Of course, in a few lines, it is impossible to do justice to the views embedded in these formative works, but Hopkins (1978) has both conveniently and perceptively summarised some of the salient points of what he calls this 'new orthodoxy'. Much of what he says is pertinent to understanding the scenario against which the pottery trade must be viewed and hence his précis is worth quoting in full.

Because most regions of the Mediterranean basin have a similar climate, in Roman times they grew the same produce. What was not grown locally, the masses of peasants and townsfolk could not afford. Therefore there was no large-scale inter-regional trade in staple foods (wheat, barley, wine and olive oil). To be sure, there were exceptions. The capital cities of Rome and later Constantinople, and perhaps the other great cities of the empire, Alexandria, Antioch and Carthage, were too large to be fed from their immediate hinterlands. But all large ancient cities were near the sea, and/or on rivers. The armies of the High Empire (300,000 men strong) also received some of their supplies from a distance: for reasons of supply as much as for defence, most of them were stationed in garrisons along rivers (Rhine, Danube and Euphrates). In any case, the army and the capital cities were largely fed by taxes, levied in wheat, so that their supply was not part of a pattern of exchange, but of taxation.

Local self-sufficiency in agriculture went hand in hand with self-sufficiency in manufacture. The Romans never developed systems of manufacture which substantially cut the costs of production through economies of scale or capital investment in equipment. The units of production were small. The largest recorded factory was a shield factory worked by 120 slaves in classical Athens; some forty government arms factories established in the fourth century A.D. may also have been large. But as far as we know the concentration of workers in these factories did not apparently involve any sophisticated division of labour. In the arms factories, for example, each armourer was responsible for the whole process of making helmets and cheek pieces. In general, then, provided there were local supplies of raw materials, goods could be made in small quantities for each local market as cheaply as they could be made in large quantities at a single centre of production, from which transport costs had also to be paid. In other words, there were no effective economies of scale. Conditions differed only when a particular town had better access to raw materials, or had a monopoly of skilled craftsmen or had a marketable reputation for certain goods (ropes from Capua, linen from Tarsus, women's clothes from Scythopolis). These premium goods, like fine wines or other prized agricultural produce, fetched premium prices, and so were bought only by the elite; and therefore, since the elite was small, trade in premium goods involved only a low volume of transport.

This minimal view of commercial activity has been labelled the new orthodoxy because it stands in contrast (and is partly a reaction to) the previous modernising orthodoxy of Rostovtzeff (1957) and his followers. Finley (1965:42) has voiced his opposition to the latter with clarity and force:

The first century of the Roman Empire offers another kind of example. The fine pottery of this period was the *terra sigillata*, rather simple, well-made red ware, with moulded decorations if any. It is often called Arretine ware because at the beginning of the period the north Italian town of Arezzo monopolized production. But not for long: the Augustan peace and the consequent expansion of population and urbanization in the western provinces saw the diffusion of the manufacture of *terra sigillata* to various centres in Gaul and along the Rhine. Arezzo was knocked out of the market and quality declined. Out of this and one or two similar developments, in the manufacture of terra cotta lamps, for example, Rostovtzeff and others following him have constructed a great theory about economic decentralization, the ruin of the bourgeoisie, the end of emergent capitalism, and the seeds of the decline of the Roman Empire. I mean no offence, but this theory is an anachronistic burlesque of the affluent society. All that had happened was that a few minor trades over-reached the market, some hundreds of craftsmen in the western Empire in a few cities were

displaced by some hundreds in a few other cities, and nothing else.

However, naturally enough the new orthodoxy has itself prompted reaction, and Hopkins has already suggested some important qualifications. Firstly he draws attention to the simple fact that farming is a hazardous business and that production varies annually whereas the demand for food does not. Some towns or parts of the empire would suffer shortage or even famine while others enjoyed a glut, and this situation would have stimulated sizeable flows of trade where transport conditions permitted. This would inevitably lead to considerable transference of goods which had to be paid for. Hopkins suggests that 'the main difference between ancient and modern marketing systems lay in the absence of any regular routes or large scale exchange between the regions specialising in the production of an agricultural surplus and regions specialising in the production of manufactures. The lines of trade in staples produced by local gluts and shortages were unpredictable'.

A second qualification relates to the trade in luxuries, which Hopkins suggests was much more important than has been allowed. Although luxuries were the prerogative of the rich, the classes able to enjoy them were spread *widely* throughout the empire and furthermore an extraordinary variety of goods was involved. The trade may have been aimed at a small section of society, but it provided a living for thousands of merchants, traders and other intermediaries such as boat-builders or hauliers and thus the economic impact can have been far from negligible. The ancient economy is thus a subject of lively debate and it is reasonable to claim that commerce is again beginning to receive more attention, but from a different viewpoint.

However, it is worth stressing that the historical texts provide but one view of the Roman economy. They were composed by and for a small section of society who controlled the power and the wealth, and it is hardly surprising that the literature should show a general predilection for the *status quo* together with lack of interest in anything that might lead to change, but they cannot be ignored since they reveal important attitudes among the men who controlled the destiny of their times. However, they are not the whole story, for beneath the apex of wealth lay a broad supporting pyramid of slaves, peasants, artisans, merchants, shopkeepers and others to whom work was a necessity and efficiency an imperative. Had this section of society generated a literature it might have given a very different view of the economy, of innovation or of social ideals. And yet it is these people who comprised the bulk of the population; their documents are the potsherds, food remains or structures which are the bread and butter of archaeology. Cintas (1950) has perhaps summed it up as well as anyone:

Les archéologues et les spécialistes d'histoire de l'antiquité ont eu tort de n'attacher d'importance qu'aux seuls objects présentant un intérêt artistique. Les humbles, le peuple, de qui il s'agit de retracer les stades de civilisation, se sont toujours contentés de vaiselle ordinaire. Dès la constitution des sociétés, telles que les humains les ont organisées, l'object de prix fut la seule propriété des riches, peu nombreux. Et c'est la vaiselle courante que l'on retrouve le plus fréquemment. Seule elle peut donc livrer un témoignage du vrai passé. Il convenait de lui rendre son importance en l'étudiant la première.

If this view is accepted, it follows that history and archaeology are in some measure complementary, the one providing evidence about the superstructure, the other about the infrastructure of the ancient world. This point need not be laboured as the foregoing chapters contain a number of examples where pottery is used to illuminate aspects of the Roman peasant economy. However, the scope of archaeology is somewhat broader, for it offers a means of assessing trade and hence of testing assertions about commerce derived from the ancient texts. In fact pottery itself has a considerable role to play in the analysis of early trade because large amounts survive and it is comparatively easy to trace sources or to assess chronology. Other artifacts can contribute something, but those of metal and glass are much rarer and it is often difficult to determine origins by either stylistic analysis or by examining the material of which they are made. Stone artifacts can be more readily characterised by scientific means but they are less common than pottery (cf. Peacock, 1980). In effect, any archaeological assessment of Roman trade must rest in large measure on the evidence of pottery. This is not to claim that the ceramic industry was of major economic importance, but simply that the distribution and concentration of potsherds will indicate the main direction and force of commercial currents, in many cases primarily concerned with more important perishable commodities. Pottery serves as an *index* of the frequency with which different routes were plied, simply because it survives, and a few sherds could be all that remains of a very considerable trade in foodstuffs, for example. This point has been admirably made by Fulford (1978) when he compared the scattered ceramic evidence for the movement of goods across the Medieval North Sea, with the very substantial documentary case for a thriving trade in wool, cloth and foodstuffs.

It is too often forgotten that the chances of finding a casual import are statistically very slight and if we have any evidence at all we could be looking at the tip of an iceberg composed of unrecovered or lost data. This point is well illustrated by Bird's (1977) meticulous study of African red-slip vessels in Britain which have now been recovered from seventeen sites throughout the length and breadth of the country. In view of the small quantities involved she plausibly argues that they entered as personal possessions of travellers from North Africa. However, the chances of finding such imports are slight and it seems reasonable to interpret the distribution as a manifestation of trade. This alternative view is corroborated by finds of North African amphorae (which were probably containers for olive oil), for these have now been recovered on some thirteen British sites (Peacock, 1977e). Since it is unlikely that such cumbersome vessels were anything other than objects of trade, it seems reasonable to see the red-slip ware arriving on the same commercial current. Similarly, we can infer that imports of German Mayen ware into late Roman Britain represent trade as originally suggested by Fulford and Bird (1975) rather than personal effects as Willems (1977) has claimed.

If these arguments are accepted, a comparatively small scatter of potsherds might indicate a fairly substantial interaction between different regions. A good example of this is to be seen in Fulford's (1977a) analysis of Britain's trade during the later Roman period. Study of pottery on the Continent and in Britain showed that three major types were imported from Gaul and Germany, while two were exported from Britain, and their respective distributions indicate the alignment of the main axes of trade. It is not excessive to claim that the ceramic evidence implies a degree of economic integration between Britain and the Continent, for this is corroborated, to some extent, by a consideration of coinage.

The study of pottery distributions offers considerable potential in testing the level of, and in assessing principal directions of, Roman commerce. It seems preferable to use it as an alternative means of studying certain aspects of the economy, rather than assuming *a priori* that trade was unimportant and therefore pottery distributions must be insignificant (*contra* Greene, 1979a). Unfortunately the study is young and the Roman empire very large, so that it is premature to attempt even preliminary synthesis. However, it is reasonable to claim that all types of

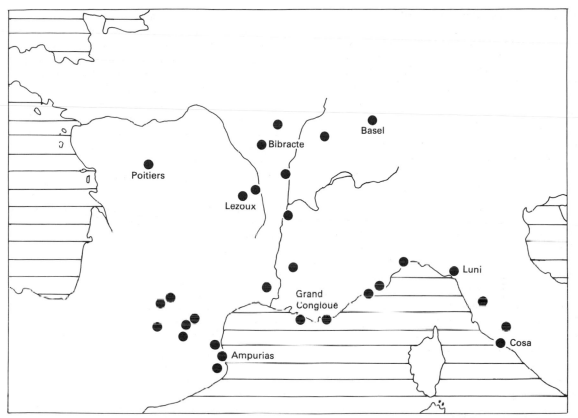

Figure 80 Distribution of Dressel 1 amphorae bearing the stamp of *Sestius*, whose kilns were probably located in the Cosa region (after Manacorda, 1978, and Lyding Will, 1979).

pottery from the humblest to the most sophisticated often appear to be transported over very wide areas and modern analysis is revealing much more extensive movement of goods than would have been thought probable a few years ago. The scope of interregional trade may well have been seriously underestimated by economic historians.

In this respect amphorae are particularly significant, for these cumbersome vessels constitute the packaging in which liquid commodities were transported the length and breadth of the empire: amphorae are not an index but a direct witness of an important facet of commerce. The study has been revitalised in the past fifteen years due mainly to the efforts of scholars such as Panella (1973), Tchernia (1967, 1971), Zevi (1966), Beltrán Lloris (1970) and many others. Careful attention to typology, stamps, painted inscriptions, together with the excavation of kiln sites has greatly enhanced our understanding of origins and contents of these vessels, so that we now have fundamental information about the main types. We are approaching the point where broad synthesis

is becoming a possibility for the first time.

Work on Dressel form 1 wine amphorae bearing the mark of *Sestius* illustrates the possibilities. These vessels have long attracted the attention of archaeologists, but it is only recently that their origin has been ascertained, and it now seems that they were produced on an estate near Cosa centred in a fertile agricultural part of Etruria. There are a large number of *villae rusticae* in the area and one, at Settefinestre, has been excavated to reveal an extensive range of presses which may have been typical of the others (Carandini and Settis, 1979; Manacorda, 1978; Lyding Will, 1979). The distribution of *Sestius* amphorae is impressive, for they are not only found in northern Italy but throughout wide areas of Gaul (Fig. 80). It is striking to note the very wide marketing of the produce of a single estate and the obvious inference is that even in the last decades of the Republic long-distance commerce was the counterpart of agricultural production. If this pattern proves to be typical, it serves to stress the potential importance of non-institutional interregional exchange.

LOCAL MARKETING METHODS

From the general we must now turn to the particular and consider the ways in which Roman pottery could have been distributed and sold. It is convenient to discuss local and long-distance trade separately, although obviously they are not entirely discrete facets.

Of all aspects of Roman commerce there is perhaps none so neglected as the arrangements for marketing within a short radius. This was true when MacMullen (1970) wrote his brief but perceptive paper and it remains true a decade later, so that much of the following discussion of markets and fairs must of necessity be based on this single source. Similarly, although we know something of the arrangement and architecture of shops in an urban setting, we know all too little about the goods they were selling. However, a handful of pottery shops have been discovered and they make a useful starting-point.

Two pottery shops appear to have been destroyed during the Boudiccan attack on the town of Colchester and although nothing is known of the structure, the contents were found as rich destruction deposits (Hull, 1958). The first shop seems to have been selling samian ware, glass, lamps, imported colour-coated cups and some Pompeian red-ware, while the second seems to have specialised in samian and a small amount of glazed ware. These assemblages can be compared with material from a store at Aquincum (Budapest) which contained Lezoux samian and lamps (Juhász, 1936) and with a crate of south Gaulish samian found in a house at Pompeii, for this also contained lamps (Atkinson, 1914). A rather similar situation is suggested by the remarkable 'gutter find' from the forum at Wroxeter. Here a series of complete samian vessels were recovered and a nest of mortaria was found a short distance away. Presumably these were being sold on stalls in the forum when it was destroyed in *c.* A.D. 155–65 (Atkinson, 1942).

All these finds are strikingly similar, for in each case the finer wares are well represented while coarse cooking-wares are virtually absent. It is a pity that there are not more discoveries to amplify this sketchy information, but the implication clearly is that shops may have been concerned with the more expensive luxury wares. If so they would have been very different to the pottery shops in present-day North Africa, for these stock virtually everything from a hand-made cooking pot to a glazed ornamental plate. The Roman shops seem to have been more akin to the china specialists of a western European High Street.

If these permanent shops are correctly seen as rather specialised outlets, presumably the coarser wares would have been distributed by potters or by itinerant merchants specialising in this type of ware. Purchases might have been made at the pottery, from peddlers or through periodic fairs and markets. Peddling, where pots are taken to the purchasers' premises will be very difficult to detect archaeologically, but in any case our ethnographical studies suggest that it is unlikely to have been a sole mode of distribution.

Periodic markets may take place in the countryside or in towns and, not surprisingly, we know most about the urban variety. MacMullen (1970) quotes an instructive description of marketing in present-day Antioch which he rightly sees as a parallel to the ancient situation.

The peasants must have not too long a journey to bring their produce to the city. It is desirable, even, that they should be able to make the round trip in one day; three or four hours' work is the maximum. They leave before dawn for the city, their donkeys laden with cereals, olives, grapes, or figs, depending on the season. Towards seven or eight o'clock the bazaar is full; souks and khans bulge with goods, animals and people. Towards ten o'clock, time to think of one's own purchases – the few items of luxury which the land does not yield: cloth bought in the city ever since rural production died, salt, sugar, soap, oil for the evenings. Towards eleven, the city is emptied and everyone starts home.

Of course, not every town supported a daily market. In Roman times, as at the present day, an attempt was made to stagger market days in the neighbouring towns so that merchants and peasants could do the rounds. There are a number of inscriptions which record market days, but the most notable is a calender used to tally markets in towns between Capua and Rome (Fig. 81). The circles are probably for decoration, but the holes would contain pegs enabling the user to keep track of town and market day.

Pottery distributed through periodic urban markets or fairs would produce a rather distinctive archaeological pattern. We might expect a concentration in the town and a thinner scatter in the countryside around. The distance travelled by the consumers and their purchased pots would depend upon the state of communications and hence the time taken to travel into the city. We might therefore anticipate a greater distribution along a road up to a maximum of *c.* 15–25 km, which would represent two or three hours' travelling. This model has already been discussed and illustrated by Hodder (1974a/b) who claims that a number of types of

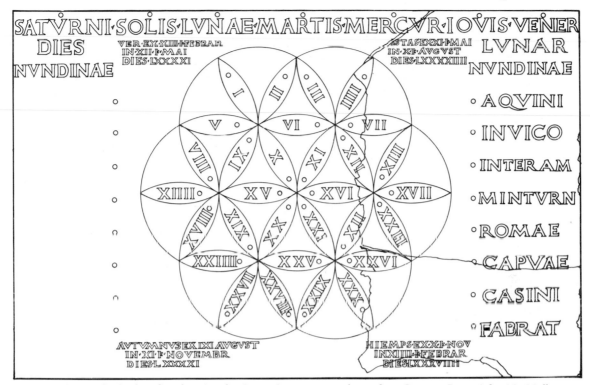

SATVRNI·SOLIS·LVNAE·MARTIS·MERCVR·IOVIS·VENER

DIES
NVNDINAE

VER·EX·XIIII·FEBRAR
IN·XII·F·MAI
DIES·LXXXXI

ÆTAS·EX·XI·F·MAI
IN·XI·F·AVGVST
DIES·LXXXXIII

LVNAR
NVNDINAE

- AQVINI
- INVICO
- INTERAM
- MINTVRN
- ROMAE
- CAPVAE
- CASINI
- FABRAT

AVTVMNVS·EX·IXI·AVGVST
IN·XI·F·NOVEMBR
DIES·L·XXXXI

HIEMPS·EX·XI·F·NOV
IN·XIIII·F·FEBRAR
DIES·LXXXXVIIII

Figure 81   Restored calender of markets (*nundinae*) covering an area northwest from Capua to Rome (after MacMullen, 1970).

Romano-British pottery were marketed in this way. The grey-wares from the kilns at Rowlands Castle in Sussex furnish an illustration, for the distribution is centred on the town of Chichester, with an extension up the Stane Street towards London (Fig. 43).

Of course, fairs and markets might be held in the country. This could be of particular importance in sparsely populated areas, but even where urban markets exist a religious or traditional event might lead to a periodic gathering in some rural spot, and whatever the primary purpose any large gathering of people would attract salesmen. Such gatherings might take place on a spot hallowed by tradition as is the case with the Portuguese *romariás* which are usually located on the outskirts of a village, but one, the *romariá de la Luz* is held on a mountain top (p. 21, Sanchis, 1977). A crossroads might form a suitable locus or alternatively an estate owner might designate part of his land for that purpose. During the empire, permission to hold such a fair had to be sought from the appropriate authorities, presumably to prevent clashes of date (MacMullen, 1970).

However, the connection between religion and commerce was very strong. There are a number of inscriptions linking merchants to the worship of Jupiter Nundinarius and Mercurius Nundinator but there is considerable evidence connecting temples with trade. Of course this was not limited to the countryside as Christ's denunciation of commerce in the temple of Jerusalem clearly demonstrates (Matthew, xxi:12). However, outside the towns a rural temple or shrine provides a likely focus for fairs and markets. Not all need have served this purpose, but those lying on tribal boundaries would be in a particularly favourable position, as Hodder (1977b) has suggested. Thus, the temple at Woodeaton seems to have lain on the boundary between two territories and the quantity of coins, pottery and other small artifacts from the surrounding fields suggests that it was the site of a fair (Lewis, 1966:130). Of course there was no practical need for such a location to be adopted in Roman times, but it may have been inherited by tradition from pre-Roman times, when it was placed on neutral ground between two tribes.

Unfortunately the relationship between temples and fairs can seldom be postulated with such confidence but in the Rhineland, northern France and Britain, temples are not uncommonly surrounded by *temenos* enclosures. These 'served as rural forums, combining in one spot the functions of sanctuary, law-court, games field, and market and social centre, as did similar enclosures in Ireland' (Lewis, 1966:5).

The distribution of pottery acquired at rural fairs and markets will be very difficult to evaluate for there may be no central nucleus from which the finds radiate. In addition, rural fairs may be held less frequently than urban so that the relatively thin spread of finds may be harder to study.

LONG-DISTANCE TRADE

Our knowledge of long-distance trade mechanisms derives largely from written sources which include both epigraphy and surviving texts. Rougé (1966) has reviewed the evidence for the Mediterranean while Hassall (1978) and Middleton (1979) have recently discussed the northwestern provinces.

The principals in long-distance commerce seem to have been the merchants, but there is a complicating factor for two classes are mentioned – the *mercatores* and the *negotiatores*. The difference between them is hard to discern, but Rougé (1966:290) has plausibly argued that there may have been a contrast in operational scale. Perhaps the *negotiatores* would charter a whole ship, while the *mercatores* were concerned with part loads. However, there is a further complication, for the term *negotiator* seems to have changed its meaning with the passage of time and in the late first century B.C. it was used to denote financial backers rather than those directly engaged in trade.

Some of the later *negotiatores* seem to have been general merchants plying a specific route. Thus from Domburg and Colijnsplaat in Holland we have inscriptions mentioning *negotiatores Britanniciani* who were presumably concerned with the British trade. On the other hand, product specialisation is attested in other cases, with merchants dealing perhaps exclusively in salt, wine, fish etc. From our point of view, the *negotiatores cretarii* are of particular interest, for these are generally regarded as traders in fine pottery or, perhaps less probably, in pipe-clay figurines (Hassall, 1978:44). Such merchants are known from inscriptions found at a number of places in Germany and eastern France: Wiesbaden, Mainz, Metz, Lorch, Sumelocenna, Cologne and Trier. At Domburg and Colijnsplaat they seem to have specialised in trade with Britain.

If the *negotiatores cretarii* are correctly seen as fine-ware traders, it is striking to compare this with the specialised nature of deposits found in shops and stores. However, although coarse-wares were probably distributed through local markets and fairs, they were certainly, on occasions, the object of long-distance trade. There is little doubt that they would generally sell for a much lower price than table-wares and it seems unlikely that they would have formed the basis of a viable business on their own. However, they might have been traded as part loads by general merchants or by the *mercatores*. On the other hand, this could have been the general rule for all types of pottery. Underwater archaeology has revealed very few Mediterranean wrecks with a cargo comprising pottery alone and even the well-known samian wreck of Pudding Pan Rock in the Thames estuary has yielded numerous tegulae as well (see Smith, 1907 (but no mention of *tegulae*) and Parker (forthcoming) for a review of Mediterranean wrecks). If this is correct, it underlines the importance of pottery as an index rather than an object of trade.

Of course traders would of necessity have worked in conjunction with shippers and sometimes their roles could have overlapped. There are three main classes of people to consider: the *nauclerus*, the *magister navis* and the *navicularius*. Rougé (1966:244) is of the opinion that the terms *nauclerus* and *magister navis* may have been more or less synonymous. They were, broadly speaking, agents of the shipowners in charge of the cargo and its sale. The *navicularii*, on the other hand, can be regarded as both the financiers and owners in shipping operations. In the late empire they had a vital role in transporting the *annona*, the tax in kind which usually took the form of corn. Pottery could well have been included in these official movements of goods, particularly as *navicularii* were apparently able to transport a proportion of their own goods duty free (Jones, 1964:828).

For example, the *annona* could well account for the high proportion of African red-slip ware at Rome, and Middleton (1979:90) has suggested that the importation of southern Gaulish samian to the Rhine frontier may have accompanied corn levied in the Aquitaine. The *annona* is clearly an important factor in the long-distance transmission of pottery and doubtless it accounts for much long-distance 'trade' as economic historians have suggested. However, it was by no means the *only* mechanism of importance as is sometimes claimed. For example, Middleton (1979) suggested this to be the case when he discussed the distribution of monuments referring to traders and shippers in Gaul. These clearly emphasise the importance of the Rhône-Rhine route and of military supply. There can be no question of the vital strategic role played by these waterways, for this is corroborated by other evidence such as that of amphora distributions (Peacock, 1978; here Fig. 84). The Rhône and the Rhine comprised the main arteries of northwestern Europe and it is not surprising that great wealth was generated there which led to a proliferation of grave monuments and inscriptions. However, it does not follow that because these are scarce elsewhere, civilian markets failed to generate significant long-distance trade. Activity would have been more dispersed and perhaps individual profits less, but cumulatively these markets could have been of great importance to producers and traders alike.

Rivers attracted many smaller boatmen of which the *nautae* seem to have been the most important group. In Gaul inscriptions referring to them are found spread widely along the major rivers (Middleton, 1979:Fig 1) They presumably operated barges which were rowed or perhaps hauled from the river bank.

All these classes of men involved in trade seem to have been organised into distinct units. At Ostia, for example, the famous Piazzale delle Corporazioni seems to have been a centre for *navicularii* working in Italy. The square has some sixty-one small rooms opening off a colonnade and in front are mosaics illustrating the occupations of the owners. Many appear to have been concerned with the African corn trade (Meiggs, 1973:283). The precise function of these *stationes* is more difficult to assess. The Piazzale delle Corporazioni could have been a centre of official control or the offices could have been rented to individual businesses to provide an operational base in Italy. Alternatively they could have been shared by independent traders or shippers of common origin. Whether people such as the *negotiatores Britanniciani* formed discrete firms or loose connections remains an open question (Hassall, 1978:45).

However, all groups could be banded together into guilds or *collegia* which had their own clubhouse or *schola*. The contrast between these guilds and those of the Medieval period has been stressed too often. They may have been primarily social or burial clubs with little interest in the improvement of professional conditions and standards, but any association between members of the same profession must have led to the exchange of economically important information, as, for example, in London clubs at the present day. It is also worth noting that in the later Roman period official control was increasingly exercised through the medium of the *collegia*.

From this discussion it will be evident that water transport played a very important role in long-distance trade. While we know all too little about the specific means of transporting pottery, it seems reasonable to assume that water would have been used where practicable. Not only would the breakage rate be lower, but there are clear indications that it was very much cheaper than land transport (Jones, 1964:841). Using the sparse figures available in the price edict of Diocletian, Duncan-Jones (1974:368) calculates that inland waterways were 4.9 times more expensive than sea transport, while road journeys were a massive 28–56 times more costly than the equivalent distance at sea. These figures compare with those of eighteenth-century England or for developing countries at the present day (Clark and Haswell, 1967), and it is reasonable to assume therefore that whenever feasible water would be preferred to land as a means of moving goods. However, these bald figures are deceptive because they take no account of the costs of loading and unloading, and if a journey was complex, involving transference from one waterway to another, the apparent economies might be seriously offset.

From this brief sketch it should be evident that the mechanisms of long-distance trade were comparatively sophisticated and it is against this background that the distribution of amphorae and widely traded pottery must be viewed. If the practical problems of construction of realistic distribution maps can be overcome (p. 166), the archaeological evidence offers great scope for understanding the changing patterns of marketing throughout the Roman period. These might be anticipated from a sophisticated appreciation of production, for the emergence of certain modes may relate to the development of marketing arrangements (p. 106). The two are inseparably linked and ideally production and marketing should be studied simultaneously.

11 The study of Roman pottery: methods and approaches

... truth will meanwhile lie concealed far below, in the bottom of her well, until patiently solicited forth by some previously unthought of process...

Hugh Miller, *Testimony of the Rocks* (1897:348)

In the preceding chapters many questions have been posed but rather fewer answered and usually any suggestions have been very tentative. This is partly in the nature of archaeology, but it also reflects the poor data-base upon which our discussions must rest. In this chapter we will consider how the situation might be improved by reviewing the uses of pottery in Roman archaeology and discussing the approaches that have been adopted. It must be stressed that the object is not to provide guidelines for field or laboratory use for that has been attempted elsewhere (Young, 1980; Peacock, 1977b). Here we will debate more general issues which are an essential prerequisite to the design of specific research strategies.

It is now almost a commonplace that the collection and presentation of data should in some measure relate to specific questions. This is particularly pertinent to the study of Roman pottery for many an excavation report has been lost to posterity in the search for a complete, comprehensive, pottery section. The majority of ceramic reports are usually addressed, albeit unconsciously, to specific problems. Thus, because Roman archaeology has developed as an aid to Roman history, chronology has naturally played an essential role in order that sites may be fitted into the established framework. Pottery reports have reflected this interest: at worst nothing but the 'dateable' finds are described, at best there is a preoccupation with the sequence and with typological evolution; the reader will usually search in vain for discussion of other aspects. Of course, such criticism is easy to level but hard to remedy and

doubtless the most comprehensive programme of today will be inadequate by future standards. It is inevitable that as knowledge advances, questions change and yesterday's data are seldom adequate to solve today's problems. This applies with some force to Roman ceramic study and no doubt as the pace of research increases we shall face continuing obsolescence of both data and the methods by which it was gathered.

At present there seem to be three principal uses of pottery in Roman archaeology:

1. the provision of site dating;
2. the analysis of site function; and
3. the evaluation of economic matters through an appreciation of production and distribution.

Other aspects, such as the recognition of cultural zones or groupings, seem less relevant than they might be in other periods, but further work might prove this to be erroneous (e.g. Hodder, 1979).

In the following paragraphs an attempt will be made to review some of the principal methods of study now available and to point to major lacunae in our knowledge.

DATING

In this book chronology has not been stressed, but rather it has been taken for granted. It is nevertheless absolutely fundamental and many of the new directions of today are only feasible because of previous preoccupation with dating. On the other hand, there are still practising archaeologists who regard ceramics merely as a means to site chronology, thus endangering interesting developments in other directions.

It is often forgotten that ceramics are rarely

dateable in their own right, although there are exceptions. For example, amphorae, found in favourable places, sometimes bear painted inscriptions (*tituli picti*) which can include the date of manufacture in terms of the consular year, and if enough have been found it is possible to establish a chronological range for the types on which they occur (e.g. Zevi, 1966). Unfortunately, as Callender (1965) has noted, amphorae do not evolve rapidly in response to fashion as they are containers and providing they serve their purpose typological change is unnecessary. Equally, as the potter is not constrained by taste there is no reason to suppose that he would take particular care with slight nuances of form. Thus, although amphorae of types which bear inscriptions can be dated accurately, they can seldom be dated precisely, except in the rare circumstances where a *titulus* is actually preserved.

Brick stamps can sometimes be dated on their own merits. We have already mentioned the consular dates on examples from Holdeurn (p. 139), but the series from Rome is better known. In A.D. 110 *M. Rutilius Lupus* introduced a consular date into his stamp for a reason as yet undetermined. Thereafter dates are found sporadically until A.D. 164, except in A.D. 123, when all bricks were dated, presumably at the behest of the government (Bloch, 1947: 13).

It is ironical that the two classes of ceramics which show least typological variation should be those bearing the most precise dates. Other wares are rarely dateable in the same way, but occasionally pieces are found bearing coin impressions. Unfortunately the latter merely provide a *terminus post quem* for the impressions could have been made at almost any time after minting. Webster (1968) has described an Oxfordshire colour-coated sherd from Cirencester with the imprint of a *follis* of Maximian I (*c.* A.D. 300), but such instances, although valuable, are rare. Rather better known are the North African lamps which are decorated around the rim with impressions from a gold coin commemorating the *vicennalia* of Theodosius II in A.D. 430 (Hayes, 1972:313).

These exceptions apart, most pottery must be dated by its associations with other evidence. Written records, which can include both historical accounts and inscriptions, are vitally important. A good example of an historically documented event is the spectacular eruption of Vesuvius on 23 August A.D. 79, which furnishes a very precise *terminus ante quem* for material used in the towns devastated by the ash falls. Atkinson's (1914) study of a crate of samian ware found in a house at Pompeii is vitally important

for fine-ware studies, but regrettably much of the pottery from both Pompeii and Herculaneum has yet to be adequately published, and the potential of these sites has been barely realised.

Military sites, particularly those occupied for a short duration, provide another opportunity for correlating ceramics with historical events, for accounts of military activity survive in some detail. For example, the fort at Oberaden in northern Germany can be assigned to the campaigns of Drusus and was plausibly occupied for the short period 10–8 B.C. (Wells, 1972:220). Similarly the legionary fortress at Inchtuthil in Perthshire can be ascribed to the Scottish campaign of Agricola and thus dated *c.* A.D. 84–90 (Frere, 1967:110). The list need not be extended for the point has been made: it is sites such as these which provide the framework upon which Roman ceramic chronology rests. Obviously fine-wares such as Arretine or samian are particularly important for they are distinctive, they often bear the stamps of individual potters, they vary considerably with the passage of time and they were spread widely from relatively few centres. Closely contemporaneous types can be readily recognised on a wide range of sites so that they are an ideal common denominator in extrapolating from well-documented to undocumented sites.

A rather less direct means of historical correlation is provided by stratified associations with coins, which furnish much useful supplementary evidence. Coins can be difficult to use with confidence because they may be hoarded and remain out of circulation for long periods or they may have a long life before being lost. However, coins are particularly plentiful in the late Roman period and if there are enough in a given deposit, the youngest is likely to be near the date when the layer was formed, providing a *terminus ante quem* for associated pottery.

The Roman period is characterised by a wealth of such indications and in consequence the chronology of the principal fine-wares is now well established. Of course, the reliability of an estimated date relates directly to the number of chronological 'pegs' available. Where they are sparse, it may be necessary to estimate intervening points by assuming a more or less constant rate of typological evolution. This is the problem that bedevilled Hayes (1972) in his study of North African and other Mediterranean red-slip wares. Because of the scarcity of firm fixed points many of his suggested dates are 'best estimates' based upon the current state of knowledge. Not surprisingly new work, such as the international programme of excavation at Carthage, is causing substantial revision and refinement. This does not detract from the value of Hayes' masterly work, but rather it is a reflection of the inevitable and rapid advance of knowledge. The important lesson for the excavator is that ceramic dates are no better than the historical correlations that have been established.

So far we have been largely concerned with fine-wares which are most amenable to dating. Certain coarse-wares, such as mortaria, are also of considerable value because they often bear potters' stamps permitting precise between-site correlations, and like the fine-wares they were widely distributed from relatively few production centres (Hartley, 1973). However, in general, coarse-wares cannot be dated with precision. Many have restricted local distributions and so even if historical associations can be established it may be difficult to extrapolate with certainty beyond the immediate region. Furthermore, even if they are found widely, it is rash to assume that their lifespan will be restricted or that the typology will develop in a consistent or logical way. If a cooking pot or other utilitarian vessel serves its purpose, there is no reason why it should change since its form is governed by function rather than aesthetics. If evolution can be detected, it may result from the unconscious modification of a typological recipe by constant copying rather than an attempt to satisfy aspirations of the market. Naturally, coarse-wares *can* display change with the passage of time, but all too often modern research is showing that they do not respond to the rules established for the finer wares and much effort has been expended in chasing a will-o'-the-wisp. Dales ware, a type of hand-made cooking pot used over wide areas of northern Britain, is a good illustration. Loughlin's (1977) comments are worth considering for they may apply to many other coarse-ware types.

Following its emergence during the latter years of the second century A.D., Dales ware cannot truly be said to have developed typologically in any logical or recognizable fashion. Niceties of rim structure and angle of neckspring, and size and thickness of fabric of vessels, for so long considered to be diagnostic factors by typologists, can be ascribed to the idiosyncracies of individual potters working from day to day as readily as to unilinear 'typological progress' through time.

Having achieved the logical shape and size that its market, and its functions, demanded, Dales ware is a case study in artefact conservatism, with a two hundred year life.

However, even when pottery can be dated with tolerable accuracy, it need not date the context in which it was found and it is necessary to consider the way in which the archaeological assemblage was formed. Schiffer (1976) has discussed this in some detail, and he has conveniently systematised and formalised many of the factors which have long been appreciated by Romanists.

At the broadest level, Schiffer distinguishes cultural formation processes (c-transforms) from natural (n-transforms) which can include factors such as natural erosion or faunal activity. C-transforms are particularly important and a number of distinct processes can be isolated. Material may be transferred directly from the cultural system to the archaeological record (S-A transforms) and here Schiffer distinguishes normal and abandonment deposits. Normal processes can be further subdivided into discard, disposal of the dead and loss patterns while discard includes both primary and secondary refuse, depending upon whether the material is left *in situ* or transferred to another location. These obviously correspond to the 'occupation deposits' and secondary refuse which a good excavator of a Roman site will try to distinguish. Thus, much of the pottery from the Avenue Habib Bourguiba site at Carthage seemed to be deposited as rubbish or make-up derived from elsewhere, so that general conclusions rather than detailed functional analysis of the site were feasible (Fulford and Peacock, forthcoming, Chapter 11).

A-S transforms, where material in a cultural system is derived from an earlier archaeological deposit, usually by scavenging, is less important in the Roman period, although this process could account for the discovery of certain flints and stone axes on Roman sites or occasionally for the presence of much earlier sherds in late layers.

On the other hand A-A transforms, where material is transferred from one archaeological deposit to another, are very important in the Roman period for earlier residual material often occurs in later deposits, and the usual cause is the digging of foundations, which cut through earlier strata bringing debris to the surface and mixing it with contemporary material. Rubbish survival is perhaps the most important and the most intractable problem facing the pottery researcher. In areas where there is a detailed knowledge of the ceramic sequence, it should be possible to recognise a majority of residual forms, but where this data-base is lacking there may be no means of knowing whether some of the rarer types are contemporary or not. Thus among the published material from Vandal and Byzantine Carthage there may well be pieces which will ultimately prove to be Roman or even Punic (Fulford and Peacock, forthcoming).

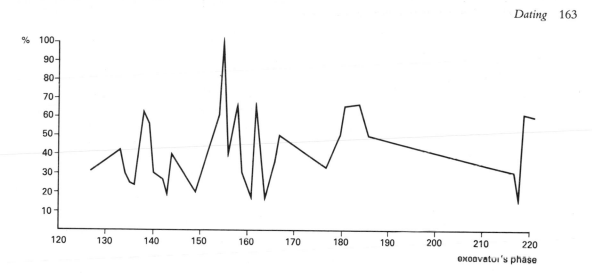

Figure 82 Quantities by weight of African amphorae recovered from part of the Avenue Habib Bourguiba site, Carthage. The deposits have not been selected and the rapidly fluctuating trend is probably a result of rubbish survival.

At present there seem to be but two sure ways of tackling the problem of rubbish survival:

1. residuality may be indicated by smaller, more abraded sherds (Bradley and Fulford, 1980);
2. if quantitative trends are plotted through time, rubbish survival may be indicated by an irregular fluctuating pattern (see Figs 82–3).

Of course, if well-dated fine-wares are present in quantity they can be used as a guide to the homogeneity of the deposit, but this presupposes a detailed knowledge of some of the pottery.

One final category worth considering is the S-S transform, where material is recycled or finds some secondary use and this clearly affects Roman archaeology to some extent. The use of amphorae as urinals or as water jars is a good example of secondary use (Grace, 1962; Callender, 1965). Also prized items can persist from one generation to another, and obviously fine pots might survive long after manufacture in use or as heirlooms. It is interesting to note that the shops and houses of Herculaneum and Pompeii contain occasional Dressel 1 wine amphorae, which should be about 80–90 years old at the time of burial if the accepted chronology is correct (Peacock, 1971).

Seriation or sequence dating has been little used on Roman pottery but it offers considerable scope for ordering material. The technique assumes regular patterns of change in the typological composition of pottery groups so the most similar assemblages will be closest in time. The method is by no means new

for it was first devised in the nineteenth century by Sir Flinders Petrie who used it to order material from certain Egyptian cemeteries dating *c.* 4000–2500 B.C. (Petrie, 1899; Kendall, 1963). Petrie's approach can be briefly summarised as follows. He firstly classified his grave goods, which were predominantly pottery, and established a type series, after which he proceeded to write the contents of each grave in order on a horizontal slip of paper or cardboard, one for each grave. The slips were placed roughly in sequence using any archaeological indications available, such as one grave cutting another, or knowledge of the broad sequence derived from elsewhere. Thereafter, the slips of paper were moved up and down by trial and error until similar graves were closest together. This is not as simple as it may seem for even with one hundred graves and the same number of artifact types, the number of permutations is astronomical and when some artifact types are brought into juxtaposition others will be thrown out of sequence. An approximation rather than perfection is the best that can be hoped for.

Of course nowadays sorting is greatly aided by the computer and new more refined methods have been devised. A full account has been given by Doran and Hodson (1975) and it would be superfluous to pursue the subject here as they have barely been applied to Roman pottery. However, it is worth noting that Millett (1975) has used seriation on groups of Farnham pottery recovered in his excavation of the small town of Neatham in Hampshire. He studied the frequency of different rim forms in each of his

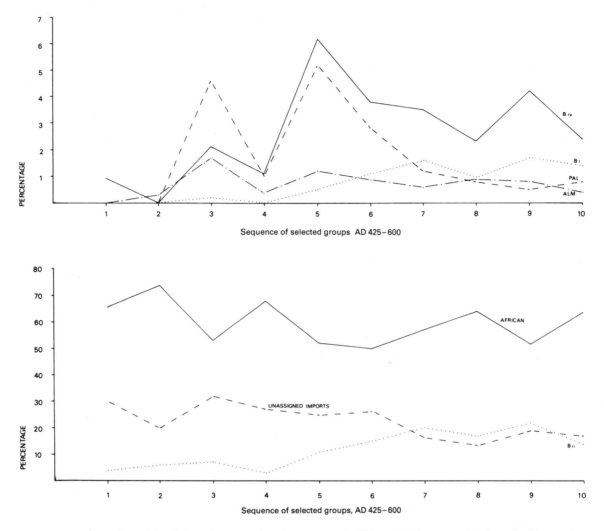

Figure 83   Quantities by weight of the main types of amphora current in fifth- and sixth-century Carthage. In this case the deposits used were selected on the homogeneity of the fine-ware assemblage and the much smoother trends probably reflect changing patterns of importation.

twenty-two groups and used a computer seriation to put them in order. The results were then checked against coin and samian evidence which suggested absolute dates for parts of the sequence, leading to an enhanced appreciation of the chronological development of Farnham ware. In this case the method seems to have produced useful results, but obviously in some situations rubbish survival could seriously interfere. In general it is perhaps best to regard seriation as a means of ordering cemetery rather than settlement data.

No account of ceramic chronology would be complete without at least a brief mention of the

methods currently being developed by archaeological scientists (e.g. Michels, 1973; Fleming, 1976). Several of these, such as radiocarbon or dendrochronology are of potential interest, for although they are not directly applicable to pottery, they can be of value in dating the contexts in which it is found. There seems little point in reiterating details of their principles, potential and limitations for these will be found in the works cited above. In any case they are of little value in Roman archaeology, since at present conventional methods offer far greater precision. The same applies to the two techniques which can be applied directly to pottery, namely thermoluminescence and archaeomagnetism, but these are worth mentioning if only because they utilise ceramic material.

Thermoluminescence (light output on heating) is a phenomenon displayed by many crystalline substances. Energy, originating in the spontaneous fission of radioactive particles, gradually accumulates in the crystal lattice until it is released by heating. Thus when a pot was fired in antiquity the geologically accumulated thermoluminescence would be 'drained off' and the clock set at zero; any thermoluminescence shown by an archaeological specimen will be proportional to the time that has elapsed since man interfered with the natural process. Most natural substances (including ceramic materials and the soils in which they are buried) contain minute quantities of radioactive impurity. If this radioactivity is measured, the susceptibility of the crystal to the accumulation of thermoluminescent energy assessed and the light output on heating recorded, an absolute date can be calculated. Unfortunately at present the accuracy is seldom better than about $\pm$ 10 per cent. Thus, in plain English, with a sample 1800 years old, there are two chances in three that the true age will lie between 1720 and 1980 years B.P.

Such a broad assessment is seldom of value in the Roman period, but the technique can be of considerable value in distinguishing forged and genuine ceramic antiquities. For example, it effectively demonstrated that certain brick stamps from the late Roman Shore Fort of Pevensey were modern forgeries. The inscriptions which read HON AUG ANDRIA were held to be the sole epigraphic mention of the activities of the emperor Honorius in Britain and hence they were of considerable historical interest. However, suspicion arose when it was realised that some of the finds were associated with Charles Dawson, discoverer of the notorious Piltdown man, and thermoluminescent tests provided a ready means of settling the matter for they showed the bricks to have been fired recently (Peacock, 1973).

Archaeomagnetic dating utilises the constantly changing direction and force of the earth's magnetic field, which remain 'fossilised' in fired materials containing minute iron oxide particles. By studying fired materials of known date it should be possible to chart the past progress of the earth's field and then to date unknown samples by comparing with established trends. Much of the early work concentrated on the direction of the earth's fields revealed by dated kilns and hearths, but in Britain the trend appears to be of little real use for during the Roman period the magnetic declination of the compass needle remained essentially unchanged while the angle of dip executed only a small oscillation. More recently, attempts have been made to study variations in the intensity of the earth's magnetism. This is of interest because artifacts need not be *in situ* and archaeomagnetic dates can be extended to pottery as well as kiln structures. However, it is perhaps unlikely that great precision will be achieved and this development may offer little real hope for the Romanist.

From this brief survey, it should be apparent that future refinements in Roman chronology are likely to emanate from archaeology rather than the natural sciences, but this could be proved wrong as archaeological science matures and develops. At present the priorities would seem to be, firstly, the excavation of more historically dated sites in the Mediterranean area using the best stratigraphical techniques and, secondly, more consideration of the problem of rubbish survival perhaps through a combination of statistical approaches and an enhanced appreciation of the way in which deposits form. Further development and investigation of seriation techniques might also be fruitful.

PRODUCTION SITES

Production sites are the key to a number of aspects of ceramic study. They are important in chronological evaluation, for a knowledge of origins can be vital, particularly if the same form is made in a number of places at different times. Conversely, production sites can produce evidence for the contemporaneity or sequence of different forms of common origin. However, above all, such sites are a guide to understanding the mode of production.

It is doubly unfortunate that our knowledge of production centres is totally inadequate to answer the questions that now seem most pressing, and this despite a very long history of research and publication. The main problems have already been mentioned, namely, the uneven spread of data and the poor quality of many published reports. However, even some of the most meticulous excavations have failed to explore more than the kiln structure, which is about as logical as merely stripping the rooms of a villa which contains mosaics or just examining the gateway of a fortress. Anyone who has visited a modern pottery will appreciate that firing is but one aspect of a complex process and the full range of activities will occupy a considerable area around the kiln. Even a minor pottery will require at least 500 square metres for the workshops, levigation tanks or for clay and fuel storage, but a majority of excavation trenches seem to cover a meagre 25–100 square metres. Although large-scale area excavations are now becoming a feature of modern archaeology, few production sites have benefited from these developments.

Our ethnographic discussion suggests that there is little hope of detecting household production or industry in the archaeological record solely by excavation. Petrological study might suggest suitable areas for the search, but it is quite possible to excavate a dwelling house where pottery was made and yet to detect no surviving traces of ceramic activity. Indeed, even today, one can visit villages which have only recently lost their household industry and be unable to see any trace of pottery-making.

However, workshop industries will normally leave very distinct traces and it is here that large-scale excavation is required with some urgency. We need an enhanced appreciation of the layout and functioning of individual workshops and if possible some knowledge of the relationship between potteries in nucleated industries. It goes without saying that the most meticulous modern methods must be adopted if we are to detect the processes recognised ethnographically.

However, even if such ventures are generally precluded by cost, much could be gained by adopting a more rigorous approach to small-scale work. For example, all too often there is no mention of how a kiln site relates to natural resources or to potential markets. Fuel remains are seldom analysed and rigorous quantitative data about products are often wanting. The study of fingerprints has rarely been attempted and yet this could furnish crucial evidence about the number of workers involved or of the relationship between potter and kiln builder. Detail of this type is vital in attempting to answer some of the questions posed by this book.

DISTRIBUTIONS

The study of ceramic distributions is the counterpart of the investigation of production and no kiln report can be considered complete unless some attempt has been made to assess the extent of the markets. In the Roman period this can present formidable problems because of the very wide distributions of certain types and the uneven spread of ceramic data. Vessels distributed solely within a given province or region are not difficult to study if reasonable comparative collections are described in the literature or housed in museums, but long-distance trade is another matter. The analysis of empire-wide distributions is hazardous because of the differential availability of data and it is all too easy to chart the intensity of archaeological work rather than an ancient phenomenon.

One way round this problem is to compare the ceramic distribution with other evidence recovered in a different manner, a point well illustrated by my recent assessment of the distribution of Gaulish wine amphorae (Fig. 84). The distribution shows a clear predilection for the Rhône-Rhine axis, raising the question whether this was really the principal way in which southern Gaulish goods were transmitted to the north or whether the distribution is basically a reflection of the concentrated work on the German *limes* (Peacock, 1978). There are two reasons for supposing that the pattern is real rather than illusory. Firstly, the same type of amphora can be seen depicted on bas-reliefs which are found in both Provence and the Rhineland, providing a control of a different nature, and secondly the distribution contrasts with that of other types of amphora such as Dressel 1 or North African cylindricals (Peacock, 1971; 1977b). In other words amphorae have been discovered in the blank parts of the map and if the Gaulish vessels had been present in quantity it is reasonable to conclude that at least some would have been recorded. Without these supporting indications it would have been hard to regard the map as a valid archaeological document.

In view of these difficulties it is not surprising that long-range distribution maps are seldom attempted for the Roman period, but regional ones are an increasingly common feature of modern research. Often the quality of the data precludes all but the simplest presentation, with merely a dot to indicate a find-spot. However, as Hodder (1974a/b) has demonstrated there is much to be gained on occasions where more sophisticated data are available. It is particularly useful to indicate quantities (usually as a percentage of the total pottery assemblage) and it is important to know whether the sample is complete or whether it has been selectively discarded after recovery. In addition, it can be instructive to indicate contemporary assemblages which have failed to produce the type being considered, and of course it is vital to know the absolute size of the groups as this can materially affect the validity of comparisons.

If all this information is considered, the distribution map becomes a very useful analytical

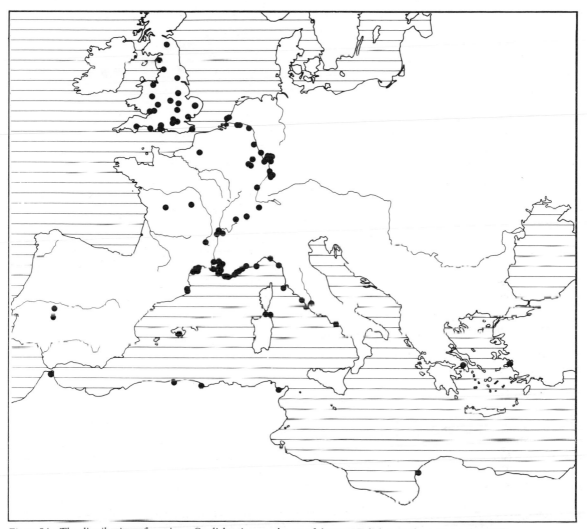

Figure 84   The distribution of southern Gaulish wine amphorae of the type Pelichet 47 (from Peacock, 1978).

tool, but at the same time interpretation and analysis becomes considerably more complex. Under ideal circumstances we might expect both the number of find-sites and quantities to diminish with increasing distance from a production centre. However, this simple relationship is rarely discernible because the ideal may be disturbed by factors such as the function of the find-site, topography and method of transport, or the situation of the markets and marketing methods. On the other hand these parameters are of greatest interest and their elucidation is often the prime objective of any spatial analysis.

If we look at the distribution in another manner and plot a graph of frequency against distance from source, more often than not the result is a

'plum-pudding' scatter of points rather than a straight line and a trend may be barely discernible. Since the deviation from the straight line is produced by the factors we are studying, it follows that statistical methods which analyse such discrepancies could produce archaeologically relevant information.

Regression analysis is one such tool and Fulford and Hodder's (1975) study of late Roman Oxford and New Forest pottery distributions provides a brilliant illustration of its potential. Figure 85 shows the percentage of Oxford pottery on sites at increasing distance from the production area. The line through the points is the best-fit linear regression, while the dotted line shows the decrease in New Forest pottery away from the New Forest kilns. The deviation from

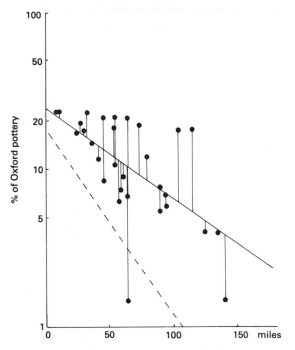

Figure 85   Best-fit linear regression line for the decrease in Oxford pottery with increasing distance from the kilns. The dotted line shows the decrease in New Forest pottery away from the New Forest kilns (after Fulford and Hodder, 1975).

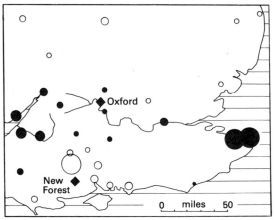

Figure 86   Regression residuals for the distribution of Oxford pottery; the size of the circles indicates the magnitude of the residuals. Filled circles, positive residuals; open circles, negative residuals (after Fulford and Hodder, 1975).

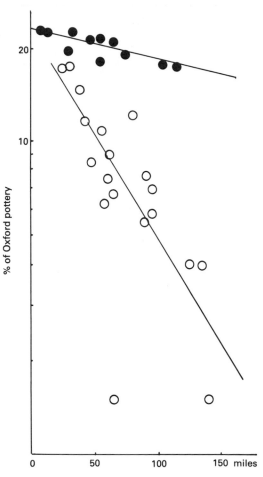

Figure 87   The decrease in Oxford pottery away from the kilns. Filled circles, sites to which water transport could have been important; open circles, sites not easily reached by water (after Fulford and Hodder, 1975).

the straight line could reflect the unreliability of the sample, but an attempt was made to search for meaningful patterning. The deviation of each site percentage from the regression line was calculated and the 'residuals' plotted on a map (Fig. 86). The result is interesting, for negative residuals are greatest around the New Forest where presumably the competition was too great for Oxford wares to make much impact, but marked positive residuals are to be seen east and west of the production area, leading to the conclusion that water transport was extensively used in distributing Oxford but not New Forest pottery. A further plot, dividing the 'by land' and 'by water' distributions, confirms this, for it produced much straighter lines (Fig. 87), the different slopes reflecting the differential cost of land and water transport (p. 159).

Figure 88 shows another aspect of the analysis, this time comparing distance and percentages for both Oxford and New Forest products. Since all the sites do not lie on a straight line between Oxford and the

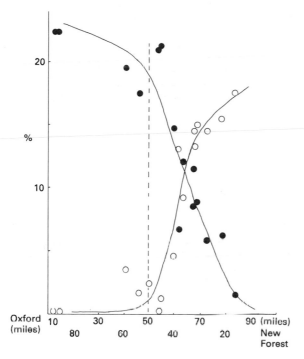

Figure 88 The decrease in Oxford and New Forest pottery in the area between the two kilns. Filled circles, Oxford pottery; open circles, New Forest pottery. The dotted line is the mid point between the two kiln centres (after Fulford and Hodder, 1975).

CONSUMER SITES

By now it should be apparent that much of our knowledge of marketing must derive from an evaluation of the consumption patterns, and there is a great need for quantitative information which will add precision to fuzzy qualitative claims and provide material for more sophisticated rigorous testing.

The ceramic worker, examining material from an occupation site, is at once confronted with the major obstacle of classification. Before he can begin quantitative assessment, he must firstly identify sources or characterise and discriminate wares of different but unknown origins. In northwestern Europe much is known of production sites and the correct identification of wares is mainly a question of knowledge and experience. In practice, however, the subject has become highly specialised and it is customary to divide material into categories such as samian, mortaria, colour-coated wares or amphorae which are then studied by experts in each field. The more local regional coarse-wares are usually described by the man on the spot who will have greater knowledge of production in the area and access to comparative material.

Of course, even under the best circumstances it will be impossible to assign all wares to their respective kilns, but some attempt will be made to subdivide on the basis of fabric and form. In studying fabric, visual classification is important but scientific analysis has a role to play and petrology is a particularly valuable tool. It may help to determine the reality of visual assessments, to furnish unambiguous descriptions and perhaps to suggest an origin if distinctive rocks and minerals are present in the fabric. Chemical analysis, particularly by neutron activation (which ranks among the more fruitful approaches), is a valuable way of characterising the finer wares and of determining the number of production centres involved. If kiln waste is available for comparison some suggestions about sources might be feasible. In general, however, chemical analysis is better suited to a regional rather than a site-by-site approach.

In the more southerly parts of the Roman empire the problems of identification are much greater for there are fewer workers and the examination of production sites has hardly begun. In Tunisia, for example, a major producer of pottery in Roman times, we know of a single kiln producing red slip ware at Oudna and an amphora kiln, as yet unpublished, at Ariana, near Tunis. In a situation such as this, much greater reliance must be placed on

New Forest, the distance from each site is expressed as a ratio of the total distance between each centre. The curves fitted by eye show a symmetrical relationship with distance. The point where the two curves cross is particularly interesting: it lies some 34 km (21 miles) from the New Forest and 62 km (39 miles) from Oxford. This is almost exactly the position predicted by Reilly's 'breaking-point formula', the calculated distance from Oxford being 61 km (38 miles). Reilly's formula seeks to relate service areas to the relative size of two centres and the distance between them. In this case the size was assessed by measuring the area containing known kilns and it is perhaps surprising that the actual and theoretical results should correspond so exactly.

There have been few further applications of regression analysis to Roman pottery, but Millett's (1979) study of Farnham ware is an exception. Regression analysis is but one of a range of statistical tools and the example discussed above serves to emphasise the power of such techniques. There is little point in further elaboration for they have yet to be applied to Roman pottery and a full account is given by Hodder and Orton (1976).

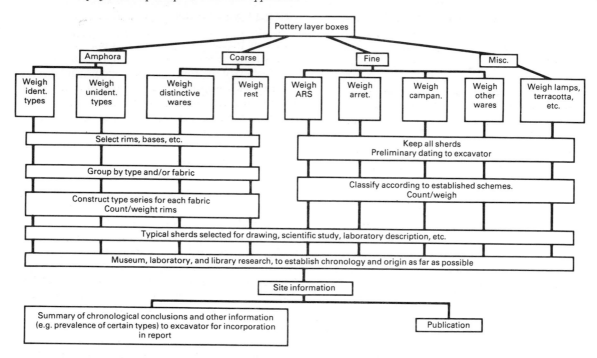

Figure 89 The pottery processing scheme used by the British team at Carthage.

fabric as a guide to origin, and for this reason petrology was an integral part of the investigation of pottery from the British excavations at Carthage (Fulford and Peacock, forthcoming). Details of the processing scheme which is summarised in Fig. 89 need not concern us for they are discussed in the first report now in press, but it is worth outlining the problems and the approaches adopted in their solution.

The fine wares, such as the African red-slip, presented little problem for they could be classified by referring to the standard works such as that of Hayes (1972), and similarly some of the amphorae were of readily recognisable types. However, the bulk of the pottery belonged to classes which have seldom been published and almost never been the subject of detailed typological analysis. The problem was approached by dividing the material into broad categories, such as hand-made wares, amphorae, mortaria, jugs, bowls, cooking pots etc. and then establishing a type series for each. This series was then used as a basis for quantification, and of course it steadily grew as the work proceeded. In addition to counting rim sherds, weights were established, and body sherds were included in this. Some of these were very distinctive and could be readily assigned to

well-known forms; others were less so and it was possible to do no more than class them as 'coarse-ware', amphora or 'fine-ware'. Thus the data are inevitably somewhat uneven, but it is possible to assess the proportion of a given type in any phase either by using weight or rim counts.

With a mass of material totalling over 15 tons, it was obviously impossible to study the fabric of every sherd, as one might hope to do in a smaller collection. Assessment of origins was therefore restricted to the type series, and sherds comprising the reference collection were carefully examined and classified under the binocular microscope after which a number of samples was selected for examination in thin-section under the petrological microscope. The objective was to construct a fabric series for each major vessel category. The final stage involved cross-referencing the individual fabrics for each category so that a master series was built up for the whole assemblage. Thus if the fabrics are taken as an indication of origins it is a simple matter to see which forms are originating in different places and from the quantitative data to assess the importance of each. Of course not all fabrics are easy to characterise; imports from volcanic areas such as Italy can be isolated without difficulty but often only the commoner rock-forming minerals are present and one fabric tends to merge with another. Firm divisions can be drawn where there are differences in the composition of inclusions but where these are absent it is necessary to make judgements on the basis of differences in texture of inclusions. This is a somewhat hazardous procedure but clear distinctions can usually be made where differences are accompanied by typological contrasts.

Of course this does not help in assessing the points of origin except where the sherds are petrologically distinctive. However, an attempt was made to define broad fabric provinces by looking at recent pottery and brick fabrics in Tunisia and by studying the variation in fabric types on ancient sites down the Tunisian coast. This is very much second best to the study of kiln material and any suggested sources must be regarded as a tentative interim statement.

Clearly the research strategy for studying assemblages of pottery from consumer sites must be dictated by the quantity and quality of the background information available. Nevertheless, whatever approach is adopted, if the pottery is worthy studying at all it is a duty of the pottery reporter to provide some form of quantified assessment. There is nothing new in this, for Hawkes and Hull (1947) long ago demonstrated the value of recording quantities when they included 'chronological tables of incidence by form' in their Camulodunum report. Without such data both intra- and inter-site comparisons are difficult and study of the economic aspects can hardly begin.

Unfortunately, quantification takes time and resources, and all too often the excavator ranks other objectives more highly. Thus, Wheeler (1972) when berated for publishing only seventy-nine sherds from 5 years' excavation retorted: 'Wheeler's task was not a rescue dig in a back garden. His subject was to put Verulamium – Belgic no less than Roman – upon the map.' This attitude, which dies hard in Roman archaeology, partly accounts for the poor quality of the Roman ceramic record. Faced with architectural and historical *richesse*, who can devote time and money to counting mere potsherds?

However, it is encouraging to record the growing number of sites for which quantitative data is now available. Portchester (Fulford, 1975a) has already been mentioned, while in the Mediterranean data are available from Carthage, Benghazi, Caesarea, Ostia and Luni (Fulford and Peacock, forthcoming; Riley, 1975a, 1981; Carandini *et al.*, 1968; Carandini and Panella, 1977; Frova, 1977). This painstaking work is a step towards a much larger goal but a framework

for more advanced thought is emerging and Finley's (1973:33) plea for a more sophisticated approach to quantification and pattern construction is gradually being realised.

Nevertheless, on the debit side, there is no doubt that the overall adoption of quantification, by whatever means, will greatly escalate excavation costs, so that conscientious pottery work must imply less excavation for the same outlay. At Carthage the British excavations alone produced 15 tons of pottery which took 500 man-days to sort in the field and at least double that figure in preparing the archive and the final report. The pottery work accounted for about 25 per cent of the excavation costs. This high input of resources can be justified, because Carthage was a great trading city and it was important to extract maximum evidence of economic activity. Since there was virtually no substantial body of data available for the area, a *total* examination of the material seemed desirable. With the wisdom of hindsight this judgement might be questioned, but there is no doubt that such massive ventures cannot be countenanced indefinitely. Not only is the cost prohibitive, but the work is tedious and there will ultimately be a shortage of suitably qualified people willing to undertake it. It is clear that if Roman pottery studies are to develop and mature, it is necessary to reduce the problem to manageable proportions by adopting an acceptable means of selecting or sampling the evidence.

There are three general types of sampling procedure: judgement sampling, haphazard sampling and probability sampling (Redman, 1974). Of these, judgement sampling is the most subjective for the selection is based on the experience of the researcher. Haphazard sampling involves the chance selection of material for study, perhaps by opening every tenth bag or 'at random'. This may be a useful preliminary guide for it will give a general impression of the material to be studied. However, 'grab samples' taken in this way are seldom truly random or representative of the whole sherd population. As Redman (1974) has said: 'The crucial misconception of grab samples is the belief that a *random* sample is one chosen haphazardly, whereas a random sample is actually one selected according to very strict mathematical rules that ensure against conscious or unconscious biases.' This *probability* sampling would normally involve recourse to devices such as a random numbers table as a basis for selection.

There is no doubt that probability sampling can be of considerable value where all the units to be sampled are of more or less equal value and bags of finds from systematic surface collection provide a good example. However, had we applied this method uncritically to excavated material from Carthage the result would have been nothing less than a disaster. We would have inadvertently selected many of the abundant deposits dominated by residual material and would probably have discarded many of the assemblages which ultimately proved most helpful. Of course excavated deposits are not all of equal value; some are useful, others less so. The excavator may have a particular interest in the data from certain crucial layers or in the evidence for site function contained in deposits which accumulated while the site was occupied. The pottery researcher might have a totally different set of priorities. He might be interested in those layers which are sealed with independent dating evidence, or he may want to build up a sequence of uncontaminated layers so that changes in the composition of the assemblage can be studied diachronically.

Any selection strategy must have two sides. The excavator must make his selection of worthwhile deposits based on the stratigraphy of the site. The pottery worker must attempt to amplify this selection by choosing ceramically homogeneous assemblages which will normally be indicated by the homogeneity of the dateable fine-wares present. What is recommended therefore is a form of judgement sampling where the selection is by archaeological criteria. This may seem a fairly obvious approach, but its adoption on large excavations will necessitate a re-evaluation of the traditional relationship between excavator and pottery worker since the two types of fieldwork, excavation and pottery-sorting, can no longer take place side by side. A worker with considerable knowledge and skill in fine-wares will be required on the dig: his function will be to supply the excavator with pottery dates and to select those deposits which appear to be homogeneous, but the main sorting will have to take place when the excavation is finished and the detailed phasing has been done so that the stratigraphically crucial deposits can be isolated.

Of course it is important not to reduce the problem too far and the above scheme can be seen as a means of selecting a basic minimum which might then be expanded by probabilistic sampling of the remaining less vital material.

In this chapter an attempt has been made to discuss some principles and outline some problems. Pottery constitutes a vast untapped reserve of data, perhaps unparalleled in any other aspect of Roman archaeology. If it is to be exploited properly and fully some careful thinking and reassessment is required now.

12 Concluding Remarks

What doth Invention but together place
The blocks of a child's game to make it whole?

Robert Underwood Johnson,
Psalm of Happiness in Nature,
1920

Since 1956, when C. P. Snow voiced misgiving about the growing gulf between the arts and sciences, archaeology has often been held as a meeting-place of the two cultures, for there can be few subjects which draw on such a wide spectrum of external disciplines. At its best archaeology can blend many strands of evidence derived from art history or linguistics on the one hand, to nuclear science, mathematics or medicine on the other. Ceramic studies are a microcosm of the discipline as a whole; the form and decoration of vessels can be a subject for the art historian, graffiti and stamps for the epigraphist, while the fabric can be analysed by the geologist, chemist or physicist. In addition, food remains or even organic matter preserved within the pores of a pot can be studied by biologists or organic chemists, and data of all types are the better for rigorous statistical treatment by the mathematician.

Unfortunately there is a gulf between reality and the ideal, in both archaeology as a whole and in ceramic studies, for instead of an integrated approach there is a tendency to spawn numerous subdisciplines characterised by insufficient intercommunication. It is as though the great divide between the two cultures has been replaced by numerous minor clouds of mutual incomprehension. For example, in the field of ceramics there are those who prefer to labour as though there was no alternative to traditional approaches, when fabric analysis might enlighten an otherwise intractable problem. On the other hand there are far too many scientists willing to analyse pottery without reference to the archaeological aspects of the material they are considering. It would

be invidious to name names, – but the literature of archaeological science abounds with papers in which both the material and the subsequent results are inadequately evaluated from an archaeological point of view. The outcome is often an interesting, and frustrating, contribution to methodology which adds virtually nothing to our knowledge of pottery and the past.

Of course, it is natural that workers should be happiest within their own discipline or techniques, for to venture into unknown fields is to risk falling into the trap of blind acceptance. It is much easier to erect defences: all too often the scientist sees conventional methods as insufficiently rigorous, while the archaeologist may cite a single dubious or erroneous analysis as grounds for dismissing the approach as a whole.

It cannot be stressed too strongly that pottery is inherently complex and no one method of evaluating it can stand alone. It is only by collecting a wide spectrum of data and weighing one piece of evidence against another that we are are ever likely to approach to the truth.

However, the problem runs deeper, for superimposed upon this picture of divided approaches is the compartmentalisation of archaeology itself, and, in Europe at least, the subject is firmly split into period specialisations. Not surprisingly, ceramic work follows suit with experts concentrating on prehistoric, Roman, Medieval and post-Medieval pottery, but seldom on more than one of these. Interchange of ideas is rare, partly because it is difficult to master more than one field, but partly because ceramic studies have been concerned with the nuts and bolts of the subject: general themes which form the common ground have hardly been formulated, let alone discussed. It is true that this book concentrates on one period, but the general processes debated will certainly have relevance in understanding the ceramic industries of complex societies of different periods and in different parts of the world. On the other hand, it might be argued that study of other systems would have brought unperceived facets into sharp relief which might in turn have enhanced our understanding of the Roman industry. There is much to be said for an approach which cuts across cultural, geographical and chronological barriers. If increasing period specialisation is inevitable from a pragmatic point of view, it needs to be tempered with greater emphasis on broader issues. At present we are in grave danger of, almost literally, not seeing the wood for the trees.

Integration and communication is a key issue in ceramic archaeology. The same problem recurs in the relationship of ethnography to archaeology, for in Europe the two subjects have unfortunately developed as separate disciplines. The ethnographical literature on pottery can be frustrating for the archaeologist, as the questions posed and the data gathered are seldom suited to answering archaeological questions. There is no doubt that new specifically ethnoarchaeological studies are required and are required with some urgency. Pottery-making is declining all over the world as piped water and modern cookers make their appearance, so that in a few years much will be lost irremediably. The threat is as great as that facing rescue or salvage archaeology and the loss to our understanding of the past just as serious – perhaps more so.

On the other hand, the flow of information between the ethnographer and the archaeologist need not always be in one direction for the latter is able to appreciate developments within a time dimension, and greater co-operation and integration could be of mutual benefit. The static nature of ethnographic information has already been stressed, but this deficiency could be overcome by the greater use of historical and archaeological methods to trace the development of a surviving industry and such an approach would be of immense value in appreciating the causes of change in ceramic industries. Similarly the demise of Roman pottery production has not been discussed in this book and at present ethnographic evidence offers few instructive insights. However, we are currently in an era where potteries are rapidly declining due to social and economic change. It would be of greatest value to know more of the process: which of the modes of production is affected first and which survives longest; at what point and why does a pottery become uneconomic; under what circumstances will a potter produce radically new lines to survive rather than turning to another career? The list of questions is considerable, but there is little data available to attempt an answer.

It is not unfair to remark, in conclusion, that ceramic studies are becoming far too parochial, and unless we can balance meticulous data gathering with broader synthetic thought, we are in danger of learning more and more about less and less. Pottery is, in itself, a small and often insignificant part of a culture, but archaeologically it is a subject worthy of the most careful scrutiny, not for its own sake, but because of the conclusions to which it can lead. In this book I have raised far more questions that I have solved, but hopefully I have conveyed something of the potential and interest in the study as a whole by concentrating on a small facet of industrial organisation within one of the greatest and most formative cultures the world has seen.

Bibliography

Adamasteanu, D. (1960) Scavi e recerche nei dintorni di Gela, *Not. Scav.* **14**, 211–46.

Adamasteanu, D. (1955) Due problemi topografici del retroterra galese, *Rend. Acc. Lincei* **10**, 205–10.

Adams, R. McC. (1974) Anthropological perspectives on ancient trade, *Current Anthr.* **15**, 239–58.

Albertos Solera, M. D., Carretero Pérez, A. and Fernández Montes, M. (1978) *Estudio etnográfico de la alfarería Conquense*, Cuenca.

Alcock, L. (1971) *Arthur's Britain*, Harmondsworth.

Amand, M. (1971) L'Industrie de la ceramique dans le site du Bois de Flinès à Howardries, *Arch. Belgica* **127**, 1–75.

Applebaum, S. (1972) Roman Britain, Ch. XII in H. P. R. Finberg (Ed.) *The Agrarian History of England and Wales*, Vol. 1, Cambridge, 223–49.

Arthur, P. (1978) The lead glazed wares of Roman Britain, in P. Arthur and G. Marsh (Eds) *Early Fine Wares in Roman Britain*, B. A. R. **57**, 293–356, Oxford.

Artis, E. T. (1828) *The Durobrivae of Antoninus*, London.

Atkinson, D. (1942) *Report on Excavation at Wroxeter (the Roman City of Viroconium) in the County of Salop 1923–1927*, Birmingham.

Atkinson, D. (1914) A hoard of samian ware from Pompeii, *J. Rom. Stud.* **4**, 27–64.

Balfet, H. (1973) A propos du tour de potier: l'outil et le geste technique, in *L'Homme hier et aujourd'hui, recueil d'études en hommage à André Leroi-Gourhan*, Paris, 109–22.

Balfet, H. (1966) Ethnographical observations in North Africa and archaeological interpretation, in F. T. Matson (Ed.) *Ceramics and Man*, Chicago and London, 161–77.

Barton, K. J. (1974) The medieval blackwares of northern France, in V. I. Evison, H. Hodges and J. G. Hurst (Eds) *Medieval Pottery from Excavations*, London, 167–82.

Beckinsale, M. and Beckinsale, R. (1975) *Southern Europe. The Mediterranean and Alpine Lands*, London.

Beltrán Lloris, M. (1978) *Cerámica romana, tipologia y clasificación*, Zaragosa.

Beltrán Lloris, M. (1970) *Las ánforas romanas en Espana*, Zaragosa.

Beltrán Martinez, A. (1949) *Arqueologia Clásica*, Madrid.

Benoit, F. (1956) Epaves de la côte de Provence. Typologie des amphores, *Gallia* **14**, 23–34.

Benoit, F. (1940) L'usine de meunerie hydraulique de Barbégal (Arles), *Rev. Arch.* **116**, 19–80.

Berger, L. (1969) *Ein römischer Ziegelbrennofen bei Kaiseraugst, Ausgrabungen in Augst III*, Basel.

Bidwell, P. T. and Boon, G. C. (1976) An antefix type of the second Augustan Legion from Exeter, *Britannia* **7**, 278–80

Bimson, M. (1956) The technique of Greek Black and Terra-Sigillata Red, *Ant. J.* **36**, 200–4.

Binford, L. R. (1968) Methodological considerations of the archaeological use of ethnographic data, in R. B. Lee and I. De Vore (Eds) *Man the Hunter*, Chicago.

Bird, J. (1977) African red slip ware in Roman Britain, in J. Dore and K. Greene, op. cit., 269–78.

Birmingham, J. (1967) Pottery making in Andros, *Expedition* **10** (1), 33–6.

Bivins, J. Jr (1972) *The Moravian Potters in North Carolina*, Chapel Hill.

Bladen, V. W. (1926) The Potteries in the Industrial Revolution, *Econ. Hist.* **1**, 117–30.

Blegen, C. W. and Lang, M. (1960) The Palace of Nestor, Excavations 1919, *Amer. J. Arch.* **64**, 153–64.

Bloch, H. (1947) *I bolli laterizi e la storia edilizia romana*, from *Bull. Comm.*, 1936–38, Rome, 64–6.

Bolton, E. G. (1968) Romano-British pottery kiln at Greetham, Rutland, *Trans. Leics. A. and H.S.* **43**, 1–3.

Bonis, E. G. (1977) Das Töpferviertel am Kurucdomb von Brigetio, *Folia Arch.* **28**, 105–42.

Boon, G. C. (1967) Micaceous sigillata from Lezoux at Silchester, Caerleon, and other sites, *Ant. J.* **47**, 27–42.

Boon, G. C. (1966) 'Legionary' Ware at Caerleon?, *Arch. Camb.* **115**, 45–66.

Bourne, G. (or Sturt, G.) (1919) *William Smith. Potter and farmer 1790–1858*, London.

Bradley, R. (1971) Trade competition and artefact distribution, *World Arch.* **2**, 347–52.

Bradley, R. and Fulford, M. (1980) Sherd size in the analysis of occupation debris, *Bull. Inst. Arch. London* **17**, 85–94.

Brassington, M. (1971) A Trajanic kiln complex near Little Chester, Derby, *Ant. J.* **51**, 36–69.

Brears, P. D. C. (1972) Techniques of the Truro pottery, *Folk Life* **10**, 47–54.

Brears, P. D. C. (1971) *The English Country Pottery*, Newton Abbot.

Breeze, D. J. (1977) The fort at Bearsden and the supply of pottery to the Roman army, in J. Dore and K. Greene, op. cit., 113–45.

Brodribb, G. (1979) Markings on tile and brick, in A. McWhirr (1979a), 211–20.

Brown, A. E. and Sheldon, H. (1975) Highgate Wood: the pottery and its production, *London Archaeologist* **2**, 222–31.

Bruno, W. (1954) Tegel industrien i mälarprovinserna 1815–1950, *Geog. skrifter Uppsala Univ.* **28**.

Bruzza, P. L. (1875) Scoperta di figuline in Pozzuoli, *Bull. dell' 1st.di Corr. Arch.*, 242–56.

Bryant, G. F. Romano-British experimental kiln firings at Barton on Humber, England, 1968–1975 *Acta praehist et arch*, **9/10** 13–22

Bryant, G. F. (1973) Experimental Romano-British kiln firings, in A. Detsicas, op. cit., 149–60.

Bryant, G. F. (1971) *Experimental Romano-British Kiln Firings*, WEA, Barton-on-Humber Branch, Occasional paper No. 1.

Buckland, P. C., Magilton, J. R. and Dolby, M. J. (1980) The Roman pottery industries of south Yorkshire: a review, *Britannia* **11**, 145–64.

Bulmer, M. (1980) An introduction to Roman samian ware, *J. Chester Arch. Soc.* **62**, 5–72.

Burford, A. (1972) *Craftsmen in Greek and Roman society*, London.

Burnham, B. C. and Johnson, H. B. (Eds) (1979) *Invasion and Response: The Case of Roman Britain*, B. A. R. **73**.

Calkin, J. B. (1935) An early Romano-British kiln at Corfe Mullen, Dorset, *Ant. J.* **15**, 42–55.

Callender, M. H. (1965) *Roman Amphorae*, Oxford.

Carandini, A. and Panella, C. (Eds) (1977) *Ostia IV* (= Studia Miscellanei 23) Rome.

Carandini, A. and Settis, S. (1979) *Schiavi e padroni nell'Etruria romana: la villa di Settefinestre dallo scavi alla mostra*, Bari.

Carandini, A. *et al.* (1968) *Ostia 1* (= Studia Miscellanei 13) Rome.

Cartier, F. and J. (1966) Four de potier gallo-romain à Aux-Marais (Oise), *Celticum* **15**, 225–52.

Casson, S. (1951) The modern pottery trade in the Aegean: further notes, *Antiquity* **25**, 187–90.

Casson, S. (1938) The modern pottery trade in the Aegean, *Antiquity* **12**, 464–73.

Castle, S. A. (1972) A kiln of the potter Doinus, *Arch. J.* **129**, 69–88.

Champion, B. (1916) Outils en fer du Musée de Saint-Germain: outils servant aux potiers, *Rev. Arch.* **3**, 244.

Charleston, R. (1955) *Roman Pottery*, London.

Chase, G. H. (1916) *Catalogue of Arretine Pottery*, Museum of Fine Arts, Boston.

Chaton, R. and Talbot, H. (1977) *La Borne et ses potiers*, La Charité sur Loire.

Chenet, G. (1927) Céramique gallo-romaine d'Argonne. Les ateliers de la vallée de la Biesme. *Bull. Soc. Arch. champenoise*, 76–96.

Chenet, G. and Gaudron, G. (1955) *La céramique sigillée d'Argonne des IIe et IIIe siècles*, Gallia Suppl. **6**, Paris.

Chiva, I. and Ojalvo (1959) La poterie corse à l'amiante, *Arts et Traditions Populaires* **7**, 203–27.

Čičikova, M. (1974) 'Firmalampen' du *limes* danubien en Bulgarie, in D. M. Pippidi (Ed.) *Actes du IXe Congrès International d'étude sur les frontières romaines*, Bucarest, 155–66.

Cintas, P. (1950) *Ceramique Punique*. Tunis.

Clark, A. J. (1949) The fourth century Romano-British pottery kilns at Overwey, Tilford, *Surrey Arch. Coll.* **51**, 29–56.

Clark, C. and Haswell, M. (1967) *The economics of subsistence agriculture*. London.

Cleere, H. (1974) The Roman iron industry of the Weald and its connexions with the *Classis Britannica, Arch. J.* **131**, 171–99.

Collis, J. (1977) An approach to the Iron Age, in J. Collis (Ed.) *The Iron Age in Britain – A Review*, Sheffield, 1–7.

Combès, J. L. and Louis, A. (1967) *Les potiers de Djerba*, Tunis.

Comfort, H. (1940) Terra sigillata, in T. Frank *Economic Survey of Ancient Rome, vol v*, Baltimore, 188–94.

Comfort, H. (1936) A preliminary study of late Italian sigillata, *Amer. J. Arch.* **40**, 437–51.

Cook, R. M. (1961) The 'double stoking tunnel' of Greek kilns, *Ann. Brit. Sch. Athens* **56**, 64–7.

Corder, P. (1957) The structure of Romano-British pottery kilns, *Arch. J.* **94**, 10–27.

Corder, P. (1950) *A Romano-British Pottery Kiln on the Lincoln Racecourse*, Nottingham.

Corder, P. (1930) *The Roman Pottery at Throlam, Holme on Spalding Moor, East Yorkshire*, Roman Malton and District Report 3.

Cortés Vázquez, L. (1958) Alfarería femenina en Moveros (Zamora), *Zephyrus* **9**, 95–107.

Cortés Vázquez, L. (1954) La alfareria en Pereruela (Zamora), *Zephyrus* **5**, 141–63.

Crawford, O. G. S. (1936) Modern red-burnished pottery in Grand Canary, *Antiquity* **10**, 86–7.

Cunliffe, B. W. (1974) *Iron Age Communities in Britain*, London.

Cunliffe, B. W. (1973) *The Regni*, London.

Cunliffe, B. W. (1970) The Saxon culture sequence at Portchester Castle, *Ant. J.* **50**, 67–85.

Cunliffe, B. W. (1961) Report on the excavations on the Roman pottery kiln at Hallcourt Wood, Shedfield, Hampshire (1960), *Proc. Hants. F. C.* **22**, 8–24.

Cuomo di Caprio, N. (1977) Una fornace a Mozia, *Sicilia Archeologica* **10**, 7–14.

Cuomo di Caprio, N. (1972) Proposta di classificazione delle fornaci per ceramica e laterizi nell'area italiana, *Sibrium* **11**, 371–464.

Curtis, F. (1962) The utility pottery industry of Bailén, Southern Spain, *Amer. Anthrop.* **64**, 486–503.

Dannell, G. (1971) The samian pottery, in B. W. Cunliffe,

Excavations at Fishbourne 1961–1969 Vol. II, Rep. Res. Com. Soc. Ant. London **27**, 260–316.

Darling, M. J. (1977) Pottery from early military sites in Western Britain, in J. Dore and K. Greene, op. cit., 57–100.

Daux, G. (1959) Chroniques des fouilles 1958, *Bull. corr. Hell* **83**, 702–3.

Daux, G. (1957) Chronique des fouilles 1956, *Bull. corr. Hell* **81**, 677.

Dawkins, R. M. (1916) *Modern Greek in Asia Minor*, Cambridge.

Déchelette, J. (1904) *Les vases céramiques ornés de la Gaule romaine*, Paris.

Delarue, T. (1974) L'implantation du tuilier à la marque QVA à Hermalle-sous-Huy, *Bull. Cercle Arch. Hesbaye-Condroz* **13**, 89–92.

Delcroix, G. and Huot, J. L. (1972) Les fours dits 'de potier' dans l'Orient ancien, *Syria* **49**, 35–95.

Detsicas, A. (Ed.) (1973) *Current Research in Romano-British Coarse Pottery*, C. B. A. Res. Rep. **10**, London.

Detsicas, A. P. (1967) Excavations at Eccles 1966, *Arch. Cant* **82**, 162–78.

Dickinson, B. M. and Hartley, K. F. (1971) The evidence of potters' stamps on samian ware and on mortaria for the trading connections of Roman York, in R. M. Butler (Ed.) *Soldier and Civilian in Roman Yorkshire*, Leicester, 127–42.

Dimbleby, G. (1962) *The Development of British Heathlands and their Soils*, Oxford Forestry Memoirs 23.

Doran, J. E. and Hodson, F. R. (1975) *Mathematics and Computers in Archaeology*, Edinburgh.

Dore, J. and Greene, K. (Eds) *Roman Pottery Studies in Britain and Beyond*, B A R , S 30.

Dowling J. H. (1979) The Goodfellows vs the Dalton gang: the assumptions of economic anthropology, *J. Anthr. Res.* **35**, 292–308.

Dragendorff, H. (1913) Tiryns, *Athen. Mitt.* **38**, 338–41.

Dragendorff, H. (1895–96) Terra-sigillata, *Bonner Jb.* **96**, 18–155; **97**, 54–163.

Dressel, H. (1891) Inscriptiones urbis Romae Latinae. Instrumentum domesticum, *Corpus Inscriptionum Latinorum* Vol **15**, 1.

Ducrey, P. and Picard, O. (1969) Recherches à Latô, *Bull. corr.Hell.* **93**, 792–822.

Dudley-Buxton, L. H. and Hort, A. V. D. (1921) The modern pottery industry in Malta, *Man* **21**, 130–1.

Duhamel, P. (1973a) *Les fours céramiques en Gaule romaine*. Thesis, Ecole pratique des Hautes Etudes, IVᵉ section.

Duhamel, P. (1973b) Les fours céramiques gallo-romaines, in P.-M. Duval *Recherches d'archéologie celtique et gallo-romaine*, Geneva, 141–54.

Duma, G. (1963) Der Brand von unglasierten schwarzen Tonwaren in Töpferbrennöfen, *Acta Ethnogr. Acad. Scient. Hungaricae* **12**, 367–405.

Duncan-Jones, R. (1974) *The Economy of the Roman Empire*, Cambridge.

Duval, P. M. (1967) Gaul tuθos = lat. Furnus, *Etudes celtiques* **11**, 314.

Duval, P. M. and Marichal, R. (1966) Un 'compte d'enfournement' inédit de La Graufesenque, *Mélanges d'archéologie et d'histoire offerts à André Piganiol* **3**, 1341–52.

Eiden, H. (1951) Römische Töpferöfen und Werkstätten bei Herforst-Speicher, *Germania* **29**, 305–7.

Eruin, T. and Tamás, R. (1977) *Búcsú a cigányteleptöl*, Budapest.

Ettlinger, E. (1977) Cooking pots at Vindonissa, in J. Dore and K. Greene, op. cit., 47–56.

Ettlinger, E. (1951) Legionary pottery from Vindonissa, *J. Rom. Stud.* **41**, 105–11.

Fabre, C. (1935) Les industries céramiques de Lezoux, *Rev. Arch.* **5** (S.6), 91–110.

Fabroni, A. (1841) *Storia delli antichi vasi fittile Arretini*, Arezzo.

Farnsworth, M. (1970) Corinthian pottery: technical studies, *Amer. J. Arch.* **74**, 9–20.

Farnsworth, M. and Simmons, I. (1963) Colouring agents for Greek vases, *Amer. J. Arch.* **67**, 389–96.

Farrar, R. A. H. (1977) A Romano-British black-burnished ware industry at Ower in the Isle of Purbeck, Dorset, in J. Dore and K. Greene, op. cit., 199–228.

Farrar, R A H (1973) The techniques and sources of Romano-British black-burnished ware, in A. Detsicas, op. cit., 67–103.

Farrar, R. A. H. (1969) A late Roman black-burnished pottery industry in Dorset and its affinities, *Proc. Dorset N. H. and Arch. Soc.* **90**, 174–80.

Ferdière, A. (1975) Notes de céramologie de la région centre: VII – Les ateliers de potiers gallo-romains de la région centre, *Rev. Arch. Centre* **14**, 85–111.

Fernando de Almeida, D., Zbyszewski, G. and Da Veiga Ferreira, O. (1971) Descoberta de fornos lusitano-romanos na região da Marateca (Setubal) *O Arqueologo Português* **5**, 115–66.

Filipović, M. S. (1951) *Żenska Keramika kod Balkanskij naroda* (Srpska Akad. Nauka. Etnogr. Inst. Posebna izdan'a **2**) Belgrade.

Fingerlin, G. (1971) Dangstetten, ein augusteisches Legionslager am Hochrhein. Vorbericht über die Grabungen 1967–1969, *Ber. R. G. K.* **51–2**, 197–232.

Finley, M. I. (1974) Aristotle and economic analysis, in M. I. Finley (Ed.) *Studies in Ancient Society*, London, 26–52.

Finley, M. I. (1973) *The Ancient Economy*, London.

Finley, M. I. (1965) Technical innovation and economic progress in the ancient world, *Econ. Hist. Rev.* **18**, 29–45.

Fleming, S. (1976) *Dating in Archaeology, A Guide to Scientific Techniques*, London.

Fletcher Valls, D. (1965) Tipología de los hornos cerámicos romanos de España, *Arch. Español de Arqu.* **38**, 170–4.

Floca, O., Ferenczi, St. and Mărghidan, L. (1971) *Micia. Grupul de cuptoare romane pentru ars ceramica*, Deva.

Forrer, R. (1911) *Die römischen Terra-Sigillata Töpfereien von Heiligenberg, Dinsheim und Ittenweiler im Elsass*, Stuttgart.

Foster, G. M. (1966) The sociology of pottery: questions and hypotheses arising from contemporary Mexican work. In F. R. Matson (Ed) *Ceramics and Man*, London, 43–61.

Foster, G. M. (1959) The potter's wheel: an analysis of idea and artifact invention, *S. West J. Anthrop.* **15**, 99–119.

Fowler, P. J. (1968) Excavation of a Romano-British settlement at Row of Ashes Farm, Butcombe, North Somerset, *Proc. Bristol Spel. Soc.* **11**, 209–36.

Franchet, L. (1911) *Céramique Primitive*, Paris.

Frank, T. (1940) *An Economic Survey of Ancient Rome: V Rome and Italy of the Empire*. Baltimore.

Frere, S. S. (1977) Roman Britain in 1976. I. Sites explored. *Britannia* **8**, 356–425.

Frere, S. S. (1967) *Britannia*, London.

Frova, A. (Ed.) (1977) *Scavi di Luni II*, Rome.

Fulford, M. G. (1978) The interpretation of Britain's late Roman trade: the scope of medieval historical and archaeological analogy, in J. du Plat Taylor and H. Cleere, op. cit., 59–69.

Fulford, M. G. (1977a) Pottery and Britain's foreign trade in the later Roman period, in D. P. S. Peacock (1977a), 35–83.

Fulford, M. G. (1977b) The location of Romano-British pottery kilns: institutional trade and the market, in J. Dore and K. Greene, op. cit., 301–16.

Fulford, M. G. (1975a) The pottery, in B. W. Cunliffe *Excavations at Portchester Castle; Roman*, Rep. Res. Com. Soc. Ant. London No. **32**.

Fulford, M. G. (1975b) *New Forest Roman Pottery*, B. A. R. **17**.

Fulford, M. and Bird, J. (1975) Imported pottery from Germany in later Roman Britain, *Britannia* **6**, 171–81.

Fulford, M. G. and Hodder, I. (1975) A regression analysis of some late Romano-British pottery: a case study, *Oxoniensia* **39**, 26–33.

Fulford, M. G. and Peacock, D. P. S. (forthcoming) *Excavations at Carthage, the British Mission. Vol. 2. The pottery from the Avenue Président Habib Bourguiba site, Salammbo.* British Academy, London.

Galetti, J. B. (1863) *Histoire illustrée de la Corse*. Paris.

Gamer, G. (1971) Über neue Funde von Töpferöfen römischer Zeit auf der iberischen Halbinsel, *Madrider Mitt.*, **12**, 153–69.

Gault, A. (1952) L'ancienne tuilerie de Civry-la-Forêt (Seine et Oise), *Bull. Folkl. d'Ile de France* **14**, 426–9.

van Gennep, A. (1911) Etudes d'ethnographie algérienne, III: Les Poteries Kabyles, *Rev. d'Ethnog. et de la Sociol.* **2**, 277–331.

Genty, P.-Y. (1980) La production d'amphores gauloises, *Archéologia* **146**, 52–63.

Genty, P.-Y. (1975) Observations sur l'habitat lié aux ateliers de potiers gallo-romains d'Aspiran (Hérault), *Bull. Soc. Et Sc. Sète* **6–7**, 45–65.

Gillam, J. P. (1973) Sources of pottery found on northern miltary sites. In Detsicas (1973), 53–62.

Gillam, J. P. (1963) The coarse pottery, in K. A. Steer, Excavation at Mumrills Roman Fort 1958–60, *Proc. Soc. Ant. Scotland* **94**, 113–29.

Gillam, J. P. (1957) Types of Roman coarse pottery vessels in northern Britain, *Arch. Ael.* **35**, 1–40.

Ginestous, P. (1947) Les poteries des Ouled Sidi Abdelkrim, *I.B.L.A.* **10**, (N.39), 237–42.

Goldman, H. (1950) *Excavations at Gözlü Kule, Tarsus* (2 vols), Princeton.

Gonzalez Anton, R. (1977) *La alfareria popular en Canarias* Santa Cruz de Tenerife.

von Gonzenbach, V. (1963) Die Verbreitung der gestempelten Ziegel der im 1. Jahrhundert n. Chr. in Vindonissa liegenden römischen Truppen, *Bonner Jb.* **163** 76–150.

Goodchild, R. G. (1951) Roman sites on the Tarhuna Plateau of Tripolitania, *Papers British School Rome* **19**, 43–77.

Goodchild, R. G. (1937) The Roman brickworks at Wykehurst Farm in the Parish of Cranleigh. With a note on a Roman tile-kiln at Horton, Epsom, *Surrey Arch. Coll.* **45**, 74–96.

Gordon, H. A. (1969) The brick kilns at Ashburnham, *Country Life*, 24 July, 240–4.

Goudineau, C. (1968) *La céramique arétine lissè*, Paris.

Grace, V. (1962) Stamped handles of commercial amphoras, in H. D. Colt (Ed.) *Excavations at Nessana I*, London, 106–30.

Green, T.K. (1970) Roman tileworks at Itchingfield, *Sussex Arch. Coll.* **108**, 23–38.

Greene, K. (1979a) Review of D.P.S. Peacock (1977a), *Britannia* **10**, 381–2.

Greene, K. (1979b) Invasion and response: pottery and the Roman army, in B. C. Burnham and H. B. Johnson, op. cit., 99–106.

Greene, K. (1978) Roman trade between Britain and the Rhine provinces: the evidence of pottery to *c.* A.D. 250, in J. du Plat Taylor and H. Cleere, op. cit., 52–8.

Greene, K. (1977) Legionary pottery and the significance of Holt, in J. Dore and K. Greene, op. cit., 113–27.

Grenier, A. (1938) Sur la 'coutume ouvrière' des potiers gallo-romains, in H. von Petrikovits and A. Steeger (Eds) *Festschrift für August Oxé*, Darmstadt, 84–9.

Griffith, R. J. (1965) Pottery of Puente del Arzobispo (Toledo) Spain, with special emphasis on methods of production and firing of popular handthrown ceramics, *Actas do Cong. Inter. de Ethnog. Santo Tirso*, 10–18 Julho 1963, Vol. II, Lisbon, 101–20.

Grimes, W. F. (1930) The works depot of the XXth Legion at Holt, *Y Cymmrodor*, **41**.

Gruner, D. (1973) *Die Berber-Keramik: am Beispiel der Orte Afir, Merkalla, Taher, Tiberguent und Roknia*, Wiesbaden.

Guery, R. (1980) L'importation de la Terra Sigillata gauloise en Afrique. Lecture to R.C.R.F. Millau, May 1980.

Hagen, J. (1912) Augusteische Töpferei auf dem Fürstenberg, *Bonner Jb.* **122**, 343–62.

Hampe, R. (1968) Eine kretische Töpferscheibe des 7. Jahrhunderts v. Chr., *Charist. Orlandou* **4**, 178–83.

Hampe R. and Winter, A. (1965) *Bei Töpfern und Zieglern in Süditalien, Sizilien und Griechenland*. Mainz.

Hampe, R. and Winter, A. (1962) *Bei Töpfern und Töpferinnen in Kreta, Messenien und Zypern*. Mainz.

Hanssen, G. (1969) The potters of Haut-Berry, *Pottery in Australia* **8**, 7–13.

Hardin, M. A. (1977) Individual Style in San José pottery painting: the role of deliberate choice, in J. N. Hill and J. Gunn (Eds) *The Individual in Prehistory*, New York, 109–36.

Harding, T. G. (1967) *Voyagers of the Vitiaz Strait*, Seattle.

Hartley, B. R. (1977) Some wandering potters, in J. Dore and K. Greene, op. cit., 251–62.

Hartley, B. R. (1970) Samian ware or Terra Sigillata, in R. G. Collingwood and I. A. Richmond *The archaeology of Roman Britain*, London, 235–51.

Hartley, B. R. (1966) Gaulish potters' stamps, *Ant. J.* **46**, 102–3.

Hartley, B. R. (1960) *Notes on the Roman pottery industry in the Nene Valley*. Peterborough Museum. Occasional Papers 2.

Hartley, K. F. (1973) The marketing and distribution of mortaria, in A. Detsicas, op. cit., 39–51.

Hartley, K. F. (1965) Mancetter, *West Midlands Archaeol. News Sheet* **8**, 12–13.

Hartley, K. F. and Richards, E. E. (1965) Spectrographic analysis of some Romano-British mortaria, *Bull. Inst. Arch. London* **5**, 25–43.

Hartley, K. F. and Webster, P. V. (1973) Romano-British pottery kilns near Wilderspool, *Arch. J.* **130**, 77–103.

Hassall, M. (1978) Britain and the Rhine provinces: epigraphic evidence for Roman trade, in J. du Plat Taylor and H. Cleere, op. cit., 41–8.

Hatt, J.-J. (1979) La chronologie de l'officine de terre sigillée de Boucheporn d'après les fouilles de 1963 à 1967, *Acta Rei Cret. Rom. Faut.* **19–20**, 72–6.

Hatt, J.-J. (1958) Les céramiques des Martres-de-Veyre (Puy de Dôme) et de Chémery (Moselle) au musée archéologique de Strasbourg, *Gallia* **16**, 251–61.

Hawkes, C. F. C. and Hull, M. R. (1947) *Camulodunum*, Rep. Res. Com. Soc. Ant. London, **14**.

Hayes, J. W. (1972) *Late Roman Pottery*, London.

Helen, T. (1975) *Organisation of Roman Brick Production in the First and Second Centuries A.D. An Interpretation of Roman Brick Stamps*, Helsinki.

Hénault, M. (1928) L'Atelier de potiers de la sablière Derome, *Pro Nervia* **4**, 74–85.

Herber, J. (1931) Contribution à l'étude des poteries Zaër (poteries à la tournette, poterie au moule), *Hespéris* **13**, 1–34.

Hermann, S. (1961) Von der Möllner Stadtziegelei, *Lauenburgische Heimat* NF **35**, 13–19.

Hermet, F. (1923) *Les graffites de La Graufesenque*, Rodez.

Heurtley, W. A. (1939) *Prehistoric Macedonia*, Cambridge.

Hill, J. N. (1977) Individual variability in ceramics and prehistoric social organisation, in J. M. Hill and J. Gunn (Eds.) *The Individual in Prehistory* New York, 55–108.

Hochuli-Gysel, A. (1977) *Kleinasiatische Glasierte Reliefkeramik*, Bern.

Hodder, I. (1979) Pre-Roman and Romano-British tribal economies, in B. C. Burnham and H. B. Johnson, op. cit., 189–96.

Hodder, I. (1977a) Some new directions in the spatial analysis of archaeological data at the regional scale (macro), in D. L. Clarke (Ed.) *Spatial archaeology*, London, 223–352.

Hodder, I. (1977b) How are we to study distribution of Iron Age material?, in J. Collis (Ed.) *The Iron Age in Britain – a review*, Sheffield, 8–16.

Hodder, I. (1974a) Some marketing models for Romano-British coarse Pottery, *Britannia* **5**, 340–59

Hodder, I. (1974b) The distribution of two types of Romano-British coarse pottery in the West Sussex region, *Sussex Arch. Coll.* **112**, 1–11.

Hodder, I. and Orton, C. (1976) *Spatial Analysis in Archaeology*, Cambridge.

Hodges, H. W. M. (1964) *Artifacts*, London.

Hofmann, B. (1971) Les relations entre potiers, fabricants de moules et artistes producteurs de poincons, *Acta rei cret faut rom* **13**, 5–20.

Holleyman, G. A. (1947) Tiree craggans, *Antiquity* **21**, 105–11.

Hollowood, A. B. (1940) The localisation of the pottery industry, *Trans. North Staffs. F. C.* **74**, 22–8.

Holwerda, J. H. and Braat, W. C. (1946) *De Holdeurn bij Berg en Dal: centrum van pannenbakkerij en aardewerkindustrie in den Romeinschen tijd*, Oud Med. Suppl. of N.R. **26**.

Hopkins, K. (1978) Economic growth and towns in Classical Antiquity, in P. Abrams and E. A. Wrigley (Eds) *Towns in Societies*, Cambridge, 35–77.

Howlett, D. R. (1961) A Roman pottery kiln at Upper Sheringham, *Norfolk Arch* **32**, 211–19.

Huld-Zetsche, I. (1972) *Trierer Reliefsigillata Werkstatt 1*, Bonn.

Hull, M. R. (1963) *The Roman Potters' Kilns of Colchester*, Rep. Res. Com. Soc. Ant. London No. **21**.

Hull, M. R. (1958) *Roman Colchester*, Rep. Res. Com. Soc. Ant. London No. **20**.

Hulthén, B. (1974) *On Documentation of Pottery*, Acta Arch. Lundenisa, Lund.

Jagor, H. (1882) Töpferei, namentlich in Ordizan (Pyrenäen) und Siut (Aegypten), *Zeitschrift für Ethnologie* **14**, 457–70.

Jandaurek, H. (1956) Ein römisches Bauwerk bei Engelhof, *Oberösterr. Heimat-Blätter* **10**, 37–57.

Jewitt, L. (1883) *Ceramic Art of Great Britain*, London.

Jobey, G. (1959) Excavations at the native settlement at Huckhoe, Northumberland, 1955–7, *Arch. Ael.* **37**, 217–78.

Johns, C. (1977) A group of samian wasters from Les-Martres-de-Veyre, in J. Dore and K. Greene, op. cit., 235–46.

Johns, C. (1971) *Arretine and samian pottery*, London.

Johns, C. (1963) Gaulish potters' stamps, *Ant. J.* **43**, 288–9.

Johnsen, A. (1912) Die Gesteine der Inseln S. Pietro und S. Antioco (Sardinien), *Abh. Preuss. Akad. Wiss. Phys. Math. Kl.* **2**.

Johnston, D. and Williams, D. (1979) Relief patterned tiles – a reappraisal, in A. McWhirr (1979a), 375–94.

Jolin, R. (1959) L'exploration archéologique de Bavai. Un quartier artisanal et résidentiel au Sud-Ouest de Bavai, *Ant. Class.* **28**, 125–31.

Jones, A. H. M. (1974) *The Roman Economy.* Oxford.

Jones, A. H. M. (1964) *The Later Roman Empire,* Oxford.

Jones, F. F. (1950) The pottery, in H. Goldman (Ed.) *Excavations at Gözlü Kule Tarsus, 1, The Hellenistic and Roman Periods,* Princeton.

Juhász, G. (1936) A Lezouxi terrasigillata gyárak Acquincumi, Ierakata, *Arch. Értesitö* **49**, 33–48.

Kendall, D. G. (1963) A statistical approach to Flinders Petrie's sequence dating, *Bull. int. stat. Inst.* **40**, 657–81.

Kenyon, K. M. (1953) Excavations at Sutton Walls, Herefordshire, 1948–1951, *Arch. J.* **110**, 1–87.

Knorr, R. (1952) *Terra-Sigillata-Gefässe des ersten Jahrhunderts mit Töpfernamen,* Stuttgart.

Knorr, R. (1919) *Töpfer und Fabriken verzierter Terra-Sigillata des ersten Jahrhunderts,* Stuttgart.

Knowles, A. K. (1977) The Roman settlement at Brampton, Norfolk: Interim report, *Britannia* **8**, 209–21.

Köpke, W. (1976) Frauentöpferei in Spanien, *Baessler Archiv* **22**, 335–441.

Kropotkin, V. V. (1970) *Rimskie importnie izdeliya v Vostochnoi Evrope (IIv po ne–V v ne),* Arkheologiya SSSR D1–27, Moscow.

La Baume, P. (1972) Das römische Köln, *Bonner Jb.* **172**, 271.

La Baume, P. (1959) Frührömische Töpferöfen aus der Lungengasse in Köln, *Germania* **37**, 293–6.

La Baume, P. (1958) Frührömische Töpferöfen aus der Lungengasse, *Kölner Jb,* **3**, 26–54.

Lamboglia, N. (1963) Nuove osservazioni sulla 'terra sigillata chiara', *Riv. St. Lig.* **29**, 145–212.

Lamboglia, N. (1958) Nuove osservazioni sulla 'terra sigillata chiara', *Riv. St. Lig.* **24**, 257–330.

Lamboglia, N. (1952) Per una classificazione preliminare della ceramica campana *Atti l Cong Int Studi Liguri (1950),* Bordighera, 139–206.

Lamboglia, N. (1950) *Gli scavi di Albintimilium e la cronologia della ceramica romana i. Campagne di scavo 1938–1940,* Bordighera.

Lamboglia, N. (1941) Terra sigillata chiara, *Riv. St. Lig.* **7**, 7–22.

Lange, O. (1945) The scope and method of economics, *Rev. Econ. Stud.* **13**, 19–32.

van der Leeuw, S. E. (1976) *Studies in the Technology of Ancient Pottery,* 2-vol. thesis, Amsterdam.

Le Patourel, J. (1968) Documentary evidence and the medieval pottery industry, *Med. Arch.* **12**, 101–26.

Leslie, K. C. (1971) The Ashburnham Estate Brickworks 1840–1968, *Sussex Ind. Hist.* **1**, 2–22.

Lewis, M. J.T. (1966) *Temples in Roman Britain,* Cambridge.

Lewis, N. and Rheinhold, M. (1955) *Roman Civilisation I,* New York.

Lisse, P. and Louis, A. (1956) *Les Potiers de Nabeul,* Tunis.

Litt, M. E. (1969) Deux fours de potiers gallo-belges à l'abbaye de Vauclair (Aisne), *Revue du Nord* **51**, 413–53.

Llorens Artigas, J. and Corredor Matheos, J. (1974) *Spanish Folk Ceramics,* Barcelona.

Loane, H. J. (1938) *Industry and Commerce of the City of Rome (50 B.C.–200 A.D.),* Baltimore.

Loeschcke, S. (1931) Die römischen Ziegelöfen im Gemeindewald von Speicher, *Trierer Zeit* **6**, 1–7.

Loughlin, N. (1977) Dales ware, in D.P.S. Peacock (1977a), 85–162.

Lowther, A. W. G. (1948) *A Study of the Patterns on Roman Flue-tiles and their distribution,* Res. pap. Surrey Arch. Soc. **1**.

Ludowici, W. (1905) *Stempelbilder römischer Töpfer aus meiner Ausgrabung in Rheinzabern,* Jockgrim.

Lung, W. (1959) Zur vor- und frühgeschichtlichen Keramik im Kölner Raum, *Kölner Jb.* **4**, 45–65.

Lutz, M. (1970) *L'Atelier de Saturninus et de Satto à Mittelbronn (Moselle),* Gallia Suppl. **22**.

Lyding Will, E. (1979) The Sestius amphoras: a reappraisal, *J. Field Arch.* **6**, 339–50.

Lyne, M. A. B. and Jefferies, R. S. (1979) *The Alice Holt/Farnham Roman Pottery Industry,* C.B.A. Research Report **30**.

MacMullen, R. (1970) Market days in the Roman Empire, *Phoenix* **24**, 333–41.

Macrea, M. (1947) Note au sujet des briqueteries en Dacie, *Dacia* **11–12**, 275–80.

McWhirr, A. (Ed.) (1979a) *Roman Brick and Tile,* B.A.R. **S.68**.

McWhirr, A. (1979b) Tile kilns in Roman Britain, in A. McWhirr (1979a), 97–190.

McWhirr, A. (1979c) Origins of tile-stamping in Britain, in A. McWhirr (1979a), 253–60.

McWhirr, A. and Viner, D. (1978) Production and distribution of tiles in Roman Britain with particular reference to the Cirencester region, *Britannia* **9**, 359–77.

Maetzke, G. (1959) Notizie sulla esplorazione della fornace di Cn Ateius in Arezzo, *Acta rei cret. faut. rom.* **2**, 25–8.

Mallowan, M. E. L. (1939) The Phoenician carrying trade, *Antiquity* **13**, 86–7.

Manacorda, D. (1978) The Ager Cosanus and the production of the amphorae of Sestius: new evidence and a reassessment, *J. Rom. Stud.* **68**, 122–31.

Manacorda, D. (1977) Testimonianze sulla produzione e il consumo dell'olio Tripolitano nel III secolo, *Dialoghi di archeologia* **9–10**, 542–601.

Manière, G. (1971) Une officine de tuilier gallo-romain du Haut-Empire à Couladère, par Cazères (Haute-Garonne), *Gallia* **29**, 191–9.

Mannoni, G. (1975) *La Ceramica medievale a Genova e nella Liguria,* Bordighera and Genoa.

Mantoux, P. (1927) *The Industrial Revolution of the Eighteenth Century,* London.

Marichal, R. (1971) Quelques graffites inédites de La Graufesenque, *Comptes Rend. Acad. Inser.,* 188–212.

Marx, K. (1918) *Capital, A Critique of Political Economy* I, Kerr edn, trans. of 3rd German edn, Chicago.

Matson, F. R. (1972) Ceramic studies, in W. A. McDonald and G. R. Rapp Jr, *The Minnesota Messinia Expedition*, Minneapolis, 200–24.

Matson, F. R. (1966) Ceramic ecology: an approach to the study of the early cultures of the near East, in F. R. Matson (Ed.) *Ceramics and Man*, London, 202–17.

Mau, A. (1898) Tituli vasi fictilibus inscripti, *Corpus Inscriptionum Latinorum*, Vol. **4**, suppl.

Mayes, P. (1962) The firing of a second pottery kiln of Romano-British type at Boston, Lincs., *Archaeometry* **5**, 80–6.

Mayes, P. (1961) The firing of a pottery kiln of a Romano-British type at Boston, Lincs., *Archaeometry* **4**, 4–30.

Meduna, J. (1970) Das keltische Oppidum Staré Hradisko in Mähren, *Germania* **48**, 34–59.

Meiggs, R. (1973) *Roman Ostia*, Oxford.

Meikle, S. (1979) Aristotle and the political economy of the polis, *J. Hellen. Stud.* **99**, 57–73.

Messham, J. E. (1956) The Buckley potteries, *Flints. His. Soc. Pubs* **16**, 31–87.

Michels, J. (1973) *Dating Methods in Archaeology*, New York.

Middleton, P. S. (1979) Army supply in Roman Gaul. An hypothesis for Roman Britain, in B. C. Burnham and H. B. Johnson, op. cit.

Miller, J. J. (1970) *Eighteenth-Century Ceramics from Fort Michilimackinac; a study in historical archaeology*, Washington.

Millett, M. (1979) The dating of Farnham (Alice Holt) pottery, *Britannia* **10**, 121–37.

Mócsy, A. (1974) *Pannonia and Upper Moesia*, London.

Mócsy, A. (1953) Das Territorium legionis und dei Canabae in Pannonien, *Acta Arch. Acad. Scient. Hung.* **3**, 179–200.

Morel, J.-P. (1965) *Céramique à vernis noir du Forum romain et du Palatin*, Paris.

Morel, J.-P. (1963) Notes sur la céramique etruscocampanienne. Vases à vernis noir de Sardaigne et d'Arezzo, *Mel. Ecole Franc. Rome* **75**, 7–58.

Morgan, G. (1979) Experiments in making and firing box-flue tiles, in A. McWhirr, (1979a), 395–400.

Müller, G. (1979) *Ausgrabungen in Dormagen 1963–1977* (= Rheinische Ausgrabungen 20), Cologne.

Myer-Heisig, E. (1955) *Deutsche Bauerntöpferei: Geschichte und landschaftliche Gliederung*, Munich.

Negev, A. (1974) The Nabatean Potters' Workshop at Oboda, (R.C.R.F. Acta Supp. 1), Bonn.

Németi, I. (1974) Cuptoare de ars ceramica din epoca La tène de la Andrid (Jud Satu Mare), *Studi si cercetari de Istorie Veche şi arheologie* **25**, 579–84.

Noble, J. V. (1969) The technique of Egyptian faience, *Amer. J. Arch.* **73**, 435–7.

Noble, J. V. (1966) *The Techniques of Painted Attic Pottery*, New York.

Nopcsa, F. (1925) *Albanien. Bauten, Trachten und Geräte Nordalbaniens*, Leipzig.

Oberlies, F. and Köppen, N. (1953) Untersuchungen an Terra-Sigillata und griechischen Vasen, *Ber. deutsch, keram. Ges.* **30**, 102–10.

Ogilvie, R. M. (1965) Eretum, *Papers Brit. Sch. Rome* **33**, 70–111.

Olton, C. S. (1975) *Artisans for Independence*, New York.

Onuzi, A. (1976) Mjeshtëria e punimit të enëve prej balte në fshatin Farkë (Tirane), *Etnografia Shqiptare* **8**, 177–89.

Onuzi, A. (1974) Një gendër e punimit të eneve prej dheu pa çark, *Etnografia Shqiptare* **5**, 195–211.

Orme, B. (1974) Twentieth-century prehistorians and the idea of ethnographic parallels, *Man* **9**, 199–212.

Oswald, F. and Pryce, T. D. (1920) *An introduction to the study of Terra-Sigillata*, London.

Oxé, A. (1933) *Arretinische Reliefgefässe vom Rhein*, Frankfurt.

Oxé, A. (1925) Die Töpferrechnungen von der Graufesenque, *Bonner Jb.* **130**, 38–99.

Oxé, A. and Comfort, H. (1968) *Corpus Vasorum Arretinorum*, Bonn.

Panella, C. (1973) Appunti su un gruppo di anfore della prima, media e tarda età imperiale. In *Ostia III* (*Studi Miscellanei* No. 21).

Paret, O. (1911) Ein römischer Gutshof mit Ziegelei bei Hoheneck OA Ludwigsburg, *Fundb. aus Schwaben* **19**, 90–118.

Parker, A. J. (forthcoming) *Ancient Shipwrecks in the Mediterranean*, B.A.R.

Parvaux, S. (1968) *La céramique populaire du Haut Alentejo*, Paris.

Pasqui, U. (1896) Nuove scoperte di antiche figuline della fornace di M. Perennio, *Not. Scavi*, 453–66.

Peacock, D. P. S. (forthcoming) Archaeological investigations on the island of Pantelleria, Italy, *Res. Rep. Nat. Geog. Soc. 1977*.

Peacock, D. P. S. (1980) The Roman millstone trade: a petrological sketch, *World Arch.* **12**, 43–53.

Peacock, D. P. S. (1978) The Rhine and the problem of Gaulish wine in Roman Britain, in J. du Plat Taylor and H. Cleere, op. cit., 49–57.

Peacock, D. P. S. (Ed.) 1977a) *Pottery and Early Commerce: Characterisation and Trade in Roman and Later Ceramics*, London.

Peacock, D. P. S. (1977b) Ceramics in Roman and Medieval archaeology. In D. P. S. Peacock (1977a), 21–34.

Peacock, D. P. S. (1977c) Bricks and tiles of the *Classis Britannica*: petrology and origin, *Britannia* **8**, 235–48.

Peacock, D. P. S. (1977d) Recent discoveries of Roman amphora kilns in Italy, *Ant. J.* **57**, 269–9.

Peacock, D. P. S. (1977e) Roman amphorae: typology, fabric and origin, *Coll. Ecole Franç. Rome* **32**, 261–78.

Peacock, D. P. S. (1973a) The black-burnished pottery industry in Dorset, in A. Detsicas, op. cit., 63–5.

Peacock, D. P. S. (1973b) Forged brickstamps from Pevensey, *Antiquity* **47**, 138–40.

Peacock, D. P. S. (1971) Roman amphorae in pre-Roman Britain, in M. Jesson and D. Hill (Eds) *The Iron Age and its Hill-forts*, Southampton, 161–88.

Peacock, D. P. S. (1969a) Neolithic Pottery Production in Cornwall, *Antiquity* **43**, 145–9.

Peacock, D. P. S. (1969b) A contribution to the study of Glastonbury ware from Southwestern Britain, *Ant. J.* **49**, 41–61.

Peacock, D. P. S. (1968) A Petrological study of certain Iron Age pottery from western England, *Proc. Prehist. Soc.* **34**, 414–27.

Peacock, D. P. S. (1967) Romano-British pottery production in the Malvern District of Worcestershire, *Trans. Worcs. Arch. Soc.* **1**, 15–28.

Perrin, R. (1977) 'Legionary' ware in York, in J. Dore and K. Greene, op. cit., 101–112.

Petrie, W. M. F. (1909) *Memphis I*, London.

Petrie, W. M. F. (1899) Sequences in prehistoric remains, *J. anthrop. Inst.*, **29**, 295–301.

von Petrikovits, H. (1960) *Das römische Rheinland*, Bonn.

von Petrikovits, H. (1959) Die Legionsfestung Vetera II, *Bonner Jb.* **159**, 124.

von Petrikovits, H. (1954) Ein Ziegelstempel der Cohors II Varcianonum aus Gelduba-Gellep, *Bonner Jb.* **154**, 137–45.

von Petrikovits, H. (1950) Zu einem Ziegelstempel der Legio XV Primigenia aus Bonn, *Bonner Jb.* **150**, 102–3.

Petrucci, J. and Poteur, J.-C. (1976) La poterie traditionelle de Vallauris. Le tournage des poteries culinaire, *Atti IX Convegno Int. della Ceramica*, Albisola.

von Pfeffer, W. (1977) Töpferöfen einheimischer Keramik im frührömischen Lagerdorf Mainz-Weisenau, *Acta rei cret. faut. rom.* **17–18**, 178–91.

Picon, M. (1973) *Introduction à l'étude technique des céramiques sigillées de Lezoux*, Dijon.

Picon, M. and Garnier, J. (1974) Un atelier d'Ateius à Lyon, *Rev. arch. Est et Centre Est* **25**, 71–6.

Picon, M., Vichy, M. and Meille, E. (1971) Composition of the Lezoux, Lyon and Arezzo samian ware, *Archaeometry* **13**, 191–208.

Piepers, W. (1971) Römische Ziegel und Töpferöfen bei Bedburg-Garsdorf, Kreis Bergheim Erft, *Rheinische Ausgrabungen* **10**, 340.

Platon, N. (1952) Anaskafai periokis stieias, *Prakt.*, 646.

Polanyi, K. (1957a) Aristotle discovers the economy, in K. Polanyi, C. M. Arensberg and H. W. Pearson (Eds) *Trade and Market in the Early Empires*, Glencoe, 64–96.

Polanyi, K. (1957b) The economy as an instituted process. *Ibid*, 243–69.

Popilian, C. (1976) Un quartier artisanal à Romula, *Dacia* **20**, 221–50.

Popović, C. D. (1959) Tekhnika primitivnog loncharstva Jugoslaviji, *Glasnik zemaljs mus u Sarajevu*, **14**, 25–59.

Pryce, T. D. (1942) Roman decorated red-glazed ware of the late first century B.C. and the early first century A.D., *J. Rom. Stud.* **32**, 14–26.

Pucci, G. (1973) La produzione della ceramica aretine. Note sull'industria nella prima etá imperiali, *Dialoghi di Archeologia* **7**, 255–93.

Rahtz, P. A. (1974) Pottery in Somerset, A.D. 400–1066, in V. I. Evison, H. Hodges and J. G. Hurst (Eds) *Medieval Pottery from Excavations*, London, 95–126.

Rahtz, P. A. and Fowler, P. J. (forthcoming) Excavations at Cadbury-Congresbury.

Rasmussen, H. (1967) Teglbrænding i Dokkedal, *Folkeminder* **13**, 209–15.

Redman, C. L. (1974) *Archaeological Sampling Strategies*, Addison-Wesley module in Anthropology No. 55, Reading, Mass.

Reusch, W. (1958) Jahresbericht 1945 bis 1958, Kreis Prüm, *Trierer Zeitschrift* **24/6**, 561–3.

Revere, R. B. (1957) 'No Man's Coast': Ports of trade in the Eastern Mediterranean, in K. Polanyi, C. M. Arensberg and H. W. Pearson (Eds) *Trade and Market in the Early Empires*, Glencoe, 38–63.

Ribeiro, M. (1972) Engenho de amassar barro. Subsídios para o estudo das técnicas da olaria popular, *O Arqueologo Português* **6**, 289–306.

Ribeiro, M. (1969) Instrumentos auxiliares de modelação. Subsidios para o estudo da olaria portuguesa, *O Arqueologo Português* **3**, 217–229.

Ribeiro, M. (1962) Contribuição para o estudo da cerámica popular portuguesa, *Revista de Guimarães* **72**, 392–416.

Richmond, I. A. (1955) *Roman Britain*, Harmondsworth.

Rieth, A. (1960) *5000 Jahre Töpferscheibe*, Constance.

Rieth, A. (1952) Die antike griechische Töpferscheibe in Jugoslavien noch in Gebrauch, *Umschau* **52**, 78–9.

Righini, V. (1971) Officine artigianili e nuclei industriale nella Villa Romana, in *La Villa romana, Giornata di Studi, Russi, 10 Maggio 1970*, 29–36.

Riley, J. A. (1981) The coarse pottery from Benghazi, in J. A. Lloyd (Ed.) *Sidi Krebish Excavations, Benghazi (Bérénice)*, Vol. II, Tripoli, 91–467.

Riley, J. A. (1975a) The pottery from the first session of excavation in the Caesarea Hippodrome, *Bull. Amer. Schools of Oriental Research* **218**, 25–63.

Riley, J. A. (1975b) Excavations of a kiln site at Tocra, Libya, in August 1974, *Soc. Libyan Stud., Ann. Rep.*, 25–9.

Ritterling, E. (1927) Skizze der Entwicklung Rheinzaberns zu Römerzeit, in W. Ludowici *Katalog V: Stempelnamen und Bilder römischer Töpfer*, 200–2.

Robinson, H. S. (1959) *Pottery of the Roman Period*, Athenian Agora Vol. 5, Princeton.

Rogers, G. (1977) A group of wasters from Central Gaul, in J. Dore and K. Greene, op. cit., 245–50.

Rostovtzeff, M. (1957) *The Social and Economic History of the Roman Empire*, 2 vols, Oxford.

Rougé, J. (1966) *Recherches sur l'organization du commerce maritime en Méditerranée sous l'empire romain*, Paris.

Rusić, B. (1957) Grncarstvo u Vranishtitsi (u okolini Kicheva), *Glasnik Etnog. inst. Srpsk. akad. nauka (Beograd)* **2–3**, 511–27.

Rutton, W. L. (1893) Sandgate Castle A.D. 1539–40, *Arch. Cant.* **20**, 228–57.

Rye, O. S. and Evans, C. (1976) *Traditional Pottery Techniques of Pakistan: field and laboratory studies*, Washington.

Sagui, C. L. (1948) La meunerie de Barbégal (France) et les

roues hydrauliques chez les anciens et au moyen age, *Isis* **38**, 225–31.

Sanchis, P. (1977) Les romarias Portugaises, *Arch. Sci. sociales Relig.* **43**, 53–76.

Sander, E. (1962) Der praefectus fabrum und die Legionsfabriken, *Bonner Jb.* **162**, 139–61.

Santrot, M.-H. and Santrot, J. (1979) *Céramiques communes gallo-romaines d'Aquitaine*, Paris.

Saraswati, B. and Behura, N. K. (1966) *Pottery Techniques in Peasant India*, Calcutta, Anthrop. Sur. India, Mem. 13.

Saunders, C. and Havercroft, A. B. (1977) A kiln of the potter Oastrius and related excavations at Little Munden Farm, Brickett Wood, *Herts. Arch.* **5**, 109–56.

Schäfer, J. (1968) *Hellenistische Keramik aus Pergamon*, Berlin.

Scheans, D. J. (1965) Evolution of the potter's wheel: the Philippines data, *Amer. Anthrop.* **67**, 1527–9.

Schiffer, M. B. (1976) *Behavioural Archaeology*, New York.

Schoene, R. (1871) Tituli vasis fictilibus, in *Corpus Inscriptionum Latinorum* (ed. C. Zangemeister) Vol. 4, *Inscriptiones Parietariae Pompeianae*, Berlin.

Schumann, T. (1942) Oberflächenverzierung in der antiken Töpferkunst. Terra sigillata und griechische Schwarzrotmalerei, *Bei. deutsch. keram. Ges.* **23**, 408–26.

von Schurbein, S. (1974) Bemerkenswerte Funde aus einer Töpferei des Hauptlagers von Haltern, *Germania* **52**, 77–88.

Seele, E. (1968) Die Ziegelherstellung im Becken von Puebla Tlaxcala, *Die Ziegelindustrie* **17(18)**, 380–6.

Serre, A. (1961) Techniques des potiers de Saint-Quentin-La-Poterie et de Saint-Victor-des-Oules (Gard), *Arts et Traditions Populaires* **9**, 309–20.

Seseña Diez, N. (1967) La alfarería de Mota del Cuervo, *Rev. Dial. Trad. Pop.* **23**, 339–46.

Sethom, H. (1964) Les artisans potiers de Moknine, *Rev. Tunisienne de Sci. Sociales* **1**, 53–70.

Shepard, A. O. (1956) *Ceramics for the Archaeologist*, Washington.

Simpson, G. (1976) Decorated Terra Sigillata at Montans (Tarn) from the Manuscript of Elie Rossignol at Albi, *Britannia* **7**, 244–73.

Smith, R. A. (1907) The wreck on Pudding – Pan Rock, Herne Bay, Kent, *Proc. Soc. Ant. London* **21**, 268–92.

Snow, C. P. (1956) The two cultures, *New Statesman*, 6 October.

Soultov, B. (1976) *Ancient Pottery Centres in Moesia Inferior*, Sofia.

Spitzlberger, G. (1968) Die römischen Ziegelstempel im nördlichen Teil der Provinz Raetien, *Saalburg. Jb.* **25**, 65–184.

Stachelin, F. (1948) *Die Schweiz in römischer Zeit*, Basel.

Stanfield, J. A. and Simpson, G. (1958) *Central Gaulish Potters*, London.

Steele, C. N. (1971) *The potters of Sorkun Village in North-West Anatolia: the study of a present-day primitive pottery industry and its relevance to archaeology*, D. Phil. thesis, Oxford University.

Steensberg, A. (1940) Hand-made pottery in Jutland, *Antiquity* **14**, 148–53.

Steensberg, A. (1939) Primitive black pottery in Jutland, *Folk-liv*, 113–46.

Steinby, M. (1975) La chronologie della *figlinae* doleari urbane della fine dell'età repubblicana fino all' inizio del III sec., *Bull. Comm. Roma* **84**, 7–132.

Steiren, A. (1952) Römische Töpferöfen im Lager Haltern, *Germania* **16**, 112–15.

Stenico, A. (1959) Ceramica Arretina a rilievi e terra sigillata Tardo-Italica, *Acta rei cret. faut. rom.* **2**, 51–62.

Stenico, A. (1958) Aretini, vasi, *Enciclopedia dell'arte artica* **1**, Rome, 608–16.

Stiles, D. (1977) Ethnoarchaeology: a discussion of methods and applications, *Man* **12**, 87–103.

Stillwell, A. N. (1948) *Corinth, XV. 1. The Potters' Quarter*, Princeton.

Stroh, A. (1934) Römischer Töpferöfen mit einheimischer Keramik von Hailfingen OA Rottenburg, *Germania*, 18, 98–102.

Strong, D. E. (1966) *Greek and Roman Gold and Silver Plate*, London.

Swan, V. G. (1978) *Roman Pottery in Britain*, Princes Risborough.

Swan, V. G. (1975) Oare reconsidered and the origins of Savernake ware in Wiltshire, *Britannia* **6**, 37–61.

Swan, V. G. (1973) Aspects of the New Forest late-Roman pottery industry, in A. Detsicas, op. cit., 117–34.

Swoboda, R. M. (1971) Der Töpfereibezirk am Südostrand von Augusta Raurica, *Helvetia Arch.* **2**, 7–21.

Szentléleky, T. (1969) *Ancient Lamps*, Amsterdam.

Szentléleky, T. (1959) Aquincumi mécseskészitö mühelyek, *Budapest Régiségei* **19**, 167–98.

Szilágyi, J. (1972) Ziegelstempel, in Pauly-Wissowa *Real-Encyclopädie der classischen Altertumswissenschaft* **2.19**, 433–6.

Taylor, J. du Plat and Cleere, H. (Eds) (1978) *Roman Shipping and Trade: Britain and the Rhine Provinces* C. B.A. Res. Rep. **24**.

Taylor, J. du Plat and Tufnell, O. (1930) A pottery industry in Cyprus, *Ancient Egypt*, 119–22.

Tax, S. (1953) *Penny Capitalism*, Chicago.

Tchernia, A. (1971) Les amphores vinaires de Tarraconaise et leur exportation au début de l'Empire, *Arch. Español de Arqu.* **44**, 38–85.

Tchernia, A. (1967) Les amphores romaines et l'histoire économique, *Journ. des Savants* (oct.–dec.), 224.

Thomas, J. (1971) *The Rise of the Staffordshire Potteries*, Bath.

Thomas, J. (1937) The pottery industry and the industrial revolution, *Econ. Hist.* **3**, 399–414.

Thompson, F. H. (1958) A Romano-British pottery kiln at North Hykeham, *Ant. J.* **38**, 15–51.

Tildesley, J. M. (1971) Roman pottery kilns at Rettendon, *Essex J.* **6**, 35–50.

Tite, M. S. (1969) The determination of the firing temperature of ancient ceramics, *Archaeometry* **11**, 131–44.

Todd, M. (1968) The commoner late Roman coarse wares of the East Midlands, *Ant. J.* **48**, 192–209.

Tomić, P. (1966) *Narodna Keramika u Jugoslaviji*, Belgrade.

Vandereuse, J. and Pinon, R. (1961) Contributions à l'étude

de la Briqueterie en Wallonie, *Ann. Comm. royale belge Folklore* **12**, 322–81.

Vegas, M. (1973) *Cerámica común romana del Mediterráneo occidental*, Barcelona.

Vegas, M. (1964) Römische Bildlampen aus einer Werkstatt des Lagers Novaesium, *Bonner Jb.* **164**, 308–20.

Vernhet, A. (1979) *La Graufesenque. Atelier de céramiques gallo-romain*, Toulouse – Millau.

Vossen, R., Seseña, N. and Köpke, W. (1975) *Guia de los alfares de España*, Madrid.

Voyatzoglou, M. (1973) The potters of Thrapsano, *Ceramic Review* **24**, 13–16.

Waagé, F. (1948) Hellenistic and Roman tableware of north Syria, in *Antioch on the Orontes*, IV, Part 1: *Ceramics and Islamic coins*. Princeton.

Waagé, F. O. (1933) The American excavations in the Athenian Agora, First Report: The Roman and Byzantine pottery, *Hesperia* **2**, 279–328.

Wacher, J. (1978) *Roman Britain*, London.

Wacher, J. S. (1969) *Excavations at Brough-on-Humber 1958–1961*, Rep. Res. Com. Soc. Ant. London **25**.

Walters, H. B. (1905) *History of Ancient Pottery*, 2 vols, London.

Warren, P. M. (1978) A Cretan pottery flask in a Minoan tradition, *Kritologia* **7**, 119–27.

Weatherill, L. (1971) *The Pottery Trade and North Staffordshire 1660–1760*, Manchester.

Webster, G. (1973) Summing up, in A. Detsicas, op. cit., 161–2.

Webster, G. (1968) A sherd of pottery from Cirencester, *Ant. J.* **48**, 102–3.

Webster, G. (1944) A Roman pottery at South Carlton, Lincs., *Ant. J.* **2**, 129–43.

Webster, P. V. (1977) Severn valley ware on the Antonine frontier, in J. Dore and K. Greene, op. cit., 163–76.

Webster, P.V. (1976) Severn Valley ware: a preliminary study, *Trans. Bristol and Glos. Arch. Soc.* **94**, 18–46.

Webster, P. V. (1972) Severn Valley ware on Hadrian's Wall, *Arch. Ael.* **50**, 191–203.

Wells, C. M. (1972) *The German Policy of Augustus*, Oxford.

Westermann, W. L. (1955) *The Slave System of Greek and Roman Antiquity*, Philadelphia.

Wheeler, R. E. M. (1972) Review of S. S. Frere *Verulamium Excavations Vol. 1*, *Ant. J.* **52**, 382–5.

Wheeler, R. E. M. (1946) Arikamedu: An Indo-Roman trading-station on the East Coast of India, *Ancient India* **2**, 17–124.

Wheeler, R. E. M. (1943) *Maiden Castle, Dorset*, Rep. Res. Com. Soc. Ant. London, **12**.

Wheeler, R. E. M. (1930) *London in Roman Times*, London.

White, W. C. F. (1971) A gazetteer of brick and tile works in Hampshire, *Proc. Hants. F. C. and Arch. Soc.* **28**, 81–98.

Whitehouse, D. (1978) Home-baking in Roman Italy: a footnote, *Antiquity* **52**, 146–7.

Wightman, E. (1970) *Roman Trier and the Treveri*, London.

Wild, J. P. (1974) Roman settlement in the Lower Nene Valley, *Arch. J.* **131**, 140–70.

Wild, J. P. (1973) A fourth-century potters' workshop and kilns at Stibbington, Peterborough, in A. Detsicas, op. cit., 135–8.

Wilkes, J. J. (1979) Importation and manufacture of stamped bricks and tiles in the Roman province of Dalmatia, in A. McWhirr (1979a), 65–72.

Willems, J. (1969) Les potiers gallo-belges de Vervoz (Clavier, Liège), *Bull. Cercle Arch. Hesbaye-Condroz* **9**, 5–21.

Willems, J. (1966) Notes au sujet de la Villa belgo-romaine d'Evelette, *Bull. Cercle Arch. Hesbaye-Condroz* **6**, 15–28.

Willems, W. J.H. (1977) A Roman kiln at Halder, gemeente St Michielsgeste N.B., in B. L. van Beek, R. W. Brandt and W. Groenman van Waateringe (Eds) *Ex Horreo*, Amsterdam, 114–29.

Williams, D. F. (1977) The Romano-British black-burnished industry: an essay on characterisation by heavy mineral analysis, in D.P.S. Peacock (1977a), 163–220.

Williams, D. and Dannell, G. (1978) Petrological analysis of Arretine and early samian: a preliminary report, in P. Arthur and G. Marsh *Early Fine wares in Roman Britain*, B.A.R., **57**, 5–14.

Williams, I. J. (1932) The Nantgarw pottery and its products: an examination of the site, *Arch. Camb.* **87**, 108–43.

Wilson, D. (1861) *Prehistoric Man: Researches into the Origin of Civilisation in the Old and New Worlds*, Edinburgh.

Wilson, R. J. A (1979) Bricks and tiles in Roman Sicily, in A. McWhirr (1979a), 11–44.

Winter, A. (1978) *Die Antike Glanztonkeramik*, Mainz.

Winter, A. (1959) Die Technik des griechischen Töpfers in ihren Grundlagen, *Technische Beiträge zur Archäologie* **1**.

Woodforde, J. (1976) *Bricks to Build a House*, London.

Woods, P. J. (1974) Types of late Belgic and early Romano-British pottery kilns in the Nene Valley, *Britannia* **5**, 262–81.

Woods, P. J. (1969) *Excavations at Hardingstone, Northampton*, Northampton.

Woolley, C. L. (1911) Some potters' marks from Cales, *J. Rom. Stud.* **1**, 199–205.

Young, C. J. (Ed.) (1980) *Guidelines for the Processing and Publication of Roman Pottery*, London, Department of the Environment, Directorate of Ancient Monuments, Occasional Paper No. 4.

Young, C. J. (1977a) *Oxfordshire Roman Pottery*, B.A.R. **43**.

Young, C. J. (1977b) Oxford ware and the Roman army, in J. Dore and K. Greene, op. cit., 289–94.

Young, C. J. (1973) The pottery industry of the Oxford region, in A. Detsicas, op. cit., 105–15.

Young, D. (1968) Brickmaking at Broadmayne, *Proc. Dorset Nat. Hist. and Arch. Soc.* **89**, 318–24.

Zevi, F. (1966) Appunti sulle anfore romane, *Archaeologia Classica* **18**, 214–17.

Index of pottery and brick making localities

General index

aegirine augite, 79
African red slip ware, 119, 121, 154, 158, 161, 170
amphorae, 3, 41, 103, 116, 129–30, 146, 151, 159, 161, 163, 166, 169–70
 Dressel 1, 155
 Gaulish, 166–7
 North African, 154
 Tripolitanian, 130
 Tripolitanian stamps, 131
annona see taxation
anorthoclase, 79
archaeomagnetism, 165
Aristotle, 81, 152
army veterans, 144
Arretine ware *see also* Arezzo, *Ateius, Perennius*, 2, 57, 63, 75, 114–28, 153, 161
 origins, 115–16
 stamps, 120–2
Ateius Cn, Arretine potter, 116, 118, 121, 124
Aust, Gottfried, 127
auxilliary instruments, potters, 28–9, 37, 59, 62
 esquinante, 23
 estèque, 13, 59
 fanadoiro, 23
 mavadero, 21
 poinçons, 57, 60, 124–5, 143, 149

baking pans, 17
Barbégal mills, 10
Beersheba, chalcolithic pottery, 26
Berber pottery, 13–15, 17, 28, 77
black-burnished ware, Romano-British, 55–7, 84–7, 94–6, 98, 103, 149
bread ovens, pottery, 21
brick clamps, 15–17, 43, 67, 73
brick-making
 migration of workers, 35, 38, 131
 rate of output, 47, 50, 143
brick stamps
 civilian, 129, 131, 133–5

dated, 161
forged, 165
imperial, 151
military, 136–7, 139, 143–4
brickyard pottery, 69, 129–30
burnishing, 13, 17, 60, 61

Cadbury-Congresbury, sherd distribution, 3
Calene ware, 115
Campanian ware, 115
carpets, Persian, 10
carriage manufacture, 9
Carthage, 1, 75–6, 79–80, 152, 161–4, 170–2
chemical analysis, 3, 101, 116, 169
Classis Britannica, stamps, 146
clay baths, 130
clay digging, 17, 19, 21, 31, 38, 42, 47, 52–3
coins, 154, 157, 161, 164
colour-coated ware, 61, 63, 99, 107–8, 156, 161, 169
contracts, pottery supply, 149
cooperation, 9, 43, 121–2
corn driers, 67
Corpus Inscriptionum Latinorum (C.I.L.), 3, 133
Cosa, 75, 79, 155
Cossyra, 79
cossyrite, 79
craft specialisation, incipient, 17
craggans, 17
Cretan flasks, modern, 12
crucible, 19
cut-glass ornament, 57, 61

Dales ware, 87, 162
dispersed manufactory, 10, 127
dolia, 130
domestic industry (Marx), 10
dominus praediorum, 133–4
drainage gullies, 53–4
drying, 9, 13, 17, 38, 42, 66–7, 107–8, 139, 141
Durotriges, 85–6, 98